THE PETROLEUM TRIANGLE

THE PETROLEUM TRIANGLE

Oil, Globalization, and Terror

Steve A. Yetiv

CORNELL UNIVERSITY PRESS   ITHACA AND LONDON

First published 2011 by Cornell University Press
Printed in the United States of America

Library of Congress Cataloging-in-Publication Data

Yetiv, Steven A.
    The petroleum triangle : oil, globalization, and terror / Steve A. Yetiv.
        p. cm.
    Includes bibliographical references and index.
    ISBN 978-0-8014-5002-0 (cloth : alk. paper)
    1. Petroleum industry and trade—Political aspects.   2. Petroleum industry and trade—Political aspects—United States.   3. Terrorism—Economic aspects.
4. Globalization—Economic aspects.   5. Globalization—Political aspects.
I. Title.
    HD9560.6Y48   2011
    338.2'7282—dc22   2011017388

Cornell University Press strives to use environmentally responsible suppliers and materials to the fullest extent possible in the publishing of its books. Such materials include vegetable-based, low-VOC inks and acid-free papers that are recycled, totally chlorine-free, or partly composed of nonwood fibers. For further information, visit our website at www.cornellpress.cornell.edu.

Cloth printing   10 9 8 7 6 5 4 3 2 1

Contents

Figures

Acknowledgments

I owe a debt of gratitude to several readers who graciously agreed to read this work. I thank Anouar Boukhars, Lowell Feld, Kurt Taylor Gaubatz, Patricia Raxter, Marc O'Reilly, and Sagar Rijal. Special thanks go to Tulu Balkir, John Duffield, Kimberly Gilligan, and Jack Kalpakian for detailed comments on earlier drafts. The work also benefited tremendously from the seasoned guidance of Cornell University Press editor Roger Haydon as well as from the input of the external reviewers. I also thank Fatmatta Deen of OPEC's library in Vienna, Austria and members of the Paris-based staff of the International Energy Agency for their assistance.

Abbreviations

Aramco	Arabian American Oil Company
CIA	Central Intelligence Agency
CRS	Congressional Research Service
FBIS	Foreign Broadcast Information Service
GCC	Gulf Cooperation Council
GPO	Government Publishing Office
IAEA	International Atomic Energy Agency
IEA	International Energy Agency
mb/d	Millions of barrels per day
NGOs	Nongovernmental organizations
NIE	National Intelligence Estimate
NSA	National Security Archives
NSC	National Security Council
OPEC	Organization of Petroleum Exporting Countries
OECD	Organization for Economic Cooperation and Development
UNMOVIC	UN Monitoring, Verification, and Inspection Commission
UNSCOM	UN Special Commission on Iraq
WMD	weapons of mass destruction

THE PETROLEUM TRIANGLE

INTRODUCTION

In August 2009, President Barack H. Obama told the annual Veterans of Foreign Wars conference that the war in faraway Afghanistan was not a war of choice but rather a "war of necessity." He believed that the U.S.-led invasion of Iraq in 2003 was a grand mistake and had run strongly on that platform during the 2008 U.S. presidential campaign, but his view of Afghanistan was different. He warned in dramatic language that those "who attacked America on 9/11 are plotting to do so again. If left unchecked, the Taliban insurgency will mean an even larger safe haven from which Al-Qaeda would plot to kill more Americans."[1] The story of transnational terror seemed to lack an ending.

This book tells the story of oil, globalization, and terrorism—what I call the petroleum triangle. It is a story in which powerful presidents from Jimmy Carter to George W. Bush have been tarnished; in which dictators from the Shah of Iran to Iraq's President Saddam Hussein have fallen; in which countries have been impacted significantly by the effects and allure of oil wealth; and in which citizens and soldiers have been killed by the thousands in wars in the Middle East and Afghanistan. This story has played out not in some isolated area of the globe as was often the case in previous centuries but in front of an international audience that is connected by the many sinews, pathways, and influences of globalization.

---

1. Obama Speech to the Veterans of Foreign Wars Conference, available at http://latimesblogs.latimes.com/washington/2009/08/obama-speech-transcript-vfw.html, accessed February 2, 2011.

Within this story of oil, globalization, and terror, this book explores a primary puzzle: how did a small band of terrorists become such a real and perceived threat to global security? I stress the difference between a "real" and "perceived" threat, because Al-Qaeda has become both a real threat based on its actual capabilities to do harm, and a perceived threat based on the fear that it has sowed, up and beyond its real capabilities.

The real and perceived threat was viewed as profound enough to motivate the strongest power in world history to declare war on Al-Qaeda, to send tens of thousands of troops abroad in order to try to destroy it, and to create a world-wide alliance to defeat it at the cost of hundreds of billions of dollars. The death of Osama Bin Laden at the hands of U.S. Navy Seals on May 2, 2011, dealt a blow to Al-Qaeda but it will take years to understand the extent of that blow and the impact on jihadi terrorism, Al-Qaeda, and Al-Qaeda's affiliates. These affiliates had splintered off from Al-Qaeda and gained some life of their own long before Bin Laden's death. Indeed, Secretary of State Hillary Clinton asserted in March 2011 that Al-Qaeda affiliates in particular were the greatest threat to the United States, describing their destruction as the "highest priority" for the Obama administration.[2] The status of these affiliates in relation to the original core organization is not fully clear, but they often appear to act like franchises of Al-Qaeda,[3] with varying levels of allegiance to, direction from, and inspiration by the core Al-Qaeda group.[4] This book treats them as part of the Al-Qaeda phenomenon.

Whatever happens in the future to Al-Qaeda, its affiliates, and transnational terrorism in the post–Bin Laden era, we should still be interested in the answers to these two puzzles. They can tell us about central issues in modern world politics, including the impact of Middle Eastern oil and oil-related issues, the effects of globalization, the evolution and nature of transnational terrorism, the U.S. role in the Middle East, global oil dependence, and the power of states.

On that score, the evidence and arguments assembled in this book strongly suggest that this small band of Al-Qaeda terrorists has become a real and perceived threat to global security because of Middle Eastern oil and modern globalization, and the many links between them. While this is an important part of the explanation, there are other dimensions to it as well. For example, as chapter 2 argues, one vital motivating force of Al-Qaeda terrorism appears to be the distorted lens through which Al-Qaeda's leaders see the world. This lens differs from but connects

---

2. ABC News, "Clinton's Biggest Fear."

3. For example, in February 2011, financial institutions in New York were told by the FBI that they face a potential terrorist threat from Al-Qaeda in the Arabian Peninsula, the Yemeni branch of the terrorist organization. Hurtado Financial Institutions. Bin Laden's role was unclear.

4. For a brief and concise argument on why their relationship to the core must be considered and understood better, see Farrall, "How al Qaeda Works."

to the petroleum triangle, and it also helps explain why terrorism has been so hard to eliminate. It's partly driven by a rigid conceptual lens and distorted narrative.

The oil era in the Middle East began in 1907 when oil was discovered in Iran. It accelerated during the two world wars, as oil became vital to the war effort, and then in the 1950s and 1960s, when power over oil slowly shifted from international oil companies to states. It assumed greater significance with the 1973–74 Arab oil embargo and successive wars, linked in differing degrees to oil, from 1980 to 2003. While the oil era was in full swing, the modern era of globalization era took off after World War II and especially in the post-1970 period.

The links between globalization, oil, and terrorism are many and varied. But they can be captured roughly in one general theme: while Middle Eastern oil has fueled terrorism, globalization has provided terrorists with global highways and side roads to traverse.

In the main, Middle Eastern oil has fueled terrorism by helping to fund the terrorist infrastructure. It has also offered the political issues, such as perceived American efforts to steal or control Persian Gulf oil and resentments against the oil-rich Saudi royal family, that have motivated Al-Qaeda, that have generated the anti-Americanism from which Al-Qaeda benefits, and that have helped Al-Qaeda recruit followers and gain sympathy in some quarters.

Meanwhile, globalization has been critical for terrorist penetration of states; for easing international travel; for exploiting modern technologies at lower cost than would have been the case otherwise; and for fundraising. In some ways, globalization has also heightened the perceived threat of terrorism via international communications and media, which have reported on the terrorist threat extensively and sometimes have even given Al-Qaeda a platform for communicating its views and amplifying its threat. The pathways and sideroads of the interconnected web of world politics have also sometimes made it easier for Al-Qaeda operatives to elude detection and the wide net of American power.

Middle Eastern oil and globalization have produced their own independent effects on terrorism. However, together, oil and globalization have also produced a noxious mix. And that mix also helped create and sustain Al-Qaeda's real and perceived threat, in a way that neither globalization nor Middle East oil could do when considered separately.

Oil and Terrorism

Middle Eastern oil is projected to grow in importance. Alternatives to oil are projected to grow faster than oil as a global energy source. Still, demand for global oil is predicted to rise significantly (see figure 1). Demand will be driven chiefly by the transportation sector, which uses 70 percent of global oil, and by

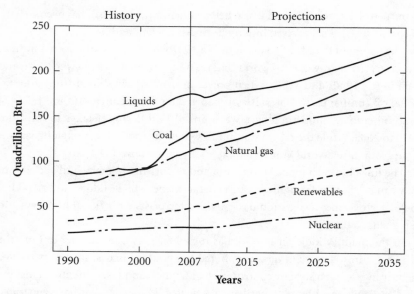

FIGURE 1.   World marketed energy use by fuel type, 1990–2035
Source: Energy Information Administration, "International Energy Outlook 2010,"
1. Available at www.eia.doe.gov/oiaf/ieo/pdf/0484(2010).pdf.

the dramatic economic growth of China and India. The conflict-prone Middle East will serve as the principal source of supply to meet rising demand over the next two decades.[5] This will make the Gulf increasingly important to global oil pricing, oil supply, and the global economy.[6]

The story of oil and terror can be captured in snapshots, but assembling them is important. Just as a movie may be interesting at any particular point, it is more meaningful when its separate parts are strung together. We gain a better understanding of how oil connects to terrorism when we also consider oil's role in the chain of events in the region—events in which U.S. foreign policy, global politics, regional developments, and terrorism all play a role. Oil is one of the few global factors that is linked to a range of terrorist activities. We can start by sketching examples of links between Middle Eastern oil and terrorism.

September 11 is so far the biggest terrorist attack perpetrated by Al-Qaeda, so it makes sense to start there. Chapter 2 divides the motivations for 9/11 into three categories: conceptual, oil-related, and non-oil-related. The conceptual level refers to the distorted religious lens through which Al-Qaeda views the world. It is an important starting point for understanding September 11 and Al-Qaeda's behavior. For example, some analysts have blamed U.S. foreign policy in no small measure for the September 11 attacks, including to some extent those responsible for the 9/11 Commission Report issued by the U.S. Congress in 2004.[7] Meanwhile, in a polar opposite view, other observers repeatedly described Al-Qaeda as motivated by a hatred for freedom and the American way of life—a notion prominently and repeatedly asserted by President George W. Bush and his Republican cohorts in the years following the September 11 attacks, as well as by many other Americans. They assert that Al-Qaeda hates what the United States is rather than what it does.

U.S. foreign policy appears to be related to Al-Qaeda terrorism, but largely by how it is interpreted through Al-Qaeda's distorted religious lens. U.S. foreign policy does not produce massive terrorist acts by other groups worldwide, so at best it is only part of the explanation. The notion that Al-Qaeda views the world through a particularly distorted lens illuminates why it has launched massive terrorist attacks against the United States and remains committed to perpetrating more attacks. Emphasizing this distorted prism also helps explain why Al-Qaeda and the millions that appear to sympathize with it do not recognize American-led efforts that clearly helped the majority of Muslims in cases such as the liberation of Kuwait, the military intervention in Bosnia, and even the reversal of the Soviet occupation of Muslim Afghanistan. Rather, it has been chiefly through Al-Qaeda's distorted prism that America's foreign policy behavior has been a motivation for terror. Seeing Al-Qaeda as hostage to its own distorted prism also helps explain why it can claim to act in the name of Islam, when in fact it distorts the religion whose genuine adherents are no more violent than those of other religions.

Illuminating the conceptual level is useful if we seek to understand how Al-Qaeda sees the world in general and how this is salient to understanding its attacks on September 11, but there is more at play than this conceptual prism. Middle Eastern oil is connected to September 11 in numerous ways, some blatant and some buried in the historical process. To put a complex story in simple terms, oil money helped create both Al-Qaeda and the Taliban, while events tied to Middle Eastern oil, including the 1990–91 Persian Gulf crisis, stoked Al-Qaeda's grievances against the United States when seen through its distorted religious lens. The timeline suggests that Osama Bin Laden had already begun to focus

---

7. See the analysis of a former intelligence officer in Scheuer, *Imperial Hubris*. The September 11 commission report recommended that the United States broadly revisit its foreign policy toward the Muslim world.

attention on America toward the end of the Soviet War in Afghanistan from 1986 to 1989, before major oil-related conflicts began in the Persian Gulf, but that he became much more radicalized from 1990 to 1996. In an interview in Afghanistan published in July 1996, Bin Laden, son of a Yemeni father and a Saudi mother, declared that the killing of Americans in the Khobar Towers bombing in Saudi Arabia the previous month marked the beginning of the war between Muslims and the United States.[8] One month later, in August 1996, Bin Laden, in collaboration with radical Muslim clerics associated with his group, issued a religious edict, or *fatwa,* in which he proclaimed a declaration of war, authorizing attacks against Western military targets on the Arabian peninsula. One central question to address concerns what happened between 1989 and 1996 to focus his attention on the United States.

Non-oil factors were also important in motivating September 11. These ranged from the ultimate goal of creating a global *ummah* to personal factors tied to the psychology of the Al-Qaeda leaders.

Ultimately, the best explanation for the September 11 attacks arises from considering how these three categories of explanation hang together. They hang together in some obvious ways, but also in more nuanced ways.

Beyond September 11, oil issues played a broader, albeit indirect, role in terrorism. For instance, the U.S. role in the Persian Gulf, critical for protecting the free flow of oil at reasonable prices, has fed a not uncommon perspective of America as imperialist, power-hungry, oil-seeking, and crusading. This perspective is borne out in many different polls conducted around the Muslim world. Some in the audience, under the influence of such views, have become more anti-American and sympathize with aspects of Al-Qaeda's agenda. In fact, opinion polls show that anti-American sentiment rose dramatically with the Iraq War of 2003.[9]

Political scientist Samuel Huntington famously predicted a clash of civilizations, involving, most prominently, Muslims and Westerners.[10] Yet it can be dangerous to make broad generalizations about civilizations, especially when relations between some Muslim and non-Muslim states are strong. And such broad generalizations, however interesting they may be, are not necessary to show that oil issues generate anti-Americanism.

---

8. "Written Statement for the Record."

9. For instance, see www.sadat.umd.edu/new%20surveys/surveys.htm, http://pewglobal. org/reports/display.php?ReportID=185, and www.usatoday.com/news/sept11/2002/02/27/usat pollresults.htm.

10. Huntington, *Clash of Civilizations.*

Oil money helped not only to create Al-Qaeda but also to sustain its operations as well as those of its affiliates from Indonesia to Chechnya. Oil money has not been important to the terrorist acts themselves. September 11 cost only half a million dollars, and the Madrid train bombings in Spain in 2004 were funded by local pedestrian criminal activity.[11] Nor is oil money critical to particular elements of the infrastructure of terror: recruitment, ideological indoctrination, salaries, housing, planning, arms, travel, logistics, communications, money for cells engaged in plots, expenses for longer-range plans such as a potential weapons of mass program, payoffs to local governments and warlords, public promotion, and adaptation to local and global counterterrorist efforts. However, oil money *has* been vital in helping to create, maintain, and expand this whole infrastructure over time, from the Afghan resistance against the Soviet occupation in the 1980s through the post–September 11 period.

Evidence suggests that oil money can also be linked indirectly to terrorism. For instance, American oil interests in the Middle East may well have decreased pressure on Arab states as well as the Taliban to take serious action against Bin Laden prior to September 11. Indeed, some evidence that I discuss later in the book suggests that oil money enhanced the ability of Osama Bin Laden to convince his key cohorts to attack the United States in the first place, as opposed to continuing *jihad* against local enemies.

As Al-Qaeda evolved, oil money appeared to become less important, with money from other activities, including trafficking in heroin, gaining in importance.[12] The relative importance of Al-Qaeda's various sources of income may change again in the future. In any case, oil was critical in its rise and in its desire to launch the 9/11 attacks in the first place.

Middle Eastern oil is tied to motivating Al-Qaeda, to provoking support outside its leadership and hard-core conscripts, and to helping it build and maintain its broader infrastructure. But oil monies are also directly and indirectly connected to the threat of weapons of mass destruction. As I discuss in chapter 4, oil monies enhanced Al-Qaeda's chances of obtaining the materials and components for weapons of mass destruction through its own auspices or via countries such as Pakistan, whose nuclear program was aided significantly by Saudi money.

Beyond the role of oil money, evidence suggests a connection between oil and nondemocracy. Although the connection between nondemocracy and terrorism remains unclear, I argue in chapter 5 that even if nondemocracy does not cause terrorism, oil resources do help prop up leaderships in the Persian Gulf that

11. Aufhauser interview.
12. Peters, *Seeds of Terror*, 3–4, 14–15.

terrorists view as corrupt and un-Islamic and therefore as targets for attack and elimination.[13] Such resources also generate other political issues to make these regimes and their allies the targets of terrorism.

Middle Eastern Oil and Globalization

The impact of Middle Eastern oil on transnational terrorism is only half of the story. Middle Eastern oil can explain only so much about terrorism. We also have to consider the broader global context for the links between oil and terrorism. The other part of the story is about the combined effects of Middle Eastern oil and globalization. To orient the reader, I briefly sketch a few sub-arguments about how globalization and Middle Eastern oil have combined in direct and indirect ways to make Al-Qaeda terrorism a real and perceived threat in world politics. The body of the book develops these and other arguments. By "combined effects," I mean two things: first, Middle Eastern oil has produced effects that have augmented the effects of globalization and vice versa. And, second, Middle Eastern oil and globalization have not only reinforced each other but have produced some new effects that probably neither could have produced alone. Both types of combined effects, in turn, have contributed to Al-Qaeda's real and perceived threat, and to that of its affiliates.

Oil money has contributed to the creation and sustenance of both Al-Qaeda and the Taliban, which provided Al-Qaeda with a safe haven in Afghanistan. Meanwhile, globalization helped the jihadis in the Afghan resistance to launch Al-Qaeda as a global organization, to make their nascent transnational force viable. Globalization became the bridge from Afghanistan to the world stage that the organization needed in order to function at long distances.

Middle Eastern oil revenues enabled industrialization, but they also helped preserve the cultural status quo. At the same time, globalization has engendered pressures for change against this status quo. The tension between these two forces is a deep fault line in many oil-rich states, contributing to social and economic dislocation—and quite probably to the types of sentiments that either generate or can be exploited by terrorists. Some of these sentiments were on full display during the revolts and revolutions that began in the Middle East in early 2011.

---

13. On the nature and implications of attacks by Al-Qaeda affiliates in Saudi Arabia post-2003, see Al-Rasheed, *Contesting the Saudi State,* 134–210; Hegghammer, "Terrorist Recruitment and Radicalisation in Saudi Arabia," 39–60; Teitelbaum, "Terrorist Challenges," 1–11; and Obaid and Cordesman, *Al-Qaeda in Saudi Arabia.*

While oil contributes to the infrastructure of and motivation for terrorism, global communications have facilitated terrorism and helped spread fear. Globalization is characterized by a web of communications, which have created a plethora of vital links among societies.[14] In previous eras, the 9/11 attacks, or any of Al-Qaeda's rhetoric, could not have been communicated worldwide in so dramatic a form. Global communications have served Al-Qaeda by spreading fear, aggrandizing it as a terrorist organization, spreading its radical message, and aiding in recruitment. They have helped Al-Qaeda project a threat that may well exceed actuality, thus enhancing its notoriety.

Working in combination, Middle Eastern oil and globalization have also contributed to a negative narrative about America and oil. Oil issues have fed anti-Americanism. Global communications have spread this negative narrative. The communications revolution has created the potential for Al-Qaeda, which would otherwise be hamstrung, to create rifts between Muslims and the West.

The oil and globalization eras have combined to make terrorist attacks more dangerous once they occur. Globalization has created interconnections in economic markets and other arenas. These interconnections, in turn, offer vulnerable nodes for terrorist attack and can augment the terrorist threat. In earlier eras, for instance, the September 11 attacks would have been a minor rather than a seismic event, but in 2001 terrorists were hitting a key node of a globalized world.[15]

As for counterterrorism efforts, Al-Qaeda would not get far if its network could be dismantled and its leadership destroyed. The effects of oil and globalization have reinforced each other to help Al-Qaeda at least to some extent avoid such an outcome, even as it has come under serious constraints due to the massive and determined U.S.-led efforts to destroy it. Oil has provided some of the funds that have made it easier for Al-Qaeda to elude attack by a U.S.-led global coalition. At the same time, globalization has provided an interconnected haven in which it can hide and become virtual, making it harder to eliminate.

Globalization also benefits the U.S.-led coalition in its fight against Al-Qaeda, of course, and that weakens Al-Qaeda. However, as I discuss in the conclusion, it appears that globalization on the whole has militated in favor of Al-Qaeda and other transnational terrorists. For example, the benefits of enhanced global communications have disproportionately favored terrorist groups, partly because

---

14. For an excellent conceptualization of the general effects of globalization, see Rosenau, *Distant Proximities,* 53.

15. U.S. Joint Forces Command in Suffolk, Virginia, has focused increasing attention on this issue. The author participated as a consultant.

they are now cheaper and easier to use. That decreases barriers to their use by poorer actors and helps level the playing field with wealthier states that could afford access even when communication and high technology were extremely expensive.

Implications of the Arguments: State Power and Energy Policy

The arguments of this book mean something for our understanding of state power and energy policy. The first is about state power, and the second is about energy policy. The combination of oil and globalization contributed to the rise of Al-Qaeda in ways that have somewhat diminished American power, and Middle Eastern oil has added its own effects as well. There is a growing literature on oil dependence and national security, as there is on globalization and national security, but little on what globalization and Middle Eastern oil mean for state power.[16]

Some political scientists see globalization as having a minor effect on state power. Most theorists of the realist or neorealist school hold such a position, as do some other scholars. For instance, T. V. Paul and Norrin M. Ripsman find that great powers (the United States, China, Russia) continue to pursue traditional nation-state strategies, that even weak states rely on their own power in a self-help world more than on regional and transnational institutions, and that globalization has not affected state power much.[17] In contrast, many globalization scholars see globalization as weakening states and making them vulnerable or forcing them to adjust significantly to new conditions.[18] For instance, Alexander Cooley hypothesizes that "globalization increases the security threat posed by non-state actors by weakening the capacity" of states to cope with transnational actors.[19] Similarly, Karl Mueller argues that globalization constrains the autonomy of states, even of the American hegemon, and their freedom of action from outside forces.[20]

Two major theoretical schools have competed for attention in the study of international relations. They are realism, to which thinkers from Machiavelli to

16. See, for instance, Kirshner, ed., *Globalization and National Security.*
17. Ripsman and Paul, *Globalization and the National Security State.*
18. Held and McGrew, *Globalization/Anti-Globalization,* 24. On this literature, see Held, *Global Transformations,* esp. 7–10; Martell, *Sociology of Globalization,* ch. 1; and Cerny, *Rethinking World Politics.*
19. Cooley, "Globalization and National Security," 208.
20. Mueller, "Paradox of Liberal Hegemony," 144.

Henry Kissinger have subscribed, and liberalism, whose adherents have included Immanuel Kant and Woodrow Wilson. Yet liberalism, realism, and their various modern progeny, while offering significant and important insights into international relations, cannot explain the effects of oil on terrorism even though oil represents the biggest sector of global trade and fundamentally shapes human and international relations, and transnational terrorism poses a serious twenty-first-century threat. In other words, they cannot explain some of the key features of our times.

For their part, realists train our attention on states as critical actors in world politics. They assume that in order to understand the world, we need to understand the actions of states dwelling in a state of nature, in a Hobbesian world of oppressive global anarchy. In so doing, they downplay the crucial connections between oil and transnational problems, because these problems are not centrally about state actors. Realists and especially neorealists have a hard time explaining even how 9/11 happened, because they so deemphasize transnational actors.[21]

Meanwhile, liberal theorists and some empiricists argue that interdependence decreases conflict between states.[22] They may be right, but what happens when we extend our purview to the issue area of global oil and to an arena beyond interstate relations? Here, the positive assumptions that liberal theory makes about interdependence and conflict only mislead us. For their part, groundbreaking scholars of transnational politics have not done much to explain how oil and globalization affect transnational terrorism.[23] Robert Keohane and Joseph Nye have come the closest. Their early work signaled the importance of transnational actors, while their model of complex interdependence allowed us to capture some of the key dynamics of our globalized world.[24] However, that model, anchored chiefly in the liberal school, allows for understanding the downside of globalization only if one explores how asymmetrical interdependence can generate conflict. More important, it does not aim to offer a theoretical explanation for the rise of transnational terrorism, nor does it illuminate how globalization and oil

21. On neorealism, see Waltz, *Theory of International Politics*; and Waltz, "Structural Realism." For a good description of the realist literature, see Layne, *Peace of Illusions*, 12–16; and Barkin, *Realist Constructivism*.

22. McMillan, "Interdependence and Conflict"; Russett and Oneal, *Triangulating Peace*; and Mansfield and Pollins, *Economic Interdependence*. On conditions affecting the link between interdependence and conflict, see Crescenzi, *Economic Interdependence*.

23. See, for example, Keohane and Nye, *Power and Interdependence*; Risse-Kappen, *Bringing Transnational Relations Back In*; Keck and Sikkink, *Activists beyond Borders*; and Rudolph and Piscatori, eds., *Transnational Religion*.

24. See, for example, Keohane and Nye, *Power and Interdependence*. Also, see Milner and Moravcsik, eds. *Power, Interdependence, and Nonstate Actors in World Politics*.

could work together to produce such an outcome. International relations theory must do more to explain the interactive effects of critical phenomena involved in the petroleum triangle. Globalization is neither positive nor negative in and of itself; rather, it depends on the issue area and dynamic with which it combines.

This book is not an indictment of the oil era. Oil has been the engine of global economic growth. But these various arguments do lead us to a policy conclusion: the greater the costs of the oil era compared to its benefits, the more quickly we should try to move beyond petroleum. A small but growing literature exists on the broader costs to the United States of oil dependence.[25] This book suggests that the costs of the oil era may be even higher than we think.

Conceptualizing Globalization

Globalization has multiple definitions.[26] For present purposes, I define it at a basic level as a high level of interconnectedness in the economic, political, cultural, and technological spheres that alters important aspects of world politics.[27]

Globalization is not one amorphous phenomenon but rather consists of different dimensions. Thus, the effects of financial, cultural, and political globalization may not all be similar. For instance, Martin Mullins and Finbarr Murphy make the interesting argument that financial globalization has actually empowered some states and bolstered their autonomy from traditional capital markets.[28] Whatever one thinks of the argument, their approach reminds scholars to unpack "globalization" into its constituent components and subcomponents. But globalization also means something beyond its parts. Globalization has produced an integration of markets, nations, and technologies—a process that is breaking down borders, even if states maintain their position as critical actors in world politics. It is creating, to borrow a term from Jan Scholte, a supraterritoriality that involves not only the intensification of links across the world but also, in some respects, a blurring of boundaries between states.[29]

Globalization is enabling individuals, groups, corporations, and states to penetrate the world more easily and quickly than ever before. This process is not just economic; it combines economic, technological, socio-cultural, and political

---

25. See, for example, Duffield, *Over a Barrel*.
26. Dreher et al., *Measuring Globalisation*, 1–5.
27. Held and McGrew, *Globalization/Anti-Globalization*, ch. 2. For how sociologists and historians define it, see Martell, *Sociology of Globalization*, 11–16.
28. Mullins and Murphy, "Financial Globalisation," 433–49.
29. Scholte, *Globalization*.

forces that generate transborder exchanges.[30] Economic globalization is often emphasized. It involves the increased interconnectedness of national economies, or, as some thinkers might say, the integration of national economies into the international economy through trade, foreign direct investment, capital flows, and the spread of technology.[31] This book views interdependence as an aspect of globalization.[32] Interdependence, which has increased significantly since World War II,[33] refers not just to broad connectedness but to mutual dependence between countries or between actors within countries. It arises when actors depend on each other for critical goods or services.[34]

Scholars debate the rise of globalization. David Held identifies three general views. Skeptics argue that globalization is not a new phenomenon, that a deep view of history reveals that it has existed for centuries and that recent developments have only accelerated its scale and scope. The hyper-globalists, in contrast, dismiss elements of widespread globalization in the past but view modern globalization as highly evolved and even as eroding the power and authority of the nation-states. A third school, the transformationalists, take a middle ground, viewing globalization as modern and novel phenomena but arguing that the nation-state is still intact, albeit transformed by globalization.[35]

Evidence strongly suggests that economic globalization has risen, based on three indicators: trade, foreign direct investment, and financial capital flows.[36] They capture, respectively, three distinct and significant dimensions of economic globalization: the cross-border flows of goods and services, production capital, and financial capital. Globalization is not a new phenomenon. More than two thousand years ago, Athens managed a large trading empire. The British Empire was a huge trading concern in the nineteenth century, and some scholars argue that the world was more globalized in the nineteenth century than it would be hundred years later. The nineteenth century is sometimes called "The First Era of Globalization," because it was characterized by high international trade

---

30. Croucher, *Globalization and Belonging,* 10; and Scholte, *Globalization,* 49.

31. Bhagwati, *In Defense of Globalization.*

32. Transnational problems occur within this context of interdependence, but they are very different from it. They occur across borders, while interdependence is about relations of mutual dependence among two or more actors. Trade between states, for instance, is a form of interdependence because states provide goods to each other, but it is not a transnational problem.

33. Key works include Keohane and Nye, *Power and Interdependence;* Russett and Oneal, *Triangulating Peace;* Rosecrance, *Rise of the Trading State;* Gartzke et al., "Investing in the Peace," 391–438; Rosenau, *Along the Domestic-Foreign Frontier;* and McMillan, "Interdependence and Conflict."

34. Keohane and Nye, *Power and Interdependence,* 7–9. For related work on defining and conceptualizing interdependence, see Kroll, "Complexity of Interdependence."

35. Held, *Global Transformations.*

36. Bhalla, *Imagine There's No Country;* and Li and Reuveny, "Economic Globalization and Democracy."

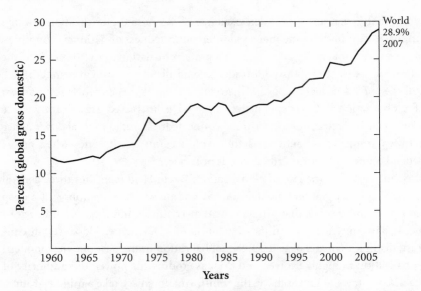

FIGURE 2. Global trade as a percentage of global gross domestic product, 1960–2007
Source: World Bank, *World Development Indicators*, last updated July 26, 2010.

and investment among the European imperial powers, their colonies, and, later, the United States. This period of globalization began to break down with World War I and then the Great Depression in the early 1930s.[37]

Since World War II, economic globalization has risen on the back of institutional efforts to decrease trade barriers and costs. These institutions, founded at Bretton Woods, New Hampshire, toward the end of World War II, include the World Bank, the International Monetary Fund, and the General Agreement on Tariffs and Trade (now the World Trade Organization), which launched various subsequent agreements to remove restrictions on free trade and increased globalization.

Numerous indicators underscore rising economic globalization after World War II right when the oil era was taking off in earnest as well. As figure 2 shows clearly, global trade, which is the sum of all exports and imports of goods and services, rose significantly from 1960 to 2007 as a percentage of global gross domestic product. The wealth of countries has increasingly come from their trade with each other as opposed to other forms of economic output.

Globalization is also reflected in the rise in foreign direct investment, from 5.8 percent of global output in 1980 to 19.2 percent in 2000.[38] Foreign direct

---

37. For a good analysis of how modern globalization differs from historical forms of globalization, see Held, *Global Transformations*, esp. 16–21.

38. Brooks, *Producing Security*, 17, graph 2.1.

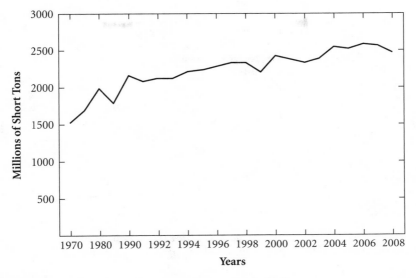

FIGURE 3. U.S. waterborne trade volume, 1970–2008
Source: Data drawn from U.S. Army Corps of Engineers, Navigation Data Center.
Available at www.iwr.usace.army.mil/ndc/wcsc/wcsc.htm.

investment refers to fixed investments, such as factories, as opposed to smaller investments abroad, such as those in stock portfolios or in shares of foreign companies. It is important beyond trade because it indicates long-term participation in the economies of other countries, usually in active advisory roles, in the management of businesses and joint ventures, or in construction or investment in other states. As such, foreign direct investment represents a greater commitment to the economies of others and a more involved level of economic interaction across borders.

The U.S. economy is a good indicator for overall global economic behavior, in part because it is such a large part of that economy. We see in figure 3 that U.S. waterborne trade increased significantly from 1970 to 2008, in a similar direction and scale as global trade and foreign direct investment.

Increases in transportation reflect a rise in globalization and are probably caused in part by globalization. In 1900, the world had 8,000 registered vehicles; by 1920, 10 million; and by 1951, a staggering 50 million.[39] As figure 4 shows, the number of automobiles has increased considerably since the 1950s. Exacerbating global oil dependence, the number of people per automobile decreased significantly, from 48.2 in 1950 to 10.6 in 2004. There are far more vehicles per person than in the past, which strongly indicates a rise in transportation

---

39. Smil, *Energy at the Crossroads,* esp. 59, fig. 1.25.

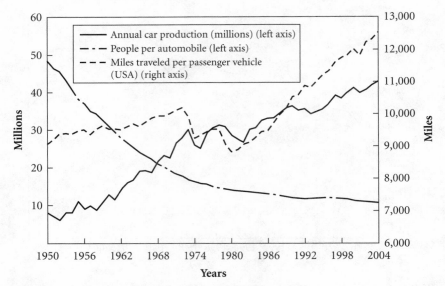

FIGURE 4. Global vehicle use indicators, 1950–2004
Source: Department of Global Studies and Geography, Hofstra University. Available at http://people.hofstra.edu/geotrans/eng/ch1en/conc1en/peoplepercar.html.

mobility. In the United States, each passenger vehicle travels around 12,500 miles (20,000 km) annually (2004 figures), up from about 9,000 miles (14,400 km) in 1980.

Economic interaction was high in the nineteenth century as well, but such interactions now exist among a far wider range of countries. For instance, the great powers of the nineteenth century exploited the less developed world in part through colonization. Now, less developed countries trade heavily with the developed world, and some of them have grown at a faster pace than developed countries.

Technological globalization has also exploded in terms of communications and information technologies. This development is quite different from the nineteenth-century version, even if we accept the notion that economic integration in that period was on the same scale and depth as it is today. It is hard to question that the rise of numerous technologies, ranging from myriad wireless gadgets to the internet, has not had a massive impact on economic, political, and cultural relations.[40]

---

40. For data on the rise of globalization, see Shapiro, *Futurecast*, ch. 3.

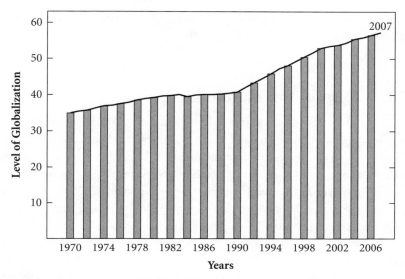

FIGURE 5. Index of globalization, 1970–2007
Source: "KOF Index of Globalization," KOF Swiss Institute of Technology Zurich.
Available at http://globalization.kof.ethz.ch.

Political globalization has expanded as well, as defined by the rising number and influence of global organizations. For instance, in 1909 there were 37 intergovernmental and 176 international nongovernmental organizations, whereas by 1996 there were 260 intergovernmental organizations and 5,472 international nongovernmental organizations.[41] Connected to this growth in global organizations is a massive rise in the number and importance of international treaties and agreements, which have shaped international interaction across business, space, conflict, energy, and the oceans.

For its part, cultural globalization can be viewed as the rise of cultural exchanges and practices among nations and peoples. Witness the impact of the rise of television, the computer, and the internet in spreading cultural ideas around the world. It is hard to estimate their effects, but these technologies have allowed people the world over to share cultural and media experiences almost instantaneously.

Figure 5 offers a complex measure of overall globalization. It accounts for the economic, social, and political dimensions of globalization, drawing on multiple

41. Held, *Global Transformations,* 53.

indicators within each of those central categories. It underscores the significant increase in globalization from 1970 to 2007.[42]

The Oil Era in the Middle East

While the globalization era was building after World War II, the oil era in the Middle East was beginning to take real shape. The oil era began in 1859 in Titusville, Pennsylvania, where the first oil well was drilled. The oil rush was on.[43] Little did the prospectors imagine that they were setting the stage for the global oil era. By 1861, one discovery met another when Nikolaus Otto invented the first gasoline engine. That allowed for the rise of the automobile as the dominant form of global transportation—a development that would revolutionize business and global life. America would be not only the first oil producer but the biggest as well, producing more oil, cumulatively, than any other country from 1918 to 1999. By the advent of the twentieth century, the Industrial Revolution and the development of large standing armies had created enormous energy needs. To fill this potentially lucrative market, the United States and Russia started producing petroleum and, by 1900, were producing 90 percent of the world supply.[44]

Oil trade now represents the single largest sector of global trade, but it took some time for Middle Eastern oil to emerge as a central, inescapable, and sometimes bewildering feature of world politics. Fifty years after oil was discovered in the United States, major oil companies began exploring the Middle East. In 1907, oil was discovered in Iran, representing the opening salvo of the oil era for the Middle East. By 1933, Standard Oil Company of California, founded in 1870, had struck a sixty-year contract with Saudi Arabia, which provided exclusive rights for exploring and producing oil from the Eastern Province—production facilities there are a major target for transnational terrorists today. In 1938, the Arabian-American Oil Company first discovered oil in commercial quantities.[45] In subsequent decades, the Saudis slowly took control of the company from Americans, forging their own power in the global oil industry and setting the stage for many vital developments to come.[46]

---

42. For details on the indicators and data for this graph, see The KOF Index of Globalization, at http://globalization.kof.ethz.ch/.

43. Yergin, *Prize*, esp. 28.

44. Andersen, *Changing Middle East*, 247.

45. On the evolution of these relations, see Pollack, "Saudi Arabia," esp. 78–79.

46. On this oil and security relationship, see Hart, *Saudi Arabia and the United States;* and Brown, *Oil, God, and Gold*. On Aramco, see Anderson, *Aramco*.

While the global oil industry was being shaped, an interesting development occurred. The oil magnates of the Gilded Age helped develop a creature that energy analyst Daniel Yergin has dubbed "Hydrocarbon Man," the prototype earthling who depends on the many benefits of the oil era, from gasoline to plastics, as if they were an entitlement. As Yergin aptly observed, oil toppled coal as the new "undisputed king," reigning over a "time of confidence, of growth, of expansion, of astonishing economic performance."[47] The explosion in the use of oil after World War II was extraordinary.[48] Oil became the undying motor of the global economy—abundant, available, quick, easy, powerful.

The oil era, accelerating in earnest after World War II in conjunction with the massive growth of the automobile, has become an entire infrastructure, a way of life built around the discovery, production, and use of oil. Oil is not just an isolated commodity to be used and forgotten. It is so embedded in our lives that it is hard to separate out. It might as well be viewed as an ecosystem of petrol, which includes symbiotic relationships between the consumers who need oil and the producers who need their business; between the global business that wants access in the Middle East and the oil exporters that need their knowhow; between the terrorists who decry elements of the oil era and their sympathizers; between the religious leaders who want to perpetuate legacies like Wahhabist Islam and their state patrons who seek their imprimatur for credibility. Like any ecosystem, the oil ecosystem is fragile.

Oil is both a prize and a problem, depending on one's vantage point, and it certainly differs from most other commodities in ways that have helped shape the oil era.[49] We depend on no commodity more than we do oil, as becomes apparent when oil prices rise and one media outlet after another runs stories on what this will mean for inflation, unemployment, and global economic health. And this dependence is a two-way street. Oil exporters also depend on oil for revenue, jobs, and possible regime existence. Both exporters and importers are buffeted by changes in oil supply and demand. The finite nature of oil is a distinguishing feature. Oil exporters will eventually begin to face diminishing oil production. This characteristic of oil differentiates it from many other products and will force hard choices on decisionmakers of all descriptions, as they face the task of reconstructing their very societies.

Over time, the allure of oil began to fade; by the late twentieth century we had become more aware of its negative effects.[50] It is not clear what has

47. Yergin, *Prize*, 541.
48. Ibid.
49. For a broad discussion, see Karl, *Paradox of Plenty*, 46–67.
50. Speth, *Red Sky at Morning*, ch. 10.

happened to the Age of Hydrocarbon Man, but it appears to be slowly yielding ground to an age of greater challenges. We may refer to it as the Age of Consequence. The real story of the Age of Hydrocarbon Man is one of conspicuous consumption, of our copious use of surfeit oil, of our love affair with the automobile. By contrast, the story of the Age of Consequence will be not about our use of oil but about the unintended consequences of that use. This is not defeatist, nor should it be construed as alarmist. But it does seek to capture an aspect of the broader tenor of our age, which is marked by key transnational problems.

Transnational Problems and Terrorism

Transnational problems cross borders and regions; affect, influence, and concern many nations and groups worldwide; usually require multilateral cooperation to ameliorate or solve; and involve at least one nonstate actor. For instance, transnational terrorism is often planned and executed across borders, it is conducted by nonstate actors organized across borders and regions, and it cannot be dealt with easily without multilateral cooperation.[51] These characteristics distinguish it from domestic terrorism, but there is no internationally accepted definition of terrorism. That is one of the key obstacles to global counterterrorism efforts. It is important, as most terrorism experts emphasize, that we consider the different groups and even individuals when analyzing terrorism.[52] For purposes of this book, I adopt an approach used in the authoritative UN Security Council Resolution 1566, which refers to terrorism as:

> criminal acts, including against civilians, committed with the intent to cause death or serious bodily injury, or taking of hostages, with the purpose to provoke a state of terror in the general public or in a group of persons or particular persons, intimidate a population or compel a government or an international organization to do or to abstain from doing any act.[53]

---

51. For analyses, see Enders and Sandler, "Patterns"; Gueli, "Bin Laden and Al-Qaeda"; Byman, *Deadly Connections;* and Kepel, *War for Muslim Minds. Milestones,* the classic work by Sayyid Qutb, is at www.globusz.com/ebooks/Milestone/index.htm.

52. Horgan, *Psychology of Terrorism.*

53. The resolution appears at www.un.org/Docs/sc/unsc_resolutions04.html. For additional discussions of definitions of terrorism, see Byman, *Deadly Connections,* esp. 8–10.

Transnational problems have become more prominent not only in our discourses but also in reality. In the post–World War II period, global pollution, poverty, transnational migration, and the proliferation of weapons across regions were submerged under the dominant tides of Cold War politics. Even after the Cold War, they were not given significant attention. For instance, the administrations of President William J. Clinton and especially of President George H. W. Bush were criticized for failing to recognize the transnational terrorist threat and for focusing too much attention on states as critical actors. Critics considered that state-centric model to be the dominant model of the past, of the two world wars and the Cold War, and even of a post–Cold War world dominated by one great power.[54] September 11 highlighted the importance of transnational actors, for the attacks were carried out not by great powers or rogue states but by a transnational terrorist organization.

Contributing to Thought

Much work exists on the links between oil and terrorism. The role of oil has become a global concern, transcending the halls of academe.[55] It is no great insight to say that oil is connected to transnational terrorism. But a number of questions remain underexplored: How is oil linked to the rise of Al-Qaeda, initially formed in 1988 from the ashes of the Soviet War in Afghanistan? To what degree has the U.S. role in the Persian Gulf been driven by oil concerns, and in what measure has its regional presence motivated terrorism? To what extent and in what way is Middle Eastern oil money related to the functioning of Al-Qaeda? To what extent did oil factors motivate the September 11 attacks and the subsequent U.S.-led invasion of Iraq? How has oil been linked to Al-Qaeda's pursuit of weapons of mass destruction? It is worthwhile trying to offer a holistic view of the links between oil and transnational terrorism.

The oil era in the Middle East has taken place in a globalized setting, but we know little about how globalization and Middle Eastern oil have affected terrorism. The notion that we live in a small, interconnected world has become a cliché, bandied about by political pundits and presidents alike, but it is not without meaning. As President Obama eloquently put it, "While the 20th

---

54. For example, this criticism appears in the 9/11 Commission Report.

55. For instance, see Moran and Russell, eds., *Energy Security and Global Politics;* Duffield, *Over a Barrel;* Klare, *Rising Powers;* Rutledge, *Addicted to Oil;* Smil, *Energy at the Crossroads;* and Speth, *Red Sky at Morning.*

century taught us that we share a common destiny, the 21st has revealed a world more intertwined than at any time in human history."[56] Globalization has dramatically altered world politics in putting states and human beings far closer together than ever before, in making territory less defining, in allowing penetration of state borders, in generating instantaneous communications, and in enabling the rise of great cities, from Istanbul to New York to London, through massive migration. But it is far less clear what all this means for key areas of world politics.

Much work explores aspects of globalization and terrorism, but this book seeks to add oil to the mix.[57] It centers not on how globalization might cause terrorism but on how it connects with oil to make terrorism a larger problem. In doing so, it also explores several sub-stories. One sub-story is about American foreign policy. Some might argue that America's regional oil interests and actions have motivated terrorism. That would be simplistic. Two questions are especially important to examine. To what extent and how have U.S. actions in the Middle East been motivated by oil? And how, when, and to what extent have its actions, insofar as they are motivated by oil, provoked Al-Qaeda? One might say that the first question does not really matter, in that terrorists may be provoked by America's actions even if they are not oil-driven. Yet it is important to understand the role of oil in American foreign policy, because it affects foreign policy actions in the first place, actions with potential links to terrorism. It is also important to understand the role of oil because Al-Qaeda identifies oil as a motivator of its actions, as do other radical jihadis.

The United States plays a critical, possibly indispensable role in protecting global oil security, mainly by virtue of its role as gendarme in the Persian Gulf.[58] To understand the potential downside of its commitment to the region, this book discusses the importance of oil in critical events such as the 1990–91 Gulf crisis, the attack of September 11, and the 2003 U.S. invasion of Iraq. It also sketches non-oil factors to highlight the role of oil and to allow readers to make sense of these critical events.

An earlier book of mine, *Crude Awakenings*, identified key economic, political, and security trends and developments from 1973 to 2003 that were related to oil security or the security of global oil supplies. I argued that the potential for serious oil disruptions had decreased from 1970 to 2003 due to numerous developments, even as oil prices rose and became more volatile and even though

---

56. Berlin Speech, July 24, 2008.
57. For example, see Cronin, "Behind the Curve"; and Moghadam, "Motives of Martyrdom."
58. Yetiv, *Crude Awakenings*.

some real threats to oil supply certainly existed. In recent years, the greatest oil disruptions have come from hurricanes and not from "geopolitical" events, lending some support to the earlier book's argument.

Crude Awakenings also argued that while concerns about oil supply disruptions tended to be exaggerated, and that the ability to mitigate them if they occurred had increased, the much bigger problem regarding oil was its connection to transnational problems. But I noted that it was unclear how the effects of the use of oil worsened some of these problems, to what extent it did so, or what this meant more broadly for world politics. This book follows up by exploring these questions with regard to a central transnational problem.

If Middle Eastern oil and globalization have combined to contribute fundamentally to transnational terrorism, will it be an inevitable, crippling feature of the twenty-first century? Not necessarily. If Middle Eastern oil and globalization have been a problematic contributors, positive changes in these two factors might help check terrorism. Some changes of this kind, which I discuss in book's conclusion, may be in the offing, but it will take time to understand if they are temporary in nature.

The Setup of the Book

This book traverses much terrain in the attempt to understand the effects of oil and globalization on transnational terrorism. Chapter 1 explores the role of oil in U.S. foreign policy toward the Middle East, while at the same time identifying key signposts on the road to the Middle Eastern oil era.

Part I of the book analyzes how and to what extent the oil era has exacerbated transnational terrorism. Chapter 2 examines the extent to which oil issues motivated Al-Qaeda terrorism, both on September 11 and in general. Drawing partly on polling data, chapter 3 examines in what measure Al-Qaeda's main conflict with the United States, and the role of oil in this conflict, has fomented anti-Americanism and generated support or sympathy for Al-Qaeda around the world. Chapter 4 explores how oil money or what some call petrodollars are funneled through states, international institutions, complex financial transactions, charities, and religious schools and directly or inadvertently fund transnational terrorism and the proliferation of weapons of mass destruction. In chapter 5, I analyze the connections between oil and democracy and between nondemocracy and terrorism.

Part II of the book argues that globalization has worsened the effects of oil on transnational terrorism. In chapter 6, I explain how globalization and Middle

Eastern oil have joined to contribute to terrorism. Chapter 7 argues that, on the whole, a globalized context tends to favor Al-Qaeda and its affiliates because it generates nodes vulnerable to attack and creates the potential that terrorist attacks will produce major consequences. The conclusion summarizes some key points and analyzes the question of how globalization has impacted the struggle between the terrorists and the United States and its allies.

AMERICA AND MIDDLE EASTERN OIL

The quest for energy starts with the mythical Prometheus, who stole fire from the gods to help shivering humans, and runs through to the modern struggle to ensure oil supplies to a global economy, whose lifeline is black crude. One American official asserted in 1944, referring to the Persian Gulf, that the "oil in this region is the greatest single prize in all history."[1] He could not have known what travails would await America, especially after it assumed responsibility from Great Britain in 1971 for the security of the Persian Gulf, a region that includes Iran, Iraq, Saudi Arabia, Kuwait, Oman, Qatar, Bahrain, and the United Arab Emirates. Nor could he have known how the use of cheap oil would at once drive the global economy and allow for industrialization and bring unforeseen problems for human beings the world over.

This chapter explains the rising role of oil in American foreign policy toward the Middle East and, in doing so, illuminates key signposts of the rise of the oil era in the Middle East. This enables a better understanding of what role American actions may play in motivating terrorism and how those actions are perceived and misperceived. We cannot understand the story of the petroleum triangle without a sense of America's role and of the broader rise of the oil era.

Oil has played an increasingly dominant role for America, drawing it into the region over time.[2] However, not all American actions have been driven by

---

1. Cited in Yergin, *Prize,* 393.
2. For extensive evidence, see Yetiv, *Explaining Foreign Policy.*

oil to the same extent, even though popular accounts may suggest as much. The 1990–91 American-led reversal of Iraq's invasion of Kuwait was far more about oil than the 2003 invasion of Iraq—although Washington would probably not have invaded Iraq in 2003 were it not for a chain of oil-related previous events. Iraq's invasion of Kuwait in 1990, which was fundamentally tied to the eight-year Iran-Iraq War (1980–88), shaped the events that contributed to the U.S. invasion in 2003.[3] Washington would not have had a case against Saddam were it not for the sixteen UN resolutions that Iraq had violated, and these resolutions were issued in response to Iraq's violations of UN Resolution 687 imposed after the 1991 Gulf War. And had Saddam not invaded Kuwait, Washington may never have had reason to fear that he could threaten American and global interests. In fact, that invasion was also linked to oil. Were Kuwaiti oil reserves not so inviting and had Iraq not fought with Kuwait over a host of oil issues, including drilling rights and quota-busting, an Iraqi invasion of Kuwait would have been less likely.

Middle Eastern Oil Discovered

In 1907, a large petroleum field was discovered in Iran. It was the opening salvo of the oil era in the Middle East, although its rapid development would come during World War II and thereafter—at a time when the globalization era was taking off in earnest. By May 1933, Washington and Riyadh made an agreement that would fashion their oil relations for the century. Standard Oil Company of California (SOCAL), founded in 1870, struck a sixty-year contract giving SOCAL the exclusive right to explore and produce oil from Saudi Arabia's Eastern Province. By 1938, the Arabian American Oil Company (Aramco), as it would later be called, first discovered oil in commercial quantities.[4]

The Persian Gulf became vital during the two world wars. The Allies viewed Iran in particular as a vital conduit for sending arms to Russia during World War I, and both the Suez Canal and the petroleum fields of Persia were perceived as critical to Allied interests. Defeating the Ottoman Empire, which had allied with Germany, meant penetrating the Middle East, much of it under direct or indirect Ottoman influence despite the weakening of the Ottoman Empire in the late nineteenth century.

In the years preceding World War I, the discovery of oil allowed Britain to shift its coal-fired navy to one that was oil-fired, allowing it greater speed, power, and maneuverability. Britain had no oil, but it did manage to exploit Iran's burgeoning

---

3. Yetiv, *America and the Persian Gulf.*
4. On the evolution of these relations, see Pollack, "Saudi Arabia," esp. 78–79.

capabilities, establishing the Anglo-Persian Oil Company in 1909 (renamed the Anglo-Iranian Oil Company in 1935 and then British Petroleum in 1954), which discovered significant oil fields in Iran. Oil allowed Britain to maintain mastery of the oceans. For its part, the United States believed it was self-sufficient in 1917 but within a few years started to become nervous that it would exhaust its oil supplies.[5]

During World War II, the oil of the region was vital to the entire Allied war effort. Unlike in World War I, armies required far greater mobility and that resulted in one hundred times the use of gasoline.[6] Oil proved crucial to mechanized warfare on a global scale, raising the specter of oil as the key fuel of the century. Had the Nazis successfully invaded the Gulf area, their control of the oil fields could have shifted the course of the war, because Germany had become oil-constrained by 1943.[7]

The Soviets occupied Iranian Azerbaijan in 1941 in the effort against Adolf Hitler, only to withdraw belatedly in 1946. Later, during the Cold War, perceptions of ongoing Soviet interest in the warm waters of the Gulf triggered Western states to secure the Gulf zealously from their erstwhile wartime ally while also jockeying among themselves for political and economic influence.

After World War II, the United States challenged Britain's key role in commercially exploiting the oil resources of the region, in conjunction with the Saudis. By 1944, U.S. output of the share of known reserves in the Gulf would for the first time overtake all competition.

Oil factored prominently during the Cold War. The West feared that Moscow or some of its clients in the Middle East would gain control over oil resources. Thus, a driving goal was to prevent this outcome. U.S. policy in various forms was to deny Moscow access to Gulf oil supplies and regional influence. In 1949, American decisionmakers even developed a plan, described in National Security Council directive NSC 26/2, to destroy the Gulf oil fields and prevent a Soviet seizure, if necessary.[8]

Countries and OPEC Assume More Power over Oil

The nature and role of outside powers in the Persian Gulf changed over time, but so did the behavior and fortunes of local actors in a way that politicized oil,

---

5. De Novo, "Movement."

6. Yergin, *Prize*, 382.

7. Sachar, *Europe Leaves the Middle East*, 176; Jensen, "Importance of Energy"; and Zubrin, *Energy Victory*, 227–37.

8. Telhami and Hill, "America's Vital Stakes in Saudi Arabia," 170.

further drew Washington into the region, and contributed to problems generated by the oil era in the Middle East. The American overthrow of Iran's popular prime minister, Mohammad Mossadegh, was related to oil. Iran nationalized oil in 1951, after the Shah of Iran was effectively stripped of his powers by the parliament in 1950. That left the Anglo-Iranian Oil Company without portfolio and threatened to make insecure a resource critical to Western fighting capabilities.[9] Washington also feared that Mossadegh was uncomfortably disposed toward the Soviet Union in a period when the Cold War was especially frigid. A U.S.-organized coup put the pro-West leaning Shah back in power in 1953, an act that has muddied U.S.-Iranian relations until the present day and contributed to the perception that Washington was seeking to exploit the region's oil resources. If Iran could kick British Petroleum out of Iran prior to the coup against Mossadegh, the thinking went, other countries in the region might follow suit, stripping the major oil companies of much largesse and influence. In fact, in the 1950s and 1960s, power slowly shifted from businesses to states in the control and pricing of oil. This would tie oil to politics even more. In the first half of the century, the world oil market was dominated by seven major oil companies, known as the Seven Sisters, composed of Exxon (the old Standard Oil of New Jersey), Texaco, Royal Dutch/Shell, Mobil, Gulf, Standard Oil of California (Chevron), and British Petroleum (there were also a few independents, most of them American). The world's proven and exploitable reserves were controlled under contract or owned outright by these companies, but with Iran's nationalization of oil in 1951, this slowly changed.

Back in 1938, the future Aramco first discovered oil in large quantities in Saudi Arabia. Between 1945 and the 1973 Arab oil embargo, the price of oil was posted largely by the big oil companies rather than being determined by the market. The price was based on the need to accommodate the interests of both oil-consuming and oil-producing countries. Historically, all international oil contracts were conducted at a fixed price between the so-called upstream producers and the downstream refiners and retailers, but that would change. By 1960, power began to shift in earnest to oil-producing nations. Decolonization and nation-building pushed many of these states to assert rights over their own resources. OPEC was formed in 1960 in this context, initially by Saudi Arabia, Kuwait, Iran, Iraq, and Venezuela, but later expanded to include Algeria, Ecuador, Gabon, Indonesia, Libya, Angola, Nigeria, Qatar, and the United Arab Emirates.

Few members thought that it would last, much less become a major institution on the global stage. But it proceeded to increase its ability to affect production

---

9. On the seven sisters and the global oil industry, see Yergin, *Prize*. Perhaps the best analysis of this effort is Elm, *Oil, Power, and Principle*.

and pricing in relation to the major oil companies. OPEC slowly took control of that role, thus signaling the weakening of the power of the majors.[10] The rise of Arab nation-state power over global oil was further aided by British decline and American misfortunes in Vietnam, which hamstrung them in the Middle East. Since the global oil order was built on the Anglo-American foundation, the shifting sands below it altered the nature of power over oil.[11]

However, while OPEC market power was rising and the influence of great powers was diminishing, it was not until the 1970s that the Arab states of OPEC demonstrated their power in the global oil arena and the propensity to use it for both economic and political purposes.[12] After the unsuccessful oil embargo during the 1967 Six-Day War, Arab states, led by Saudi Arabia, launched the infamous oil embargo during the 1973 Arab-Israeli War. The sharp rise in oil prices emblazoned the Middle East on the American political psyche and underscored rising dependence on Persian Gulf oil.

Oil during the Cold War

Washington understood the importance of Saudi oil at least as early as the 1930s and began to make informal commitments to Saudi security in the early 1940s. In 1947, President Harry S. Truman and King Abdul Aziz Ibn Saud, the founder of the modern Saudi kingdom, made a pact. Described in a U.S. State Department cable, the United States pledged that if Saudi Arabia were attacked by another power or under threat of attack such as the one that Iraq would later pose in 1990, Washington would take "energetic measures under the auspices of the United Nations to confront such aggression."[13] To Washington, Gulf oil would be vital to prosecuting a war in Europe and possibly beyond against Moscow.[14] Good relations with Arab states were important. Maintaining them while also supporting the state of Israel would become a recurring challenge, one that would become more complex as American involvement in the region increased.

After World War II, the British economy was unable to handle significant foreign commitments. Throughout the entire period between 1945 and 1971, key British statesmen warned that Britain must reduce its foreign commitments to avoid economic crises. By 1965, opposition to the British role in the Gulf had

---

10. This generated a change from a vertically integrated market structure to a deintegrated one. Ait-Laoussine, "Pricing of Oil."
11. Yergin, *Prize*, ch. 28.
12. On the development of OPEC, see Amuzegar, *Managing the Oil Wealth,* ch. 3.
13. Pincus, "Secret Presidential Pledges."
14. McCullough, *Truman,* 541, 599–605.

spread well outside the Labour Party and included a number of influential Tories.[15] Between 1966 and 1970 Britain was hit by serious financial crises that sapped its economic strength.[16] The British regional role had been quasi-hegemonic, although the British left much up to the locals.[17] When Britain withdrew from the Gulf in 1971, responsibility for its security devolved to the United States. But the United States preferred to avoid protecting Gulf stability directly. Rather, Iran and to a much lesser extent Saudi Arabia formed the pillars of President Richard M. Nixon's "twin pillar" strategy, also known as the Nixon Doctrine.

British departure increased America's influence in the Gulf and heightened the USSR's fears that Washington would either seize control of Gulf oil or use the region to undermine Soviet security. In particular, on April 9, 1972, the Soviet Union and Iraq signed the Soviet-Iraqi Treaty of Friendship and Cooperation. It provided for the qualified Soviet use of the Iraqi base at Umm Qasr and increased Soviet-Iraqi economic and especially military cooperation. Moscow became Iraq's top arms supplier and helped create the Iraqi army that invaded Iran in 1980 and Kuwait in 1990. Article 9 stipulated that the parties would continue to "develop cooperation in the strengthening of their defense capabilities," a defense stipulation so strong that it was not even in Soviet treaties with critical countries such as Egypt and India.[18]

The Soviet-Iraqi treaty was of much concern to Washington because it appeared to challenge all of its interests in the region. During the Cold War, the primary aims of the United States in the region were to achieve stability, to limit Soviet influence while avoiding confrontation with Moscow, and to assure access to Persian Gulf energy.[19] One month after the Soviets and Iraq signed this treaty, President Nixon and National Security Advisor Henry Kissinger visited Iran and made a fateful agreement in which Washington promised to provide the Shah of Iran with unrivaled access to U.S. weapons in exchange for his role in protecting U.S. regional security.[20] At the end of the meeting, Nixon stated that the United States would continue to cooperate with Iran in strengthening its defenses as the best hope for regional stability and security.[21]

---

15. Abadi, *Britain's Withdrawal from the Middle East, 1947–1971*, 39, 203.

16. Pickering, *Britain's Withdrawal East of Suez*, esp. ch. 7.

17. Lawson, "Hegemony," 317–37.

18. On the nature of the agreement, see Central Intelligence Agency, "Moscow and the Persian Gulf."

19. U.S. Department of State, "South and Southwest Asia: New Policy Perspectives," IR01136, December 31, 1976, National Security Archive (NSA).

20. Bill, *Eagle and the Lion*, esp. 200–204.

21. U.S. Department of State, "Evolution of the U.S.-Iranian Relationship," IR03555, January 29, 1980, NSA.

Enunciated at Guam in 1969, the famous Nixon Doctrine called on states in Asia to assume greater responsibility for their own security, thus relieving the United States of direct involvement in the region.[22] In line with that doctrine, Washington delegated responsibility for Persian Gulf security to Iran and, to a much lesser extent, Saudi Arabia so that it could avoid post-Vietnam regional conflicts. In exchange for Iran's stabilizing role, Washington sold the Shah copious amounts of conventional weapons, following Nixon's promise to do just that when he visited Iran in May 1972.[23] In the words of Kissinger, the United States "adopted a policy which provided, in effect, that we will accede to any of the Shah's requests for arms purchases from us (other than some sophisticated advanced technology armaments, and with the very important exception, of course, of any nuclear weapons capability."[24] The Shah was entirely right to note, without a hint of understanding that his connection to America would prove controversial with his people, that these arms sales, "whose vastness may prove astonishing," served partly as an indicator from Tehran of strong U.S.-Iran relations.[25] However, these arms sales also underscored just how critical Washington saw its relations with Iran for protecting regional oil and for checking Soviet influence.[26] Arms sales to Iran accounted for one-third of American sales to the world between 1973 and 1978.[27]

From Iranian Revolution to Afghanistan Invasion

The events of 1979 were critical in shaping the oil era, because they left the security of the Persian Gulf at its very nadir and put the United States on a trajectory to becoming the outright regional gendarme. The Islamic zeal of Iran would now overlap a region that was central to the global economy. The United States could not have known that its reliance on Iran would leave it highly vulnerable after the Shah of Iran fled Iran on January 16, 1979, and American hostages were seized by Iranian militants in November. The Iranian Revolution of 1979 destabilized oil-rich Iran and heralded the rise of Ayatollah Khomeini as leader. Khomeini

---

22. Nixon, "U.S. Foreign Policy in the 1970s," 55–56.

23. On these sales, see Bill, *Eagle and the Lion*, 200–201; Sick, *All Fall Down*, 13–15; and Vance, *Hard Choices*, 315.

24. Memo from Henry Kissinger to President Gerald Ford, "Strategy for Your Discussion with the Shah of Iran," IR00955, May 13, 1975, NSA, 3.

25. Memo from American Embassy in Tehran to Secretary of State, "Iranian Involvement in World Affairs Deepens," August 22, 1974 (1974TEHRAN07081), National Archives.

26. Memo from Kissinger to Ford; and Kissinger, *White House Years*, 1263–64.

27. Bill, *Eagle and the Lion*, 202–3; and Ramazani, *United States and Iran*, 47–48.

sought to overthrow politically the oil-rich Arab monarchs whom he considered to be corrupt lackeys of the United States and to reengineer the politics of the Arab Gulf to make it look like Iran's. As such, the Iranian Revolution coincided with, and to a considerable extent spurred, a period of Islamic revivalism.

In December 1979, the Soviets invaded Afghanistan, an act that brought its troops about 320 miles closer to the Gulf and stoked fears that Moscow might try to gain influence over the Persian Gulf that lay beyond Afghanistan. The Russians, it was said, had always wanted a warm water port as well as influence in the Persian Gulf.[28] The perception of Soviet political and military gains in Angola, Ethiopia, South Yemen, and now Afghanistan, coupled with Washington's loss of Iran as an ally and the unending hostage crisis, further damaged U.S. credibility. Not long after the invasion, on January 23, 1980, President James E. Carter issued the Carter Doctrine, which raised the American role in the region to an unprecedented level, adding yet another dimension to the evolving oil era in the Middle East. Largely in response to the Soviet invasion, the Carter Doctrine committed the United States to deter or respond to "outside" as opposed to internal threats to Gulf security.[29] Washington was determined not only to improve its capability to deter "outside" pressure on the Gulf but also to deal with pressures arising within the Gulf.[30] In that spirit, President Ronald W. Reagan stated in October 1981 that there was "no way" the United States could "stand by" and allow Saudi Arabia be threatened to the point that the flow of oil could be shut down.[31] This statement and others of a similar kind later became known as the Reagan Doctrine, which was a U.S. commitment to protect Saudi Arabia against not only external but also internal threats within the Gulf and against domestic threats to the regime. The United States made a tacit agreement to protect the Saudis in the 1940s and the Carter Doctrine asserted a U.S. commitment to protect the free flow of oil from threats outside the region; now Reagan was elevating the U.S. commitment one more notch. Saudi Arabia would become the linchpin of U.S. security in the Gulf region.

Middle Eastern Oil and American Intervention

In the midst of the momentous events of 1979, Saddam Hussein, after a decade as the de facto dictator of Iraq, would become president of the country in July

---

28. Curzon, *Russia in Central Asia;* and Hauner, "Last Great Game."
29. On the Nixon and Carter doctrines, see Palmer, *Guardians of the Gulf,* 85–111.
30. Veliotes, "U.S. Policy toward the Persian Gulf," 9.
31. Reagan, *Public Papers,* 873, 952.

1979. In September 1980, Iraq invaded next-door Iran, triggering one of the century's bloodiest wars with more than one million casualties. Neither side ultimately won—an outcome many in the world wanted—but Saddam Hussein was not done. In many ways, the bloody and lengthy Iran-Iraq War (1980–88) set the stage for Iraq's invasion of Kuwait in 1990, which was fundamentally tied to oil but had multiple causes.[32] The Iran-Iraq War devastated Iraq's economy and left it heavily indebted to Kuwait and Saudi Arabia. They had loaned Saddam considerable amounts for the war against revolutionary Iran, which they feared more than Iraq. Estimates suggest that Iraq began that war with $35 billion (U.S.) in reserve and ended the war $80 to $100 billion (U.S.) in debt. Iraqi Foreign Minister Tariq Aziz claimed shortly after the invasion of Kuwait in 1990 that Baghdad had to "resort to this method" of invasion because Iraq's economic situation had deteriorated and it had no alternative.[33] Kuwait was quite a tempting economic prize.

Iraq also emerged from the first war a much stronger military power than Iran. That Iraq did not have to contend with a powerful Iran on its border presumably made an invasion of Kuwait more plausible.[34] Moreover, Iraq's huge standing army, expanded during the Iran-Iraq War, could not be effectively reintegrated into the shaky Iraqi economy after the war. And like Napoleon, Saddam may have understood that an idle, restless army poses a greater threat to the regime than one kept busy in war. The invasion also appealed to Iraqis who viewed Kuwait as a part of historical Iraq.[35] The merger of Iraq and Kuwait after the 1990 invasion wed the two countries and, in Iraq's mind, fixed history.[36] Under Ottoman rule, Iraq was not a unified or independent state. Rather, it consisted of three disparate provinces—Mosul, Baghdad, and Basra. From Iraq's perspective, Kuwait was always part of Basra under the Ottoman Empire. Iraq's Baathist Party ideology also may have played a role. It sought to sweep away artificial borders, and Saddam wanted to unite the Arab world behind Baghdad. He would even assert

32. See Yetiv, *America and the Persian Gulf.*
33. Cairo MENA, in Foreign Broadcast Information Service (FBIS): Near East and South Asia (NES), August 13, 1990, 5.
34. In a letter to Iran's President Hashemi Rafsanjani on August 15, Saddam even called on Iran to help Iraq confront the "evil doers who seek to inflict evil on Muslims and the Arab nation." Baghdad, Republic of Iraq Radio, August 15, 1990, in BBC Summary of World Broadcasts, August 16, 1990.
35. For excellent background analysis, see Schofield, *Kuwait and Iraq.*
36. On Iraq's view, see the Aziz statement in Baghdad AL-THAWRAH, FBIS: NES, September 12, 1990, pp. 26–32. Also, see FBI interviews with Saddam Hussein, Interview Session no. 13, March 11, 2004. Saddam asserts that Kuwait is Iraqi and that the Kuwaitis were arrogant prior to his invasion. Available at www.gwu.edu/~nsarchiv/NSAEBB/NSAEBB279/index.htm, accessed September 10, 2010.

that it was during war that the Iraqi army "rose to the level of the [Islamic] mission," trying pass off Baathist Party ideology as something holy.[37]

Saddam's personal ambitions, above and beyond state or institutional interests, further pushed Iraq to invade Kuwait. A few months before the outbreak of the war, he spoke in typical terms of Iraq achieving great "glory," calling on the faithful to play a role in this unfolding of history.[38] However, the more immediate cause was Iraq's growing tensions with Kuwait. At the Arab League summit meeting in May 1990, Saddam attacked Gulf states, particularly Kuwait, for not treating oil production quotas seriously, keeping oil prices down, refusing to forgive Iraq's war debts from the Iran-Iraq War, and failing to provide war reconstruction credits.[39] Even though Iraq had attacked Iran in September 1980, Baghdad repeatedly argued that it had sacrificed treasure and blood to check Iran's fundamentalist Islamic threat to all Arab states, especially the Gulf monarchies, which Iran's Ayatollah Khomeini had wanted to overthrow through political means. Thus, from Iraq's perspective at least, Iraq deserved Arab allegiance and economic support, and Kuwait could not expect to get a free ride on Iraq's military back.[40] Because the Kuwaitis and Saudis were not particularly forthcoming with postwar economic support and because Iraq's economy was devastated, Saddam sought to raise money for economic recovery by limiting OPEC production and trying to increase the price of oil. To add to tensions, Kuwait may well have indirectly lowered oil prices by pumping too much oil, some from the Rumaila oil field, over which Iraq laid joint claim. Iraq also accused Kuwait of slant drilling into this oil field. By starting oil wells on their side of the Iraq-Kuwait border and angling their oil equipment under the border, the Kuwaitis could draw on oil from Iraqi sources. Interestingly, in January 2001, Aziz asserted that Kuwait "got what it deserved" in 1990 because it was undermining Iraq's oil prices and slant drilling.[41]

Kuwait was reluctant to bend to Saddam's brinkmanship, perhaps not recognizing his seriousness despite the massive Iraqi presence on Kuwait's borders. On July 25, U.S. Ambassador to Iraq April Glaspie met with Saddam Hussein. In responding to Saddam's queries about U.S. intentions, she made

37. Quoted in Bengio, *Saddam's Word*, 37.

38. Quoted in ibid., 155.

39. Speech by Saddam Hussein to the Arab Summit Conference in Baghdad, in FBIS: NES, May 29, 1990, p. 5. On the quotas, Iraq recognized that Kuwait did change its position but said that Kuwait's behavior suggested it was a ploy. See interview with Iraqi First Deputy Prime Minister Taha Yasin Ramadan, in London AL-TADAMUN, FBIS: NES, October 30, 1990, p. 24.

40. On Iraq's view, see the Aziz statement in Baghdad AL-THAWRAH, FBIS: NES, September 12, 1990, pp. 30–31.

41. Quoted in "Saddam Says He Won the War," *APS Diplomat Recorder*, vol. 54, January 20, 2001.

the now-infamous statement that the United States had "no opinion on the Arab-Arab conflicts, like your border disagreement with Kuwait."[42] Saddam asserted in an interview in 1992 that he saw her statement as providing a green light to invade Kuwait. Whether or not this is true, he certainly did not expect such a strong response from Washington. On August 2, Iraq invaded Kuwait and added yet another dimension to the oil era in the Middle East: one Arab state, for the first time ever, would invade and annex another—and in the heart of the world's biggest oil region no less.

The American-led Response

Washington was concerned centrally by the threat that Iraq's invasion posed to global and, in turn, U.S. economic interests through the potential domination of the regional oil.[43] After invading Kuwait, Iraq controlled 19 percent of the world's oil. A potential invasion of Saudi Arabia would raise that to approximately 44 percent. If left unopposed, Iraq might gain enough capability to blackmail other Arab states into supporting its inflated foreign policy agenda, to threaten Israel, and to push global oil prices higher, which would allow it to build weapons of mass destruction (WMD). Thus, while the United States received only 8.7 percent of its oil from Iraq and Kuwait combined, Iraq's invasion still posed a serious threat in a world of global interdependence.

After some discussions with Washington, Riyadh accepted the U.S. view of the potential Iraqi threat. As General Khalid bin Sultan, the commander of Saudi forces, put it, Saudi Arabia may have been targeted, but even if it were not, Iraq could dictate terms on "all important matters—particularly oil policy and foreign affairs."[44] Meanwhile, the United States was anxious to deter a possible invasion of Saudi Arabia, and King Fahd did not want to wait for an "unambiguous" threat from Iraq, as some of his advisers counseled, noting that the Kuwaitis had done just that.[45] Photographs from America's Central Intelligence Agency (CIA) revealed to him that Iraq's forces were less than 250 miles from Saudi oil fields and within striking range of Riyadh.

---

42. For the transcript of the Glaspie meeting, see "Excerpts from Iraqi Document on Meeting with U.S. Envoy," A19.

43. For extensive evidence, see Yetiv, *Explaining Foreign Policy,* ch. 2.

44. Sultan, *Desert Warrior,* esp. 19.

45. Fahd was also aware of Saddam's Machiavellian nature. After all, he suggested to Fahd twice in the 1980s that they divide the small Arab Gulf states between them. "Road to War."

President George H. W. Bush was convinced that Iraq had Saudi Arabia in his sights, which added urgency to his counteroffensive.[46] After obtaining Saudi agreement for U.S. access, he began to inform the public of the U.S. approach. In an August 8 national address, he asserted that U.S. goals included the unconditional withdrawal of all Iraqi forces from Kuwait, removal of a puppet regime put in place by Iraq and restoration of Kuwait's legitimate government, the long-standing and historical role of protecting oil, and the protection of the lives of Americans abroad.

The United States sent a massive army to kick Iraqi forces out of Kuwait. The U.S.-led alliance of twenty-eight members grew to thirty-seven by war's end and included more than half a million soldiers, with a 10,000-soldier brigade from the Arab Gulf states, 7,000 Kuwaiti soldiers, and 15,000 Syrian troops fighting only on Kuwaiti soil. On the European side, the British sent 43,000 troops and significant military equipment, while France sent 16,000 soldiers. By January 1991, an incredible 50 percent of all U.S. combat forces worldwide would be deployed to the Gulf theater.

War became even more likely because of a particular dynamic that was in play. The United States believed that even if Iraq were to withdraw peacefully, it would just return another day. Meanwhile, Iraq must have considered what the United States would do if it withdrew. And since Iraq could not have known U.S. intentions, it presumed the United States might attack, even if Iraq withdrew unconditionally.[47] Saddam Hussein asserted in 2004 that he believed that the United States would have attacked anyway.[48] The U.S.-led coalition evicted Iraqi forces from Kuwait, but Saddam did not fall from power, as many had expected—including President Bush—thus adding a wild card to global oil markets.

Iraq's Defiance of UN Resolutions

After the war, Iraq faced containment under UN sanctions. UN Resolution 687 in particular mandated full disclosure of all of Iraq's ballistic missile stocks and production facilities over 150 kilometers in range, all nuclear materials, all chemical and biological weapons and facilities, and cooperation in their destruction. Paragraphs 10 through 12 required Iraq to "unconditionally undertake not to use, develop, construct, or acquire" WMD. UN Resolution 687 also forced Iraq to

---

46. Bush interview with Sir David Frost, PBS, January 16, 1996.
47. For extensive analysis of this dynamic, see Yetiv, *Explaining Foreign Policy.*
48. See NSA, Interview Session no. 4, February 13, 2004, available at www.gwu.edu/~nsarchiv/NSAEBB/NSAEBB279/index.htm.

accept the UN demarcated border with Kuwait, the sovereignty of Kuwaiti territory, and UN peacekeepers on the Iraq-Kuwait border.[49]

For its part, the Clinton administration executed a policy toward the Persian Gulf called "dual containment," referring to the containment of both Iraq
and Iran. Washington believed that previous efforts to placate Iran and Iraq in
the 1980s in the effort to moderate their behavior had failed. Iran was already
under numerous military and economic constraints that extended back to the
1979 hostage crisis. All military exchanges were prohibited and most economic
forms as well, although trade between the two states was higher than one might
expect. Diplomatic relations were severed in 1980, and Iran was placed on the
State Department's list of state sponsors of terrorism in 1984.

Dual containment aimed not only to impede the ability of Iran and Iraq to
threaten neighbors but also to undermine their ability to build military capabilities. Washington explored how the Iraqi opposition might overthrow Saddam
and also took a tougher line on Iran than had the Bush team. As one official points
out, Brent Scowcroft, National Security Advisor under Bush, was trying to create
an opening to Iran in the early 1990s, but the Clinton administration dropped
that approach rather clearly.[50] The United States took measures to unseat the
dictator. For instance, in 1996 the CIA tried to overthrow Saddam in cooperation
with the Iraq National Congress and the Iraq National Accord, two major opposition groups, but Saddam defeated them in August 1996 when the United States
proved incapable of protecting anti-Saddam forces against his military forces.
American policy toward Iran was much less openly hostile, but nonetheless, it
was also based on the notion that its regime needed to be changed.

By 1998, the United States started to see Saddam's removal as a more pressing
necessity for generating stability in the Persian Gulf. That type of thinking, which
emerged slowly, represented a shift in previous policies. Indeed, during the Iran-
Iraq War, the United States bolstered Iraq and placated Saddam after it. In the
1991 Gulf War, it hoped to kill Saddam but would not venture into Iraq to do so.
Then in the 1990s, it decided to contain him in every way possible, but its official
policy was not regime change. That would shift in earnest in 1998.

Sanctions were doing less than the United Nations intended, and Iraq's failure
to abide by UN Resolution 687 raised suspicions that it had WMD capability. Such
suspicions solidified over time and created the potential for the George W. Bush
administration to push for the ouster of Saddam's regime by force in 2003. Iraq's
defiance peaked in particular in 1998. In mid-January, Baghdad blocked a series

---

49. For the texts of major UN resolutions adopted in 1991, see Congressional Research Service,
"U.N. Security Resolutions on Iraq."

50. Off-the record, August 10, 2009.

of planned inspections of Saddam's presidential sites, which it believed should be off-limits. It then demanded a three-month moratorium on inspections and a six-month deadline for lifting sanctions altogether, irrespective of its disarmament status and in violation of the basic thrust of UN Resolution 687 and subsequent UN resolutions requiring that the UN give Iraq a clean bill before sanctions could be lifted. Such conflicts with Iraq continued throughout the year, forcing the United States to try to shore up its support in Europe and the Persian Gulf.[51]

In August 1998, Saddam, angry that UN Special Commission on Iraq (UNSCOM) would not give Iraq a clean bill of health, ceased cooperating with UN inspectors, although he did allow some monitoring activities to proceed. However, on October 31, 1998, Iraq raised the stakes by shutting down all international inspection and monitoring activities. UNSCOM came to an end on December 16, 1998, when it withdrew from Iraq. The United States responded with Operation Desert Fox in December 1998. A total of forty ships participated, with ten of them firing over three hundred Tomahawk missiles and ninety cruise missiles over a period of several days. Saddam was now free of UN inspectors, and Washington feared that he would be even more able to pursue his WMD programs. It had grown tired of playing games with Saddam, trying to contain him, enforcing no-fly zones, and trying to keep the international coalition intact. As U.S. Secretary of State Madeleine Albright pointed out, the United Nations had been "given the job of doing something never before done—disarming a country without militarily occupying it."[52] That very fact allowed Iraq to try to elude sanctions and presented Washington with a significant, perhaps unbridgeable, problem.

Over time, it became clear that containing Iran and Iraq would be no easy task. The policy of dual containment began to falter, given the rising international criticism, global noncooperation with Washington's approach, enduring Iraqi intransigence, and Iran's resurgence in the region.[53] Iran and Iraq defied sanctions with some efficacy, but Iraq's case gained more public and official attention in Washington, raising the prospect for regime change one more notch in decisionmaking circles.[54]

The U.S.-led Invasion of Iraq

With the perennial issue of how to contain Iran and Iraq still in the minds of American policymakers, the attacks of September 11, 2001, galvanized the nation

---

51. Albright, *Madam Secretary,* 357–62.
52. Ibid., 349.
53. For a detailed account, see Pollack, *Threatening Storm,* 77–108.
54. On Iran, see Alikhani, *Sanctioning Iran,* esp. ch. 10.

and the administration of George W. Bush to take action against Al-Qaeda. In October 2001, the United States launched Operation Enduring Freedom, which involved attacks on the Taliban regime in Afghanistan. By the end of September, efforts had failed to pressure the radical Taliban, which ruled Afghanistan, into giving up Osama Bin Laden and Al-Qaeda militants. By late October, Taliban strongholds were under heavy attack, but the regime remained defiant behind the leadership of the Mullah Mohammed Omar, the Commander of the Faithful of the Islamic Emirate of Afghanistan and a close associate of Bin Laden. The Taliban regime soon fell, all known Al-Qaeda training sites were destroyed, and a number of Al-Qaeda and Taliban leaders were captured or killed. Evidently anticipating an American attack, many in Al-Qaeda scattered to fight another day. Even as the war in Afghanistan was being waged, speculation emerged about whether the United States would turn its guns on Iraq.

Immediate Background to the 2003 Invasion

As a pivotal moment in the crisis, President Bush addressed the United Nations on September 12, 2002. He demanded that Iraq immediately comply with the previous sixteen UN resolutions passed between 1991 and 2002. Bush believed that Baghdad was continuing to pursue WMD and missile delivery systems, which represented a "grave and gathering danger" to American and global security and hurt UN credibility. In a letter sent to Congress in late September 2002, the White House enumerated Iraq's failure to meet numerous UN Security Council resolutions and asked Congress to pass a resolution allowing the administration to "use all means" to "defend the national security interests of the United States against the threat posed by Iraq and restore international peace and security to the region."[55] Congress obliged, and the UN Security Council, after some political wrangling, also unanimously passed Resolution 1441 on November 8, 2002, by a vote of 15 to 0.[56] It required Baghdad to admit UN inspectors from the UN Monitoring, Verification, and Inspection Commission (UNMOVIC) and the International Atomic Energy Agency (IAEA) and to comply fully with all foregoing resolutions. The resolution held that Iraq "has been and remains in material breach" of its obligations under previous UN resolutions, gave Iraq thirty days to declare its WMD to the UN Security Council, and underscored that false statements would constitute a further "material breach" for which Iraq could face serious consequences.[57]

---

55. Excerpted in Wald, "Approval."

56. For the text of the resolution, see *Arms Control Today* 32 (December 2002): 28–32.

57. Major UN resolutions adopted in 1991 appear in Congressional Research Service, "U.N. Security Resolutions on Iraq."

However, the consequences of committing another "material breach" were interpreted differently among the Security Council members, which may have led them to believe that it had some room for maneuver. Iraq did move to comply with UN Resolution 1441 by allowing UN inspectors back into the country and by submitting twelve thousand pages and several compact discs of information to the UN that supposedly described its capabilities. Baghdad asserted that it lacked WMD programs and had no WMD in storage. Chief UN weapons inspector Hans Blix issued a report in January 2003 that was critical of Iraq's efforts to disarm or cooperate with UN inspectors.[58] He observed that serious questions remained about Iraq's chemical and biological weapons capability, some of which he believed was unaccounted for in Iraq's disclosures to the United Nations.

As Colin Powell explained to the UN in his famous appearance on February 5, 2003, "We haven't accounted for the anthrax, we haven't accounted for the botulinum, the VX, bulk biological agents, growth media, 30,000 chemical and biological munitions."[59] On February 10, Blix offered a more optimistic account of Iraq's cooperation, seeing in Iraq a new "positive attitude," and requested additional time for inspections.[60] Russia, Germany, and France in particular seized on Blix's report to try to impede the American and British drive toward war, to no avail.

The United States and Great Britain may well have concluded that Saddam was simply engaging in more games with UN inspectors and that Iraq did not meet the conditions of UN Resolution 1441 or previous UN resolutions. They moved to present the eighteenth resolution against Iraq, which, in essence, called for war. To pass this resolution, the United States needed the support of nine of the fifteen Security Council members while avoiding a veto by any of the four other permanent members of the Security Council. The Security Council had unanimously supported the seventeenth resolution, but the underlying differences about going to war complicated U.S. efforts to pass the eighteenth resolution. Russia, and especially France, threatened to veto it, though Moscow avoided an open breach with Washington.[61] Washington and London offered somewhat different justifications for war but argued similarly that Iraq's violations of the previous seventeen UN resolutions gave them sufficient basis for using force. As a result, they gave Saddam, his sons, and key elites the opportunity to leave the country within forty-eight hours or face war. Saddam rejected the ultimatum, possibly fearing that the United States would eventually track him down

---

58. Hans Blix, "Update on Inspection," Report of the Executive Chairman of UNMOVIC to the United Nations Security Council, New York, January 27, 2003, available at www.un.org/Depts/unmovic/Bx27.htm.

59. Excerpted in *New York Times*, February 23, 2003.

60. Linzer, "Iraq Approves."

61. Gustafson, *Changing Course?* 2–3.

wherever he went or that he could survive the American-led onslaught to fight another day. Some strong evidence also suggests that he did not expect a massive American onslaught but rather a more limited attack and preferred to maintain the myth of his WMD potential as a deterrent chiefly against Iran but also against a broader American invasion.[62] In another interpretation, it is possible that he and his generals planned to disperse into a guerrilla movement, with greater chances of evicting American forces from Iraq through a war of attrition. Minutes of a meeting of his top commanders chaired by Saddam underscores this interpretation.[63] Whatever the case, Operation Iraqi Freedom was launched against Iraq on March 19, 2003. Saddam and his regime soon fell, though he survived the onslaught.

Non-Oil Factors in Going to War

The United States offered three key reasons for going to war, which at least point to its motivations.[64] An examination of this case suggests that oil was not a primary motivation of the U.S.-led invasion, but it was not irrelevant either.

We now know that Iraq had destroyed its WMD well before the United States invaded in 2003.[65] However, as of August 14, 2002, National Security Advisor Condoleezza Rice chaired a principals meeting that laid out U.S. goals in Iraq in a draft of a National Security Presidential Directive entitled "Iraq: Goals, Objectives and Strategy," which the president signed into effect on August 29. It emphasized the desire to free Iraq in order to eliminate WMD, to end its regional threat, to create democracy in Iraq, and to limit the chance of a WMD attack on the United States or its friends and allies.[66]

The intelligence to which the Bush administration was privy was contained chiefly in a top-secret document that was made available to all members of Congress in October 2002, days before the House and Senate voted to authorize Bush to use force in Iraq. This National Intelligence Estimate (NIE), which reflected the combined U.S. intelligence community's most authoritative judgments, was titled "Iraq's Continuing Programs for Weapons of Mass Destruction." It asserted, "Iraq has continued its weapons of mass destruction programs in defiance of UN resolutions and restrictions. Baghdad has chemical and biological weapons as well as missiles with ranges in excess of UN restrictions; if left unchecked, it probably

---

62. Gordon and Trainor, *Cobra II,* 64–65, 121.
63. Bodansky, *Secret History of the Iraq War,* 5.
64. On the war's motivations, see Freedman, "War In Iraq."
65. On Saddam's views on this matter, see NSA, "Casual Conversation."
66. Woodward, *Plan of Attack,* 155.

will have a nuclear weapon during this decade."[67] President Bush claimed that if the Iraqi regime is "able to produce, buy, or steal an amount of highly enriched uranium a little larger than a single softball, it could have a nuclear weapon in less than a year."[68] In September 2002, he cited a British intelligence report indicating that Iraq could launch a chemical or biological attack forty-five minutes after the order was given to do so.[69] The administration also described Iraq as capable of using WMD against the United States, a position that was not shared by the intelligence analysts who had written the NIE.

For their part, senior U.S. officials repeatedly asserted that Iraq was seeking to rebuild its nuclear program and to obfuscate the use of facilities by placing them underground or camouflaging them. In this view, inspections could not stop these activities, and even if they could, Iraq would resume them once the inspectors had left the country.[70] In the case that Iraq did not possess actual capabilities, the administration believed that it had the intellectual infrastructure and intent to produce them. That alone was enough of a threat after September 11 to motivate U.S. action against Iraq. The administration did not trumpet this argument because it was less marketable than other arguments for war.[71] Yet in August 2002, Vice President Richard Cheney asserted, "If the United States could have preempted 9/11, we would have, no question. Should we be able to prevent another, much more devastating attack, we will, no question."[72] The view was that Saddam had given the administration enough reason to have serious doubts about his intentions in a post-9/11 environment. As Bush asserted in his January 28, 2003, State of the Union speech, a "brutal dictator, with a history of reckless aggression, with ties to terrorism, with great potential wealth, will not be permitted to dominate a vital region and threaten the United States."[73]

The Bush administration also asserted that it was concerned about Iraq's ties to terrorism. This concern played to, or was buoyed by, the fact that a majority of Americans (53% to 64% in an August 2002 Gallup poll) believed that Saddam Hussein was directly involved in the 9/11 attacks. Prior to the 9/11 attacks, the administration was not especially concerned about Al-Qaeda. Evidently, Bush did not receive even one brief from Richard Clarke, his chief counterterrorism

---

67. Central Intelligence Agency, *National Intelligence Estimate: Iraq's Continuing Programs.*

68. The White House, "President Bush Outlines Iraqi Threat," October 7, 2002.

69. Remarks by the President on Iraq in the Rose Garden, September 26, 2002, available at http://georgewbush-whitehouse.archives.gov/news/releases/2002/09/20020926-7.html.

70. Katzman, *Iraq,* 10–11.

71. On how the war was sold, see Kaufmann, "Threat Inflation."

72. "Risks of Inaction Are Far Greater Than the Risk of Action," Address to the 103rd National Convention of the Veterans of Foreign Wars, August 26, 2002.

73. The full text of the State of the Union is available at www.gpoaccess.gov/sou/index.html, accessed September 10, 2010.

expert prior to 9/11.[74] In Clarke's account, the administration was stuck in bureaucratic inertia and politics and unable to make sensible adjustments to the Al-Qaeda threat until the 9/11 shock wave, and Rice was slow to respond to his suggestions to take action against Al-Qaeda.[75] Ironically, on September 10, 2001, she was in the process of preparing a National Security Directive on how to eliminate Al-Qaeda.[76] After September 11, the administration appeared to be concerned about, even obsessed with, the connection between WMD and terrorist organizations, as suggested in many speeches by top American officials, including Cheney.[77]

To what extent the administration manipulated intelligence to support the war may not be fully known for some time. However, it seems clear that it was concerned that Iraq could conceivably support Al-Qaeda. Evidence for this interpretation came in the now-famous Downing Street Memo, which summarizes a July 23, 2002, meeting of British Prime Minister Tony Blair with his top security advisers. In the memo, which are the actual minutes of the meeting, the head of Britain's MI-6 intelligence service reports on his high-level visit to Washington that "Bush wanted to remove Saddam through military action, justified by the conjunction of terrorism and WMD. But the intelligence and facts were being fixed around the policy."[78]

The argument that Iraq was linked to Al-Qaeda proved faulty.[79] Saddam Hussein emphasized in interviews with the FBI what we had already suspected: he and Bin Laden had sharply contrasting ideologies and goals and were uncooperative.[80] Nonetheless, in describing Saddam after 9/11, Bush asserted that "all his terrible features became much more threatening. Keeping Saddam in a box looked less and less feasible to me."[81] In the words of Secretary of State Donald Rumsfeld, "We acted because we saw the existing evidence in a new light, through the prism of our experience on September 11th," which highlighted America's vulnerability to states with WMD and connections to terrorists.[82]

74. Clarke, *Against All Enemies,* 26, 237–38.

75. Ibid.; and Memorandum from Richard A. Clarke to Condoleezza Rice, National Security Council, Washington D.C., January 25, 2001.

76. Woodward, *Bush at War,* 34–35.

77. Dick Cheney, "Speech to the Council on Foreign Relations," Washington, D.C., February 15, 2002, available at www.cfr.org/publication/4346/launch_of_the_maurice_r_greenberg_center_for_geoeconomic_studies_with_vice_president_dick_cheney.html.

78. Downing Street Memo Text, available at http://downingstreetmemo.com/memos.html.

79. Kaufmann, "Threat Inflation." For a view that the Al-Qaeda connection to Iraq was real, see Bodansky, *Secret History,* ch. 3.

80. National Security Archive, "Casual Conversation."

81. Quoted in Woodward, *Plan of Attack,* 27.

82. "Testimony by Secretary of Defense Donald H. Rumsfeld."

Some scholars have argued, as has Saddam Hussein in his interviews with the FBI, that the administration used the WMD threat to justify a war that it had already decided to launch even before 9/11.[83] That does not seem likely. September 11 not only gave the administration a basis for garnering public support for war it had lacked, but it also affected its strategic calculations decisively, animating it to take major actions against even a very small chance that terrorists could obtain WMD.[84]

Bush made it known early on that he thought Iraq was involved in the 9/11 attacks, and he repeated the mantra that Iraq was linked to dangerous terrorist groups.[85] He had Iraq on his radar screen but wanted to wait for the right time to get Saddam, although he did order the creation of contingency plans for forceful regime change.[86] For his part, Rumsfeld, having been advised that Al-Qaeda may well have planned the 9/11 attacks, reportedly asked for plans to invade Iraq in the hours following the attacks.[87] Bush sought contingency plans for such an attack, although he was slow in forming his decision.[88]

The United States was also motivated by an interest in democratizing Iraq and sowing democratic seeds in the Middle East. It did not fixate on democratization initially as a motivation for war, but it would be a mistake to consider it simply an afterthought.

Oil, Perceived National Interests, and the Iraq War

The United States has viewed access to Persian Gulf oil as vital to U.S. and global security, but, as discussed elsewhere in this book, little evidence exists that it sought to steal this oil by invading Iraq in 2003.[89] The invasion of Iraq was not fundamentally about oil, but, in several ways, oil may well have been one of the motivations. If the September 11 attacks presaged the 2003 invasion, and if these attacks were partly tied to oil, then that is one indirect connection.

---

83. National Security Archive, "Casual Conversation."

84. For some inside information on this point, see Suskind, *One Percent Doctrine*.

85. Woodward, *Bush at War*, 99; and Radio Address by the President to the Nation, Office of the Press Secretary, December 7, 2002.

86. This paragraph is based on Gordon and Trainor, *Cobra II*.

87. Clarke, *Against All Enemies*, 30.

88. Rice, "Testimony." See also Freedman, "War in Iraq," 18–19. On the impact of 9/11, see Woodward, *Bush at War*, 34–35. On the decisionmaking process, see "U.S. Decision on Iraq Has Puzzling Past: Opponents of War Wonder When, How Policy Was Set," *Washington Post*, January 12, 2003.

89. As even some critics of U.S. foreign policy acknowledged. Rutledge, *Addicted to Oil*; National Security Directive 54, The White House, Washington, D.C., January 15, 1991; and Yetiv, *Explaining Foreign Policy*.

In addition, both Bush and Cheney expressed concern that Iraq had a considerable portion of the world's oil reserves and that if Saddam Hussein obtained WMD, he would attempt to dominate the rest of the oil-rich Persian Gulf.[90] Of course, his aggressive and violent track record in the region bolstered such views. Iraq invaded both Iran and Kuwait at least in part to achieve greater regional influence and possibly hegemony. After 9/11, the Bush administration saw special dangers in allowing him to gain such power.

In this sense, oil was tied to the fear of a dictator obtaining WMD. Oil could fund such weapons, and such weapons could be used to dominate regional oil. Thus, on September 17, 2002, the White House published a document titled "The National Strategy to Combat Weapons of Mass Destruction." Bush asserted again that America would not "permit the world's most dangerous regimes and terrorists to threaten us with the world's most destructive weapons."[91]

The 9/11 attacks also led many in Washington and around the world to question Saudi stability and its role as a global oil anchor.[92] Questions about Saudi stability had been in the air for decades, with scholars predicting the fall of the regime, even its near-imminent demise.[93] However, the fact that fifteen of the nineteen hijackers came from Saudi Arabia heightened concerns about the Saudi regime's stability. People wondered whether hatred for the United States was a more severe problem in the kingdom than previously believed. If Al-Qaeda loathed the regime and enjoyed some sympathy in Saudi Arabia, how stable could the regime be? Might it fall to religious zealots who might use oil as a weapon or change Saudi oil policies? The 9/11 attacks also raised questions about whether Al Qaeda's attacks were intended to create a schism in U.S.-Saudi relations, thus hurting the legitimacy of the Saudi regime, which, after all, was one of their primary targets.

Not only were the terrorists from oil-rich Saudi Arabia, but their extremist views were shaped in the Saudi political and religious milieu. Concerns also arose in Washington, which proved exaggerated in many ways, about whether or not elements in the Saudi regime actually supported the terrorists, suggesting a radical element within the royal family itself. Or possibly that the regime had turned a blind eye to the terrorists either because it did not want to confront them or because its own religious system had hatched them.

---

90. Mann, *Rise of the Vulcans,* 341.

91. White House, "National Strategy to Combat Weapons of Mass Destruction," September 17, 2002.

92. Klare, *Blood and Oil,* 84–90.

93. As was evident in an intelligence briefing in which this author participated. Meridien Center, Washington, D.C., 1996.

By raising fears of oil insecurity in the Middle East, September 11 pushed the United States to seek alternative suppliers of oil. Russia figured prominently in this effort, as did Africa and the Caspian Basin—and quite possibly Iraq. Following the 9/11 attacks, Russia repeatedly let Washington know that it would be willing to offer its oil fields as a secure alternative to Mideast oil. President Vladimir Putin, in fact, asserted in October 2001 that as "instability in the world directly impacts world markets, Russia remains a reliable and predictable partner and supplier of oil."[94] This sentiment continued into 2002. Shortly after Putin met Bush in late May 2002, reports surfaced that Russia had offered to supply the United States with oil to make up for any shortfalls arising from a disruption of Mideast oil.[95]

The invasion of Iraq may have, in some measure, been driven by a similar interest to diversify global sources of oil. With both Saudi Arabia and the U.S.-Saudi relationship less stable, securing Iraq's vast oil resources made more sense. Iraq's oil production could be in friendlier Iraqi hands. This would give the West some greater leverage for obtaining oil in the event of political or security problems in Saudi Arabia. Even if the Saudi regime was initially stable, U.S.-Saudi tensions might mount over time, thus making Iraq more important in diversifying oil supply.

The Iran-Iraq War, the Gulf War, subsequent UN sanctions, periodic American military attacks, and Saddam's own mismanagement and corruption had curtailed Iraq's potential and left its oil infrastructure in disarray. Various UN resolutions, including UN Resolution 1284, allowed for Iraq to open its industry to foreign investors and to increase production significantly, provided that Baghdad permitted UN inspectors to rid it of WMD. But its cooperation was never viewed as satisfactory by the UN and, of course, by the United States.

Iraq has an estimated 112.5 billion barrels of known reserves, which places it second only to Saudi Arabia's 262 billion barrels. With a totally rebuilt oil infrastructure and political stability, it could increase oil production to an estimated 6 to 12 mb/d within a decade.[96] In early 1990, prior to the invasion of Kuwait, Baghdad had planned to raise production and export capacity to 6 mb/d by 1996.[97]

Another possible oil motivation was that an invasion could liberate Iraq's oil resources in other ways. Under Saddam, foreign investment from outside the

---

94. Quoted in Wines and Tavernise, "Russian Oil Production," A3.
95. Williams, "OPEC Restraint," 76.
96. Iraq could eventually triple its current production capacity. EIA, *Annual Energy Outlook 2002.*
97. Al-Chalabi, "Iraqi Oil Policy."

Arab world was outlawed, thus denying Iraq the knowledge, experience, capital, and management to exploit its oil potential.[98] Washington may have thought that it could shape and control most investment decisions following a successful invasion of Iraq. New foreign investors could employ more sophisticated technology for oil exploration and production, thus yielding cheaper products, in a post-Saddam environment.[99] Moreover, the more privatized Washington could make Iraq's oil industry, the more likely it could rehabilitate itself based on more efficient market factors instead of less efficient government realities. That would be predicated on the notion that the new Iraqi government would accept the importance of privatization and could be stable enough to spur this effort. Privatization, moreover, could bolster oil security because it would make it harder for Iraq to control the behavior of its oil companies. Privatized companies, less affected by pressure within OPEC, would be more likely to make decisions that maximize their own profits and, at a minimum, would complicate OPEC's efforts to cut production. They would also probably attract more foreign investment, thus creating the types of economic relations that produce interdependence and a greater sense that all benefit from supply stability.

A successful invasion could also lead to a different role for Iraq in OPEC. If Iraq had assumed a more dovish policy, Washington could have expected its production to be higher, creating downward pressure on oil pricing and complicating efforts by OPEC hawks, such as Iran, to generate enough cooperation within OPEC to cut global oil production and push oil prices higher. Some observers even believed that Iraq might leave OPEC, thus complicating its ability to gain consensus on production cuts and, in turn, making it less likely that it could keep oil prices at higher levels than consumers would want.

Another possible oil-related motivation for invading Iraq deserves some consideration, albeit it is highly speculative. In the post-9/11 period, questions about global oil markets were amplified. For instance, prior to 9/11, China was seeking oil security chiefly through global markets. This meant that it was willing to pay the global market price for oil in order to obtain its oil supplies in lieu of seeking bilateral deals to obtain oil. But after 9/11, new fears arose in China about the risks of global oil market volatility.[100] American security was rattled,

---

98. On how Iraq should view foreign investment and OPEC, see "Political Economy of Iraqi Oil," Deutsche Bank, July 1, 2003.

99. "Technology Key to Enduring Depressed Crude Prices," *Oil and Gas Journal,* March 29, 1999, pp. 20–22. See also Verleger, *Adjusting to Volatile Energy Prices,* 183, table 6.4.

100. Gilboy, "China's Energy Security," 3.

and perceptions of its power may have been undermined by the brazen attacks on symbols of its key economic, political, and military might. This may have left Washington interested in taking strong action to restore its reputation and to reassert its ability to protect global security, including the free flow of oil from the Persian Gulf and global oil markets.

Invading Iraq would serve a larger goal of meeting the expected rising American and global demand for oil. In May 2001, the National Energy Policy Development Group emphasized the problem of rising oil demand and may have laid the foundation for the argument that liberating Iraq could serve American and global energy security by allowing global oil companies to exploit its massive oil reserves.[101]

One or more of these reasons may very well have added to the Bush administration's interest in invading Iraq. Administration officials could not have underestimated the importance of oil to the American and global economy and to potential problems with Saudi Arabia. Nor could they have overlooked that Persian Gulf oil would only become more important as other sources of oil around the world began to peak and then dry up.

Oil and Nonnational Interests

The national interest in protecting American oil security was likely salient, but so were nonnational interests. Bush may have sought to finish his father's work. Saddam's longevity proved to be a source of embarrassment to the George H. W. Bush, not just because he survived the 1991 war when many thought he would fall but also because he continued to be perceived as a major threat to global oil in the region and as an actor who sought WMD in contravention of UN resolutions. The 1991 operation against Iraq was a success—but the patient lived. An invasion of Iraq might just kill him or result in his capture or at least eliminate his regime. In the process, his father's legacy would benefit, and the world would be more secure to boot, by removing a threat that could prove more serious in the future if Saddam actually did have WMD and connections to terrorists. Bush repeatedly asserted that he would have been held accountable if the United States did not do anything to undermine Iraq's threat and then Iraq was involved in a major WMD attack on American interests.[102]

George W. Bush may have also sought to avenge Saddam's effort to assassinate his father in Kuwait in 1993, while he was on a visit there. After all, he did say

---

101. For such an argument, see Klare, *Blood And Oil*, chs. 3–4.
102. For instance, President Bush and First Lady Laura Bush, CNN interview with Larry King, July 7, 2006.

that Saddam Hussein was "a guy that tried to kill my dad," suggesting an overt hostility toward the dictator.[103]

According to some thinkers, the vested interest of the "military-industrial complex" of business and military organizations is to enter into war so that those within the complex can gain prestige and money. Wars result in bigger military sales, military research budgets, and influence.[104] As a twist on this, it might also be argued that a potential oil explanation for invading Iraq is that Cheney and his close contacts in the oil world would benefit. They could gain large oil contracts after Iraq was liberated by American forces.[105] With America dominating or influencing Iraq, the United States could vie for such contracts much more effectively with countries such as France, Russia, and China, which already had a foothold in the region.

This view of American motivations is cynical and may have been motivated by the administration's detractors to embarrass it, but the Bush team did lay out plans of Iraqi oil fields, sorting out which major American companies might exploit them after the fall of Saddam.[106] And the administration made involved preparations to occupy Iraqi oil installations, which it carried out at the onset of the war, seizing oil-export facilities north of Kuwait, two major Iraqi oil terminals, Iraq's southernmost oil fields of Basra, and the Oil Ministry in Baghdad.[107] To what extent these actions represented a coordinated plan to dominate Iraq's oil sources is not fully clear, nor do these actions mean that Washington sought to steal these sources—a motivation that in any case is not supported by its subsequent behavior in Iraq. However, these actions are suggestive of oil interests as part of the motivation for invading Iraq. For his part, former secretary of the Treasury Paul O'Neill believed that interest in controlling Iraqi oil was a factor in the war decision.[108]

Of course, the Bush family has a reputation of advancing its oil interests.[109] And Cheney's previous role as CEO of Halliburton fed into views that oil was a dominant factor in the invasion of Iraq.[110] The Bush administration's Energy Task Force presented a draft report in April 2001 recommending that the United States reconsider sanctions against Iran, Iraq, and Libya that prohibited U.S. oil

103. Remarks by President Bush on September 26, 2002.

104. For a polemical argument that the Pentagon shaped American foreign policy to its own interests, see Carroll, *House of War*, esp. 434–38.

105. For an argument in this vein, see Phillips, *American Theocracy*.

106. On these views, see, for instance, Ratner et al., *Against War in Iraq*.

107. On these events, see Klare, *Blood and Oil*, 99–102.

108. Suskind, *Price of Loyalty*, 96.

109. Phillips, *American Dynasty*.

110. On the war's motivations, see Freedman, "War In Iraq," esp. 9.

companies from "some of the most important existing and prospective petroleum-producing countries in the world."[111] Halliburton itself was given a monopolistic $15 billion contract by the Army to provide services such as delivering food and fuel to American troops, a contract that was controversial partly because its critics charged cronyism in the Bush White House.[112] Analysts such as Geoff Simons drew specific attention to Bush's past as a failed Texas oilman, Cheney's stint as CEO of Halliburton, Rice's work on the board of Chevron, and Rumsfeld's former post running a pharmaceutical company with ties to the oil industry, suggesting that U.S. foreign policy was shaped by a clique of oil interests, driven by America's oil dependence.[113]

However, it is not very likely that Cheney would risk a national and global scandal to help a company for which he no longer worked, when he must have known that he would be suspect. Some have argued that he still had Halliburton stock from which he could benefit, but we would still have to argue that he would risk a high-profile scandal for money, and Halliburton was under much scrutiny, including government investigations, during this period.[114] It is likely that oil companies as a group saw major benefits in invading Iraq and then exploiting the vast business deals that could arise from a successful venture. Mining Iraq's energy resources could benefit companies like Halliburton that support the infrastructure for oil production, although an invasion of Iraq could have had a split impact on the big oil producers. This is because as more oil flowed from Iraq, the price of oil would likely decrease based on the law of supply and demand. Big oil companies could benefit if the value of additional contracts in Iraq outweighed the losses they would face from decreased oil prices. Moreover, American oil giants have fared poorly. Reflecting the general state of affairs, on December 11 and 12, 2009, in one of the largest auctions held anywhere in the 150-year history of the oil industry, not even one U.S. oil company secured a contract to shape Iraq's oil industry in the next two decades. Two of the best contracts went to countries that opposed the invasion—China and Russia. Even France's companies performed better than those of the United States, and France played little role in helping reconstruct Iraq. One would think that if the United States had had a major plan to corner the Iraqi market, it would have had more success, unless we argue that it was incredibly inept in doing so—which is not likely given the success of its oil giants in general.

---

111. Quoted in Unger, *House of Bush*, 225.
112. Glanz, "Army Plans," A6.
113. Simons, *Future Iraq*.
114. Driody, *Halliburton Agenda*.

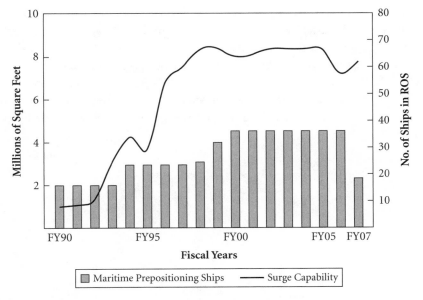

FIGURE 6. American sealift capability, 1990–2007
Source: Based on data provided by, and correspondence with, Chief of Naval Operations, Director, Strategic Mobility/Combat Logistics Division (N42), October 2007.
Note: The decrease in prepositioning ships in 2007 resulted from their addition to surge capability.

Of course, we should recall that the United Nations lifted economic sanctions on Iraq following the 2003 war. UN Resolution 1483 was approved in May and not only required that Iraq's oil profits be placed in a fund to benefit the Iraqi people but also called on all members to assist in Iraq's reconstruction.

The invasion of Iraq would prove another milestone in the rise of the American profile in the region. The Iranian Revolution and the previous wars and conflicts had already put this development in motion, and it was accelerated in stark relief by the U.S. invasion of Iraq. As figure 6 shows, the significant rise of American sealift capability mirrored and reflected the rise of the American regional profile and underscored its rising military capability as well, capability that made an invasion of Iraq possible.

The rise of oil in American foreign policy in the Middle East, as we shall see in the next chapter, is related to the attacks of September 11. It rose significantly by virtue of a number of developments, which were described in this chapter. Control over oil shifted from global companies to oil-producing states, thus mixing oil and politics and making oil security a larger issue. Moreover, the Iranian Revolution and radical Islam began to overlap with the geography of the oil-rich Gulf, and America's regional security framework collapsed in 1979. The Iran-Iraq War and Iraq's invasion of Kuwait further drew Washington into the region and raised the specter of threat to regional oil supplies. The American-led invasion and subsequent occupation of Iraq put Middle Eastern oil front and center in U.S. national security, even if Washington was not motivated primarily by oil factors.

Part I

OIL AND TRANSNATIONAL TERRORISM

2

EXPLAINING SEPTEMBER 11
The Oil Factor

Few events have received greater global scrutiny in the annals of history than the attacks of September 11, 2001. Those events came as a shock to Americans and non-Americans alike, not only because they were barbaric, sudden, and bizarre and struck American sites of symbolic importance but also because they clashed with the times. The Cold War was over, dictators had recently fallen all across Europe, and some scholars were even celebrating the end of history—the notion that, since major conflicts are driven by ideological disagreements and since American liberalism had triumphed over Soviet-style authoritarianism, it followed that serious conflicts would slowly become less prominent in world politics.[1] In this global context, the 9/11 attacks were an anachronism, because they seemed to presage a long fight against shadowy elements that appeared impossible to appease and capable of just about anything.

There is no justification for the 9/11 attacks, but we should try to understand why they occurred. This chapter analyzes what motivated those acts and what has motivated Al-Qaeda more broadly, with an eye toward answering a particular question: to what extent has Al-Qaeda been motivated by American actions related to Middle Eastern oil?

---

1. Fukuyama, *End of History*.

Terrorism is a complex phenomenon. In searching for the causes of the September 11 attacks, we need to employ multiple levels of explanation.[2] This chapter divides the motivations of, and enabling factors for, the 9/11 attacks into three categories: conceptual, oil-related, and non-oil-related. In brief, the conceptual level refers to the distorted religious lens with which Al-Qaeda views the world. That is an important starting point for understanding September 11 and Al-Qaeda's behavior, partly because some observers have blamed American foreign policy for the 9/11 attacks.[3] Yet it cannot explain why others around the world have not attacked America on such a scale. Nor can it account for smaller-scale terrorism in such places as Russia, India, and China. The foreign policy explanation also cannot account for the Manichean element of Al-Qaeda's views, nor for its systematic distortion of American behavior. Why didn't it see that Washington had helped Muslims in places such as Bosnia, Kuwait, and Albania, and largely backed Pakistan against India? Why did it lambast the United States for supporting Arab dictatorial regimes in the Arab Gulf but not even note that it eliminated the quintessential Iraqi dictator who had murdered tens of thousands of Muslims? Part of the reason may well have to do with Al-Qaeda's distorted lens.

Meanwhile, many have described Al-Qaeda as loathing freedom and the American way of life, rather than American policy. But this explanation cannot account for why only Al-Qaeda appears to hate democracy enough to use brutal terror on America, nor does it account for the timing of its attacks or the high volume of Al-Qaeda statements on its own motivations, which often do not include the need to destroy democracy.

A better explanation is that through the distorted prism of hijacked religion, America's sometimes positive and sometimes muscular foreign policy was viewed as aggressive and oppressive, a threat to Muslims and to Al-Qaeda's radical Islamic vision. These two elements are crucial: the lens that was shaped by distorted religion, and the way that these actions and events looked through that lens.

Middle Eastern oil–related events, including the 1990–91 Gulf War and American intervention in the region, contributed to the motivation for and helped enable the actual attacks. These factors do not appear to be necessary to Al-Qaeda's interest in launching a broader *jihad*. Toward the end of the Soviet War in Afghanistan, Bin Laden began to assert the desire to extend the jihad beyond Afghanistan to get rid of Arab governments and to create Muslim governments, but it is not clear that he intended to attack America. So what drove him in that

---

2. On these studies, see Moghadam, "Motives of Martyrdom," esp. 51–54. See also Cronin, "Sources of Contemporary Terrorism," ch. 1.

3. The September 11 commission report recommended that America assess its foreign policy toward the Muslim world. *9/11 Commission Report.*

direction between 1989 and 1996? As we shall see, the oil-related Persian Gulf crisis of 1990–91 and its ongoing effects were major turning points, as were a series
of personal events related to the fact that the Saudis stripped him of citizenship
in 1994, partly for becoming increasingly vocal against the regime.

Non-oil issues also motivated and enabled the 9/11 attacks. Assessing the
motivations of terrorists is, of course, a guessing game in which many people
have partaken, but it is worthwhile providing a sense of these broader causes
in this chapter, so as to put the oil-related causes in better perspective.[4] We can
now turn to an analysis of these three categories of explanation: conceptual, oil-
motivated, and non-oil-motivated.

Distorting Islam: The Crucial Conceptual Lens

A great deal of analysis has focused on why Al-Qaeda terrorists undertook the
September 11 attacks. Robert Pape, for his part, has found that suicide terrorism
is highly linked to the rejection of foreign occupation and that religious factors contributed insignificantly to terrorism.[5] But the two things need not be
mutually exclusive. An important driving force of Al-Qaeda terrorism is the lens
through which Al-Qaeda sees the world and factors such as foreign occupation.
This also explains, in connection with the petroleum triangle, why it has become
such a real and perceived threat and has been hard to defeat.

The religious underpinnings of violence and the growth of religious terrorism have been discussed by many scholars.[6] Mark Juergensmeyer, for instance,
notes that religion often provides the motivation, justification, organization, and
worldview that allows for public acts of violence and that jihadi terrorism is a
religiously framed act, often justified in terms of good versus evil.[7] Graham Fuller
describes an Islamist broadly as "anyone who believes that Islam has something
to say about how political and social life should be constituted and who attempts
to implement that interpretation in some way."[8] But Islamism is not a monolith.
It refers to many different strands and versions of Islam. And jihadism and Islamism are sometimes falsely conflated. Among other things, jihadism is transnational, often rejecting the state or nationalism, while Islamism can support

---

4. For a good review of the literature on terrorist motivations, see Anderson, "Shock and
Awe," 303–25.

5. Pape, *Dying to Win.*

6. Juergensmeyer, *Terror in the Mind of God,* 263–78; and Stern, *Ultimate Terrorists.*

7. Juergensmeyer, *Terror in the Mind of God.*

8. Fuller, *Future Of Political Islam,* 47.

religious nationalism. There is little point trying to negotiate with jihadists such as Al-Qaeda, but it is possible with other, less radical groups.

Bin Laden, a jihadi radical, was not a Wahhabist, but Wahhabism is important inasmuch as it shaped the environment in which he operated. As is widely known, the Saudi body politic largely subscribes to Wahhabism, sometimes referred to as Saudi Islam, which is perpetuated and enforced by the state. It is a form of fundamentalist Islam and an offshoot of one of the four schools of Islamic legal theory—the Hanbali school of law. Wahhabists differ from traditionalists who are not Islamists in that they are not actively seeking political change.[9] Traditionalists accept existing political authority and seek continuity within the context of Islam as it has evolved in each local culture. Fundamentalists, contrary to popular views, seek political change, although they are socially conservative. They want to reinvigorate a literal interpretation of Islam based on the Qur'an and Hadith, the sayings of the Prophet Muhammad. Many of them seek an Islamic state or, at a minimum, a significant role for Islam in governance.

Wahhabism is the strictest fundamentalist strain and is intolerant of other faiths and even of other strains within Islam that do not accept the notion that Islam is a total way of life and should govern all affairs. Wahhabism draws inspiration from the teachings of Muhammad ibn Abd al-Wahhab (1703–92), who called for a return to the pure and orthodox practice of Islam and literal renderings of the Qur'an and the Hadith.

Wahhabism takes different forms, but prominent among them is the notion that non-Muslims are infidels, that they should not be present on Saudi soil, and that aggressive jihad against them can be justified or even mandated.[10] Al-Wahhab himself launched an unsuccessful jihad against the Ottoman Empire in order to wrest control of Muslim holy sites, which he believed were defiled with tainted Islam. These tenets of Wahhabism do not mean that it should spawn terrorism, as Saudi authorities have been quick to point out. However, we do know that Bin Laden quoted generously from the teachings of al-Wahhab when interviewed.[11] And that he quoted in many of his justifications for terrorism the works of Ibn Taymiyyah (1263–1328), a political theorist of legendary status revered by Wahhabites.[12]

Bin Laden, however, was not a Wahhabist, nor are the lines clear that separate different Islamic schools and traditions. He appeared to use some admixture of Wahhabist thought, which suspects foreigners and emphasizes fundamentalist

---

9. On the different schools within Islam, see ibid., ch. 3.

10. On the multiple meanings of Jihad, see Esposito, *Unholy War*, ch. 2.

11. Fandy, *Saudi Arabia*, 190–92.

12. Sivan, *Radical Islam*, 84–100. On Bin Laden's views, see Bodansky, *Bin Laden*; and Fandy, *Saudi Arabia*, ch. 6.

Islam, and Salafism. Salafism, which forged a basis for Wahhabite thought, is sometimes used interchangeably with Wahhabism. However, Wahhabism is associated with Saudi Arabia, while some see Salafism as tied to a broader puritanical Islamic movement, although the Saudis sometimes refer to themselves as Salafis rather than Wahhabis.[13]

Salafism, of which there is an innovative and a conservative kind,[14] emerged in the second half of the nineteenth century in response to the rise of European influence; it promoted a return to ancient Islamic traditions or to Islam's original condition based on a literal reading of the sacred texts.[15] Bin Laden's hybrid concoction may be described as jihadist Salafism, in its combination of religious doctrine and terrorism, or as one school within the broader realm of Islamic radicalism. Islamic radicalism accepts the basic precepts of the fundamentalists, but with several twists, some of which Bin Laden adopted. He advances notions of a pan-Islamic state. As the quintessential extremists, radical Islam and its jihadists seeks a universal, unified *ummah* or religious community rather than its division in nation-states. And it sees the struggle with the West as implacable and as one requiring violence.[16]

Mainstream Islam does recognize a division of the world into an abode of Islam and an abode of war. It also differentiates believers from nonbelievers. However, it does not imply that the nonbelievers should be destroyed. This is Bin Laden's interpretation.[17] Even Saudi Wahhabism is not enough to explain acts of terror, because few Wahhabists are terrorists. Saudi leaders such as Foreign Minister al-Faisal are quick to assert that Bin Laden "had not followed the terrorist path as a result of teachings he received at the Saudi schools…but that he was misled once he went to Afghanistan."[18] That is partly true in that he was considerably influenced by Muslim thinkers outside of the Saudi kingdom.

One of Bin Laden's central teachers and co-jihadists in the Soviet War in Afghanistan, Abdullah Azzam, asserted that holy war or jihad in this context was "every man's duty" in the event that foreigners took Muslim lands.[19] Azzam, who was born in Palestine but emigrated to Saudi Arabia to teach at King Abdul Aziz University in Jeddah before going to Pakistan to join the jihad against the Soviets,

---

13. On Salifi Islam, see Moghadam, "Motives of Martyrdom," 62–78.

14. Lacroix, "Between Islamists and Liberals," 349–50.

15. Wiktorowicz, "New Global Threat."

16. Fuller, *Future Of Political Islam*, ch. 8. For Bin Laden, Jihad is a holy war against the infidels; in mainstream Islam, Jihad means a struggle against oneself for self-improvement.

17. Esposito, *Islamic Threat*; Esposito, *Unholy War*; Huntington, *Clash of Civilizations*; and Bodansky, *Bin Laden*.

18. See his news conference, Al-Arabiyah Television in FBIS: NES, May 4, 2004 (WNC# 0hx8szx02t2gi5).

19. Quoted in Kepel, *Jihad*, 318.

embraced a central notion. Jihad against the West for purposes of liberating an oppressed Muslim world was a religious duty, and only force would allow the ummah to gain victory; for him it was "Jihad and the rifle alone: no negotiations, no conferences, and no dialogues."[20] The jihadists see a profound incompatibility between the Islamic and Western worlds and anticipate and want to bring about a confrontation between Islamic and Western civilizations. In one of Al-Qaeda's most important documents, which was either written by or authorized by Bin Laden, Al-Qaeda justifies aggressive jihad. In fact, as Raymond Ibrahim notes, Al-Qaeda's aggression is ultimately rooted in what it believes to be principles intrinsic to Islam.[21]

More broadly, Al-Qaeda radicalism is built fundamentally on the writings of Sayyid Qutb, who was imprisoned by Egyptian president Gamal Abdel Nasser and executed in 1966, and Hassan al-Banna, who founded the Muslim Brotherhood in 1928 and sought to oust British control from Egypt, as al-Wahhab had tried to do to the Ottomans in Arabia and Bin Laden sought to do to the Americans.[22] The views of Bin Laden were shaped by these ideas as well as by those of numerous clerics from various countries, such as Sheikh Abdul Majeed al-Zindani, a prominent Yemeni cleric, who is widely viewed as one of Bin Laden's spiritual mentors. The same can be said of Ayman al-Zawahiri. He was an Egyptian doctor who had been tortured in Cairo prisons for his antiregime activities, became leader of the Egyptian Al-Jihad Group, and then became Bin Laden's right-hand man.[23]

Qutb emphasized that the West seeks to dominate and destroy the Islamic world and to replace Islam with its own model of how to govern human affairs.[24] Qutb stressed that Islamic jihad is an offensive movement. In one of his writings, "Jihad in the Cause of God," he asserted that those who see jihad as defensive are lacking "understanding of the nature of Islam and its primary aim."[25] He emphasized a world divided into the Dar-al-Islam (House of Islam) and the Dar-al-Harb (House of War), into a world of the believers and the nonbelievers; while his writings appeared to be measured and philosophical, his message was clearly divisive, confrontational, and aggressive against the nonbelievers.[26] Al-Qaeda documents and statements are littered with this Manichean worldview.

---

20. Quoted in Bodansky, *Bin Laden*, 11. For his views, see www.ict.org.il/articles.
21. Ibrahim, *Al-Qaeda Reader*, esp. 20.
22. Qutb, *Milestones*. On the writings of extremists, see Schweitzer and Shay, *Globalization of Terror*, ch. 1. For a brief argument that Qutb has been misunderstood, see Khan, "Radical Islam."
23. Wright, *Looming Tower*, ch. 2.
24. Qutb, *Milestones*.
25. Translated in Laqueur, ed., *Voices of Terror*, 394.
26. Qutb, *Milestones*, 79, 97, 101–2.

For example, in one prominent essay, "Loyalty as Enmity," al-Zawahiri lays out a black-and-white world of infidels and believers and describes September 11 as the peak of the struggle between infidels and the Islamic ummah.[27]

In offensive jihad, Qutb viewed martyrdom as the highest calling, as a great honor and emphasized its importance.[28] Not surprisingly, Al-Qaeda has justified martyrdom at length, sometimes twisting the sayings of the prophet Muhammad in lengthy essays on the subject.[29] Whatever the exact form of extremist religion to which Al-Qaeda subscribes, we do know that martyrdom was preeminent in the minds of the 9/11 hijackers and is a central leitmotif of Al-Qaeda as an organization. Radical interpretations of religion are a special case. They allow for and spawn fanatical and homicidal behavior because they make it possible for individuals to place a greater premium on death than on life. Mohamed Atta, who headed the 9/11 team and flew American Airlines Flight 11 into the North Tower of the World Trade Center, was carrying his will as well as the Spiritual Handbook for the Suicide Attack on the World Trade Center. They were found in his travel bag. They are both threaded with references to meeting God in Heaven, the after life, and serving God against infidels: "As soon as the Faithful take on the fight against the Unfaithful, the Faithful shall remember that God is with them and that they shall prevail."[30]

In the Qur'an, it says that to die for one's faith is the highest form of witness to God, but this can be twisted to mean martyrdom in suicide attacks. Meanwhile, Islam prohibits suicide but, as John Esposito points out, suicide can be defined to exclude martyrdom, thus getting around this prohibition.[31] Interpretation and distortion is key. Al-Qaeda distorts the Qur'an to promote violence. Bin Laden's messages drew heavily on religious verses and passages that, he asserts, command Muslims to attack the infidels.[32] He and other Al-Qaeda leaders convinced their disciples that great rewards awaited them in Heaven, with the pain and sorrows of life replaced by the eternal bliss of paradise and marriage to seventy-two beautiful virgins.

The Al-Qaeda leadership turned its errant view of Islam into a force for destruction. Al-Qaeda followers were brainwashed into believing that their enemy was the crusader, an actor that threatened their very way of life, an infidel whose nonbeliever status was worthy of repugnance and could not be reconciled with their views and that martyrdom would serve Islam. The brainwashing of Al-Qaeda

---

27. For this document and a cogent analysis of it, see Ibrahim, *Al-Qaeda Reader*, 66.
28. Murawiec, *Mind of Jihad*, esp. 37.
29. Ibrahim, *Al-Qaeda Reader*, 137–74.
30. From the Manual, a translation of which can be found in *Inside 9-11*, 308.
31. Hafez, *Why Muslims Rebel*, 99.
32. Ibid., 188.

operatives helps explain why young men would send themselves to a senseless death, bringing down thousands of innocent people, many of them Muslim. Brainwashing and indoctrination help explain why others that hate the United States have not engaged in the barbarism epitomized by September 11. They may hate America, but they are not driven by intense religious indoctrination to commit mass murder.

One additional notion of vital importance shapes the lens of radicals. The separation of church and state is enshrined in Western culture. The American and French Revolutions capped a period in which ideas about separation of religion from politics gained ground. In both cases, religion was vital in the private sphere but was kept separate from the public sphere, thus preventing religious fervor from spilling over into public affairs.[33]

It cannot be overemphasized that Islamists of Bin Laden's kind believe that separation of mosque and state deviates significantly from the divine nature of authority that flows from Allah and Allah alone. Allah cannot be preeminent if fundamental areas of human life are governed by temporal, man-made institutions. Dictatorships or tyrannies exercise control over and demand allegiance from the people whose true allegiance can only be to Allah.[34]

It is no mistake that Bin Laden, building on the ideas of al-Banna and Qutb, described the abolition of the Ottoman caliphate in March 1924 as an abomination. In a video broadcast on October 7, 2001, Bin Laden, appearing with al-Zawahiri, tried to justify 9/11 as revenge for Muslim pain, observing that "since nearly eighty years we have been tasting this humiliation."[35] He was evidently referring to the Muslim calendar and the abolition of the caliphate and to all that it conjured in the minds of radical Islamists. In conjunction with abolishing the caliphate, Mustafa Kemal, referred to as "Ataturk" or "the Great Turk," also abolished the ministry that dealt with the application of Muslim canon law and the administration of pious foundations and created a unified education system. That action implied the closure of *madrassas* or religious schools and replaced them with Turkish secular schools. In fact, the institutions of Islam, which had enjoyed some level of autonomy from the sultans of the Ottoman Empire, would be nationalized and subject to secular criteria,[36] by a man Winston Churchill described as an "enlightened dictator consecrated to the transformation of his homeland into a modern state,"[37] a man whose victory at Gallipoli

---

33. Bell, *Cult of the Nation*.
34. This notion may well be shared by Islamicists and liberals as well in Muslim countries. Wedeen, *Beyond the Crusades*, 58.
35. CNN, October 8, 2001.
36. This paragraph is based on Mango, *Ataturk*, ch. 20.
37. Churchill, *Visions of Glory, 1874–1932*, 708.

represented one of Winston Churchill's greatest failures, while elevating Kemal to iconic status among Turks. Kemal, who displayed reverence for Western progress, put Turkey on precisely the opposite path that Bin Laden and other Islamists would seek for the Muslim world in the twenty-first century. For them, Kemal had eliminated the center of Islamic community, undermined Muslim unity, undermined the role of religion in modern life, and mimicked the West.

While we can guess that distorted religion is an important part of the puzzle of terrorism, hundreds of extreme ideologies are practiced around the world, but terrorism does not often happen on the scale of 9/11. And so we know that extremist ideologies alone cannot explain terrorism, even though the significant emphasis on martyrdom may distinguish Islamic radicalism from other types of radicalism.

Contributing and Enabling Motivations

A conceptual lens is crucial for creating the type of terrorism that we saw on 9/11, but it is not a sufficient explanation. The distorted lens of Islam was both a motivator in and of itself and a vital starting point. Presumably, through that lens, the world looked different, including the Saudi regime, secular rulers, critical events, and the role of the United States. U.S. foreign policy, especially in the Middle East, assumed a sinister, oppressive tone. Aggressive jihad, with the key ingredient of martyrdom, became a compelling option. Were it not for this lens, for example, jihadists may have disliked America's role in the Middle East but seen it in different terms, reacting to it like others around the world who find it problematic—without violence.

As we shall see, oil played a large role in motivating and enabling the September 11 attacks. In part, as discussed in chapter 1, oil factors also motivated some of America's actions in the Persian Gulf, and they were seen, with a jaundiced eye through the religious lens of extremists and likely also contributed to anti-Americanism. But the picture is more complex than just the nature of U.S. foreign policy and the terrorist response to it.

The Role of the Soviet War in Afghanistan

The role of oil in the Soviet War in Afghanistan was significant. Oil appears to have contributed to the rise and development of Al-Qaeda. Oil money facilitated the rise of the Afghan resistance, which believed that evicting the godless communists from Muslim Afghanistan was a sacred duty. The resistance included thousands of foreign militants. The Pakistanis had been enrolled in perhaps twenty-five hundred Saudi-funded madrassas and were indoctrinated with Wahhabist ideology, all of which Saudi oil money enabled. Pakistani and foreign militants were urged in some radical mosques and madrassas to pursue jihad and to prepare for exalted death in the form of martyrdom.[38] Massive Saudi funding for these schools and for mosques continued throughout the 1990s. In fact, in the early 1990s, the kingdom's Ministry of Pilgrimage and Religious Trusts asserted that the regime had spent about $850 million on mosque construction world-wide, with an emphasis on Afghanistan and the wider region.[39]

The United States, of course, also played a key role in supporting the Afghan rebels. America viewed the conflict in Afghanistan through the prism of the Cold War, and was concerned about a potential Soviet threat to the oil-rich Persian Gulf. The Soviet invasion of Afghanistan shocked Washington, motivating it to take action on various fronts, including in Afghanistan, where Afghan Marxists and Soviet troops were allied on one side, while the native Afghan *mujaheddin* and a much smaller cadre of foreign fighters were on the other.

On the whole, it is estimated that while America committed some four to five billion dollars between 1980 and 1992 in aid to the mujaheddin, Saudi Arabia matched that amount to fund the resistance.[40] Much of the support that Bin Laden and his cohorts received, which eventually helped them build Al-Qaeda, came from oil-rich states and donors, as we shall see. For instance, Saudi Arabia established and funded the Ittihad-i-Islami faction, which became one of the seven Sunni factions based in Peshawar, Pakistan; in turn, the leader of that faction would become central in establishing the Al-Qaeda training camps.[41]

In essence, Washington wanted to fell the Soviet bear, while Riyadh sought to support the Muslim resistance and spread Wahhabism. While 250,000 Afghan mujaheddin fought the Soviets and the communist Afghan government, it is estimated that there were never more than several thousand foreign mujahed-din in the field at any one time. Nonetheless, the number of jihadis that par-ticipated in the Afghan movement is reported to have been around thirty-five thousand, coming from forty-three countries in the Middle East, North and East Africa, Central Asia, and the Far East. Thousands more foreign Muslim radicals came to study in the hundreds of new madrassas along the Afghan border.[42] They gathered in camps near Peshawar and in Afghanistan, forging battle-hardened

---

38. Murawiec, *Mind of Jihad,* esp. ch. 2.

39. Bronson, *Thicker Than Oil,* 222.

40. Rashid, *Taliban,* 18.

41. Brisard, *Zarqawi,* 25. See also Johnson, "Financing Afghan Terrorism," 109–11.

42. This paragraph is based on Rashid, *Taliban,* 129–32.

and ideological ties with fighters from around the world that extended beyond nationalities and became the basis for transnational terrorism.

The Saudis were especially critical to funding the Afghan Arabs, a smaller part of the resistance that would form the core of Al-Qaeda and that attracted Bin Laden's special attention starting in 1986.[43] This organization was founded by Bin Laden and Palestinian militant Azzam. The Makhtab al-Khadimat (Office of Order) or Afghan Services Bureau as it was called, trained and recruited non-Afghan Muslims to join the resistance. According to the court testimony on February 6, 2001, of Al-Qaeda operative Jamal al-Fadl, a Sudanese militant and former Bin Laden associate in the early 1990s who became an informant for the United States after he clashed with Bin Laden, "Azzam, he runs office, and Bin Laden, he gives them the money for that."[44] The Makhtab channeled funds from charities in the Middle East and North America but also from Saudi intelligence and private donations from Saudi princes and mosques, among other organizations.[45] Bin Laden earned his spurs among many Muslims in recruiting and indoctrinating the Afghan Arabs, which included four thousand volunteers from Saudi Arabia alone.[46]

Little did the Saudis, Americans, or other benefactors know that these Afghan Arabs would form the core of a terrorist group capable of committing massive atrocities on September 11.[47] Al-Zawahiri argued that the jihadist movement found an "incubator" in the war in Afghanistan, "where its seeds would grow and where it can acquire practical experience in combat, politics and organizational experience."[48] By the end of the Soviet War in Afghanistan, Bin Laden consciously wanted to use his fighters for conflicts worldwide. He established Al-Qaeda ("the base") as an outgrowth of the Makhtab, where Al-Qaeda's worldview began to take shape. Although the notion of launching a global jihad was controversial within the movement, he eventually triumphed in promoting it. His Rolodex of contacts developed during the war became critical, as some of them later became financial supporters of Al-Qaeda.

Oil money was also critical to the rise of the Taliban, which, in turn, allowed Al-Qaeda to develop and operate in Afghanistan. The connection between the mujaheddin and the Taliban is not exactly clear, but it appears that the Taliban's role in the Afghan resistance was minor. The Taliban, who are ethnic Pash-

---

43. Scheuer, *Through Our Enemies' Eyes*, 100–105.

44. "Court Testimony of Al-Qaeda Operative Jamal al-Fadl."

45. Rashid, *Taliban*, 131–32.

46. Johnson, "Financing Afghan Terrorism," esp. 101–4.

47. On such effects, see Coll, *Ghost Wars*. The case is replete with what some call "blowback," or the unintended effects of great power intervention abroad. See Johnson, *Blowback*.

48. Al-Zawahiri, "Importance of Afghanistan," 48–49.

tuns, came largely from the Afghanistan-Pakistan border areas and in particular the Helmand, Kandahar, and Uruzgan provinces. In Peshawar there were seven mujaheddin parties that were recognized by Pakistan and received a share of CIA aid. However, the most extreme mujaheddin factions arose from the broader Afghan resistance, including that of Mullah Mohammed Omar, who later emerged as the Taliban's supreme leader.

The Taliban emerged in Pakistan in late 1994 as a militia of Pashtun Islamic fundamentalist students. These students, many of whom were orphans drawn from Afghan refugee camps just over the border in Pakistan, had received training in Pakistan's religious schools, which were funded with Saudi money. These schools were also attended by refugees who had fought as the CIA-backed mujaheddin. Omar's followers were deeply disillusioned with infighting and corruption in the mujaheddin leadership and sought a return to what they had learned in madrassas—a radicalized version of Islam.[49] The Taliban, whose leadership was indigenous to Afghanistan, captured Kandahar City in October/November 1994; by September 1996, they had taken control of Afghanistan's capital, Kabul.

To some extent, the Taliban acted as a proxy for Pakistan and, to a lesser degree, Saudi Arabia.[50] Riyadh viewed the Taliban as a route to influence in Afghanistan and as an important asset in its rivalry with Iran, which had ongoing tensions with the Taliban, but it was the Wahhabi *ulema* in Saudi Arabia that most pushed the regime to support the Taliban. The ulema was devoted to exporting Wahhabism, and the regime was reluctant to ignore its views. As a result, the Saudis began to fund the Taliban as they had the Afghan resistance, to a significant degree. But elements in Afghanistan proved difficult to control. Just as the Saudis, Americans, and others could not have guessed that the Afghan Arabs would form the backbone of Al-Qaeda, they could not have known that the Taliban would play a critical role in making the September 11 attacks possible. Of course, the basic story is now well known. Al-Qaeda gained a foothold in Taliban-controlled Afghanistan and from there planned and coordinated the attack of September 11. Its Taliban patrons or allies facilitated the necessary freedom of action that terrorists would have severe difficulty achieving in other states. The Taliban aided Bin Laden in many ways. It protected him from extradition to the United States in 1998 when the international community sought to extradite him after Washington indicted him in 1998 on 319 criminal counts, including conspiracy to murder U.S. citizens. It provided him a security detail, established communications facilities for him and Al-Qaeda, facilitated recruitment efforts, and enabled him to build and maintain terrorist camps. In return, he invested in Taliban projects and offered

---

49. Rashid, *Taliban*, ch. 1.
50. Johnson, "Financing Afghan Terrorism," 96–97.

his well-trained fighters to support Taliban efforts to take and maintain control of Afghanistan.

American intelligence authorities estimate that between 1996 and 2001, as many as twenty thousand Al-Qaeda recruits from all over the world passed through its training camps; one scholar estimates that 66 percent of them came from Saudi Arabia, heavily financed by the same Saudi charitable foundations that had funded the Afghan resistance in the 1980s.[51] This link suggests just how important the oil connection is to Al-Qaeda.

Middle Eastern Oil and a Potential Missed Chance

Oil plays another possible role in this story. One memo from Al-Qaeda military chief Mohammed Atef, found by the FBI in 1998 during its investigation of the 1998 African embassy bombings, suggests that Al-Qaeda had detailed knowledge of negotiations between the ruling Taliban and the American government over an oil and gas pipeline that Unocal, with Washington's blessing and support, wanted to build across Afghanistan. The pipeline was to connect the oil fields of Turkmenistan and possibly other Central Asian nations with the coast of India and Pakistan, allowing for shipping to global destinations. Such a pipeline would also help Washington exclude rivals, such as Russia, China, and Iran, from Asian pipelines; decrease the drawbacks of not being able to transport oil and gas through Iran; and enhance alternative routes for oil, which could increase American and global oil security.[52] It is conceivable that the United States tolerated the Taliban and even Bin Laden because it wanted the Taliban's support in this venture. The memo reveals that the Taliban viewed the pipeline as a way to reduce American pressure on it to alter its behavior and to control or even extradite Bin Laden.[53] We can surmise that were it not for this pipeline interest, Washington may have been tougher on the Taliban and may have gone to greater lengths to eliminate Bin Laden. American oil interests, especially in Saudi Arabia, may well have made Washington less interested in pressuring the Saudis to help the United States check Bin Laden.[54]

As I will discuss, the Saudis became far more cooperative with America after Al-Qaeda unmistakably started to target the royal family around 2003. However, such cooperation was always very weak, whether before or after September 11. In

---

51. Bronson, *Thicker Than Oil*, 225.

52. On the value of this pipeline to Washington and on this episode in general, see Coll, *Ghost Wars*, esp. 305–13, 342–45.

53. This paragraph is based on Brisard and Deasquie, *Forbidden Truth*, 141–43. See also Napoleoni, *Terror Incorporated*, 117–18, 196–98.

54. Coll, *Ghost Wars*, 511–12, 571.

this sense, the oil factor may be indirectly linked to Al-Qaeda. It allowed it greater freedom of maneuver than it otherwise would have had. It helped the Saudis stonewall the United States prior to September 11, when their aggressive support may have made a difference—a clear missed opportunity.

Afghanistan and the Global Turn

The Soviet War in Afghanistan is related to 9/11 in a manner not linked to oil, which is important to understand. The Afghan insurgency lasted until the Soviets' ignominious withdrawal in 1989. It may well be that the fall of the Soviet Union at once emboldened Al-Qaeda to act against the United States and raised fears among some of its leaders, as well as other notables in the Muslim world, that America could now threaten them more easily. For his part, Saddam Hussein feared that America could now put the Arab Middle East under its hegemonic thumb, and such a view gained currency among many Muslims.[55]

The Muslim resistance took much credit for the Soviet failures. The Afghanistan experience was related to 9/11 not only in that it helped form the Taliban and Al-Qaeda but also because it led Bin Laden to believe that he could bring down a superpower. Bin Laden started to think of spreading jihad globally in the period around 1986 or 1987, when he began to split with Azzam and when he first met al-Zawahiri and spoke openly of the need for a global jihad, not just against corrupt secular governments in the Middle East but also against the United States and Israel.[56] The eviction of Soviet forces led Bin Laden repeatedly to say that the "myth of the superpower was destroyed," and to "now predict...the end of the United States."[57] In one interview, he observed that "God used our holy war in Afghanistan to destroy the Russian army and the Soviet Union, and now we ask God to use us one more time to do the same to America and make it a shadow of itself.... The Americans are a paper tiger."[58] Al-Fadl's testimony suggested that Bin Laden sought to spread the jihad to the global level as the next step following the Soviet War in Afghanistan.[59]

There is further evidence that Bin Laden began to focus on the United States by the end of the war in Afghanistan—an important point in trying to

---

55. Saddam Hussein's speech to the Arab Cooperation Council, in FBIS: NES, February 27, 1990. See also Aziz statement in Baghdad AL-THAWRAH, FBIS: NES, September 12, 1990; and "Excerpts from Iraqi Document on Meeting with U.S. Envoy." On Saddam's concerns about U.S. hegemony, see text of interview with Saddam, Mexico City XEW Television Network, FBIS: NES, December 26, 1990, p. 20.

56. Coll, *Ghost Wars*, 156, 163.

57. Wright, *Sacred Rage*, 250, 257.

58. Quoted in Schweitzer and Shay, *Globalization of Terror,* 118.

59. "Court Testimony of Al-Qaeda Operative Jamal al-Fadl."

understand the role of oil. On November 8, 1990, the FBI raided the New Jersey home of El Sayyid Nosair, an associate of Ali Mohamed, a former Special Forces sergeant stationed in North Carolina. In 1989, Nosair traveled to Afghanistan and Pakistan and became "deeply involved with bin Laden's plans."[60] Nosair was eventually convicted in connection with the 1993 World Trade Center bombing.

Westerners in Saudi Arabia

While it appears that Bin Laden had begun to focus on the United States by the end of the Afghan war, it is not clear how serious he was about launching a massive attack on the order of September 11, or to what extent Al-Qaeda had the capability to engage in such an attack at that time. However, evidence suggests that subsequent events would ratchet up his intensity and commitment and increase his ability to raise the funds to run Al-Qaeda. In the year following the Soviet withdrawal from Afghanistan, the Persian Gulf crisis of 1990–91 erupted; it would ignite one of Bin Laden's chief grievances. Seeing the world through a particular religious lens, Bin Laden repeatedly asserted that it is "not permitted for non-Muslims to stay in Arabia."[61] Of course, we should note that American troops never entered Mecca and Medina and were isolated from Saudi society for fear of offending some of its citizens. Leading Saudi religious scholars, not wearing Bin Laden's extremist lenses and beholden to the House of Saud, gave their imprimatur to an American military deployment.

That the Saudi regime allowed U.S. forces entry in 1990 and let some forces stay thereafter strongly motivated Bin Laden and other Saudis who opposed the regime.[62] Occupation of Arab land played a key role.[63] In meeting with Saudi Defense Minister Prince Sultan, Bin Laden offered the services of his Afghan Arabs in the effort to protect the kingdom against Saddam Hussein but was rebuffed. Sultan said, "There are no caves in Kuwait," and Bin Laden responded, "We will fight them with our faith."[64] By "caves," he meant that in Afghanistan, Bin Laden's rebels could succeed because they had a complex network of caves in which to hide, which wasn't the case in the desert. In any case, the Saudis trusted the United States far more to perform militarily, and they also were concerned

---

60. Wright, *Looming Tower,* 181.

61. This section is based on several Osama Bin Laden videos shown on CNN in the period of September 15 to October 15, 2001. Also see his interview with Peter Arnett, Afghanistan, CNN, March 1997, available at www.anusha.com/osamaint.htm.

62. Baghdad INA, in FBIS: NES, October 10, 1990, p. 27.

63. Pape sees suicide terrorism as fundamentally a response to foreign occupation. Pape, *Dying to Win.*

64. Quoted in *New York Times,* December 27, 2001, p. B4.

that Bin Laden might turn his forces on their regime. The regime's rejection of his genuine offer and its allowance of Americans into the land of the two holiest cities of Mecca and Medina turned Bin Laden and other radicals against the Al Saud, led the regime to place him under surveillance, eventually forced him into exile, and left him with a serious grievance against the royal family.[65] In fact, Prince Turki, the Saudi intelligence chief, viewed the meeting as a watershed, indicating that it caused "radical changes" in Bin Laden's personality away from a "calm, peaceful, and gentle man."[66] Subsequently, Bin Laden moved to Sudan and continued to build the vast network of militants that would form Al-Qaeda and to denounce the Saudi government for allowing Western forces into the kingdom.

The regime understood that allowing U.S.-led forces into the kingdom was controversial, so they sought and received a religious sanction from the establishment clerics. This, in turn, further aggravated Bin Laden and may have been the cause of his split, along with other radicals, from the traditional Wahhabi establishment.[67] Bin Laden's issue with the Saudis, which is directly tied to events arising from the need to protect Middle Eastern oil, may well have been a significant motivation for him.

Upon his return to Afghanistan, Bin Laden became more openly hostile against the West and the Saudi regime. But it was only following Al-Qaeda's bombing of American embassies in Kenya and Tanzania in August 1998 that the Saudis and Americans made serious, albeit uncoordinated and ineffective, attempts to coerce the Taliban to turn over Bin Laden.[68] That effort failed despite the threat of an American military attack.

Since at least 1992, Bin Laden focused much attention on challenging the United States, suggesting a direct connection to the Gulf War. In Afghanistan, to which he had fled Sudan to take refuge under Taliban rule, he wrote a vitriolic fatwa. He issued his "Declaration of Jihad against the Americans Occupying the Land of the Two Holy Places" in August 1996. Evidently, still heavily influenced by the Gulf War, his rejection by the Al Saud regime, and his eviction from Sudan under American pressure, he focused much attention on Saudi Arabia and the United States. In the main, he asserted that to "push the enemy—the greatest *kufr* [infidel]—out of the country is a prime duty. No other duty after Belief is more important than [this] duty.... Utmost effort should be made to prepare and instigate the Ummah against the enemy, the American-Israeli alliance."[69] In his

---

65. Springer et al., *Islamic Radicalism,* 14–16; and Gerges, *Far Enemy,* 147–50.

66. Quoted in Coll, *Ghost Wars,* 223.

67. Springer et al., *Islamic Radicalism,* 27.

68. Pollack, "Saudi Arabia and the United States," 85.

69. See PBS Web site, Bin Laden's Fatwa on www.pbs.org/newshour/terrorism/international/fatwa_1996.html.

second paragraph, following typical praises for Allah, he asserted that the "Arabian peninsula has never—since Allah made it flat, created its desert, and encircled it with seas—been stormed by any forces like the crusader armies spreading in it like locusts, eating its riches."[70] After describing a variety of aggressions against the Muslim world by the Zionist-Crusader alliance, the Declaration referred to the occupation of the "two holy places"—a reference to Mecca and Medina— as the most serious transgression of all.[71]

In February 1998, six months before the U.S. Embassy bombings in East Africa, Bin Laden issued a fatwa under the banner of the "World Islamic Front for Jihad against Jews and Crusaders." This fatwa again highlighted what appears to have been Bin Laden's chief grievance, the presence of American troops in Saudi Arabia; this grievance involved his two main targets, Saudi Arabia and the United States. The fatwa lambasted the Saudi regime for allowing infidels to occupy the most sacred lands of Islam, asserted that America had declared war on Allah and on Muslims, and called the faithful to attack American interests.[72]

After failing to claim responsibility for 9/11 but noting American transgressions, Bin Laden issued various statements. In a mid-November video, he spoke to a room of supporters, possibly in Kandahar, Afghanistan, with a video camera running. At the end of his exchange with a follower in which he had not yet explained his motivations for 9/11, he offered a glimpse into his mind by reciting a somewhat odd poem that emphasized how Muslims had been subjected to territorial aggression and invasion.[73]

The 1993 World Trade Center Bombing

The World Trade Center bombing may or may not have been connected to Bin Laden's grievances regarding the Gulf War, but it is an important event to understand, given that it was the first attack in the United States with links to Al-Qaeda. On February 26, Ramzi Ahmed Yousef, who was born to Pakistani-Palestinian parents in Kuwait in 1968, and his accomplices drove a rented van into the garage underneath one of the North Tower of the World Trade Center. Yousef set the bomb before leaving the garage in another vehicle. He later told interrogators that his goal was to topple one building and have it crash into the other, causing mass casualties, but only six people were killed as the explosion did not fell the

---

70. For more analysis, see Bergen, *Holy War, Inc.*, esp. 95–96.

71. Robert Pape finds that the U.S. military presence in the Middle East accounts for forty-three of sixty-seven Al-Qaeda suicide attacks (including the one from Lebanon), or 64%. Pape, *Dying to Win*, 114.

72. For more analysis, see Bergen, *Holy War, Inc.*, esp. 95–96.

73. For the transcript, see FindLaw Legal News on http://fl1.findlaw.com/news.findlaw.com/ hdocs/docs/binladen/binladenvid121301rls.pdf.

towers. It is not clear when Yousef began to plan the 1993 attack, but the best evidence indicates late 1991 and 1992. He asserted that he was motivated largely by his hatred of Israel and the United States. His turn toward terrorism chiefly came in 1991 when he established ties with elements from the Philippine terrorist group, Abu Sayyaf, and proposed the attack.[74] During his trial for the bombing after his 1995 arrest, he testified that he had planned the 1993 bombing at an Abu Sayyaf base in the Philippines with other veterans of the war in Afghanistan.[75]

To what extent the 1993 bombing increased Al-Qaeda's interest in conducting the September 11 attacks is not clear. Bin Laden's connection to the 1993 bombing is likewise not clear. None of the U.S. government's indictments against him suggested a link to this bombing, but evidence at least suggests an indirect link. Sheikh Omar Abdel Rahman, the militant cleric convicted in the 1993 plot, once led an Egyptian group now affiliated with Al-Qaeda; two of his sons are senior Al-Qaeda officials. And Yousef, who was convicted of masterminding the 1993 attack, spent time at Al-Qaeda training camps in Afghanistan.[76] Yousef's uncle is none other than Khalid Sheikh Mohammed, the architect of the 9/11 attacks, who provided advice and, on November 3, 1992, wired $660 from Qatar to the bank account of Yousef's co-conspirator, Mohammed Salameh.[77]

Oil-Stealing Infidels

Bin Laden asserted in his November 2001 confession to the 9/11 attacks that the Twin Towers were "full of supporters of American economical power which is exploiting the world."[78] He repeatedly claimed that Americans have been stealing Arab oil, sometimes subtly and sometimes less so;[79] that "[oil] production is restricted or expanded and prices are fixed to suit the American economy." However, he did not exhort his followers to attack the Saudi oil infrastructure in the 1990s, because he wanted to be able to exploit it in order to fund his ambition of creating a pan-Islamic superstate.[80]

---

74. See The Investigative Project on Terrorism, Individual terrorists on www.investigativeproject. org/profile/105.

75. Labeviere, *Dollars for Terror,* 220–21.

76. Wright, *Looming Tower,* ch. 9.

77. "Khalid Sheikh Mohammed," GlobalSecurity.org, available at www.globalsecurity.org/ military/world/para/ksm.htm.

78. For the transcript of this video, see http://purl.access.gpo.gov/GPO/LPS16430 (PDF).

79. Jacquard, *In the Name of Osama Bin Laden,* 110–11; and Schweitzer and Shay, *Globalization of Terror,* 29.

80. Daveed Gartenstein-Ross, "Al-Qaeda's Oil Weapon," *Daily Standard,* October 3, 2005, available at http://daveedgr.com/publications/internet-journals/Al-Qaedas-oil-weapon/, accessed September 9, 2009.

In typical fashion, he asserted in 1998 that the Muslim world and Islam are under siege, noting that others "rob us of our wealth and of our resources and of our oil. Our religion is under attack."[81] Instead of allowing this to happen, Bin Laden asserted that such resources should be protected in order to fund an Islamic state.[82] This depiction of oil-stealing Americans increased in prominence in the statements by Al-Qaeda and its affiliates well after September 11. In fact, the organized campaign to target Saudi oil facilities beginning in 2003 or 2004 gave this new emphasis teeth.[83] For Al-Qaeda and its sympathizers, oil is seen as an Arab resource controlled by a few greedy and corrupt families across the Gulf who serve America's interests and power, power which is then used to oppress Muslims around the world. Al-Qaeda not only resents American intervention in the Persian Gulf, it also sees oil as serving U.S. global power. Low oil prices buttress the global and American economy, while high oil prices hurt U.S. power. If Bin Laden had his wishes, he would have lead a radical regime in Saudi Arabia, evicting all Western influence from the region, and trying to raise oil prices. Thus, it is no surprise that Al-Qaeda affiliates attacked residential compounds and took hostages in late May 2004 in Saudi Arabia's Al-Hasa oil province. They did so days after Saudi Arabia indicated that it would tap its excess capacity from this area in order to lower global oil prices.

Loathing the Saudi Regime

While the 9/11 attacks were visited on the United States, it would be a mistake to believe that Bin Laden was focusing only or perhaps even primarily on the United States. Saudi Arabia was also a key target of the 9/11 attacks and of Al-Qaeda terrorism. The most persistent aspects of Bin Laden's statements were that non-Muslims should be expelled from the land of Mecca and Medina, that the un-Islamic House of Saud run by illegitimate royals should be overthrown, that such regimes are the main betrayers of Muslim causes (sometimes in cahoots with the Americans), and that they are hypocritical. When the Soviet War in Afghanistan came to a close in 1989, Al-Qaeda's goal was to keep its fighters together around the world to overthrow Arab governments, "because there's no Muslim government."[84]

---

81. *Frontline* interview with Osama Bin Laden, "Hunting the Enemy," May 1998.

82. Zambelis, "Attacks in Yemen."

83. On the nature and implications of attacks by Al-Qaeda affiliates in Saudi Arabia after 2003, see Al-Rasheed, *Contesting the Saudi State,* 134–210; Hegghammer, "Terrorist Recruitment," 39–60; Teitelbaum, "Terrorist Challenges," 1–11; Obaid and Cordesman, *Al-Qaeda in Saudi Arabia;* and Fattah, "Suicide Attacks Foiled."

84. Court Testimony of Al-Qaeda Operative Jamal al-Fadl."

Al-Qaeda also sees the Saudi regime as corrupt. In 1996, Bin Laden asserted that the Saudi people know that their country is the biggest oil producer in the world but realize that they are "suffering from taxes and bad services" and that Saudi Arabia is "a colony of America."[85] And he promoted the view that Saudi policy is controlled by the United States and Great Britain—two countries that "bear the greatest enmity toward the Islamic world."[86] He has repeatedly said that the Saudis serve American energy interests, allowing the United States to plunder the oil resources of the Arab nation, selling oil at prices favorable to the West, depriving the Muslim nation of these vast energy resources, and adding to its poverty and weakness around the world.[87]

Al-Qaeda also resents the U.S.-Saudi strategic relationship. This is partly because in Bin Laden's view, those who befriend the nonbelievers have disbelieved in Allah and His Prophet." He saw the Saudi regime as betraying Muslims by siding with those who wish to undermine the Muslim world. Bin Laden's grandiose plans were also disrupted by U.S. support for the Saudi monarchy. Using Saudi men to attack the United States could split the United States and Saudi Arabia and weaken the Al Saud, thus serving Al-Qaeda's goals. That may well be how the Saudi regime interprets Al-Qaeda's goals. As Saudi Prince Bandar argued, "Al-Qaeda will never control the Islamic world unless it controls Saudi Arabia because Saudi Arabia is home to Mecca and Medina and has great oil resources."[88] And if the United States weakens, then so will the various regimes, such as Saudi Arabia, that it helps keep in business.

Bin Laden also thought that the Saudis and Americans betrayed the Afghan resistance at the end of the war. In his view, they, and especially the United States, denied the Islamists their rightful control of Afghanistan. To him, Washington did not want Al-Qaeda or Islamists to have significant control but rather preferred a secular regime, so it instigated divisions among the Muslim rebels to try to achieve this end.[89]

We should also not underestimate Bin Laden's probable personal vendetta against the regime, discussed earlier in the chapter.

UN Economic Sanctions against Iraq

After the war, the United Nations imposed economic sanctions on Iraq. The invasion was partly oil-motivated, while the American-led response in Operations

---

85. "Saudi Oil Industry and Terrorism," United Press International, November 17, 2003.
86. See his interview with the magazine, *Nida'ul Islam*, available at www.fas.org/irp/world/para/docs/LADIN.htm.
87. Scheuer, *Through Our Enemies' Eyes*, 49–51.
88. CNBC interview by Chris Matthews, April 25, 2004.
89. This paragraph is based on Scheuer, *Through Our Enemies' Eyes*, 51–52.

Desert Shield and Desert Storm in 1991 was fundamentally linked to the abundant oil resources in the region.

The sanctions were targeted at a secular despot who had tortured Muslims and killed tens of thousands of his countrymen, but they also hurt the Iraqi economy and its people, who were seen increasingly as innocent victims, dying by the thousands, while Saddam built one palace after another and the United States ignored their problems. Recognizing this problem in early 2001, Washington sought to strengthen UN sanctions against Iraq by replacing the existing sanctions with "smart sanctions." Rather than letting Iraq off the hook, the United States aimed to ease economic sanctions while tightening sanctions against military and dual-use goods. For his part, Secretary of State Colin Powell asserted that through smart sanctions, "we have kept Saddam…in a box."[90] But such moves certainly did not appease Bin Laden. He repeatedly railed against UN economic sanctions, which he claimed had killed more than one million Iraqis. He also claimed that they were an American-imposed tool of domination and exploitation. Referring to the 9/11 attacks in his October 7, 2001, video statement, Bin Laden asserted that "there are civilians, innocent children being killed every day in Iraq without any guilt, and we never hear anybody. We never hear any fatwa from the clergymen of the government."[91]

Al-Qaeda's response to UN economic sanctions appeared to be part of a broader theme about perceived Western and especially American abuse of Muslims, under the guise of democracy and freedom. That theme appears repeatedly in statements by both Bin Laden and al-Zawahiri, both of whom cite a wide range of alleged American atrocities worldwide.[92] For instance, in a statement reflecting its own policy of preemption, al-Zawahiri asserted in a tape in early October 2004 that Muslims not wait to strike, or "we will be devoured one country after another."[93]

Oil Money and Al-Qaeda

As we shall see in chapter 4, oil money was critical in Al-Qaeda's continued development, and it may well have been linked fundamentally to the decision to attack the United States on 9/11, but not because the attacks were expensive to mount. Rather, there is reason to believe that al-Zawahiri, a critical player in the September 11 attacks, would not have agreed to Bin Laden's decision to attack the United

---

90. Colin Powell, Press Briefing, February 23, 2001.

91. For the transcript, see CNN.com WORLD "Bin Laden: America filled with fear" on http://archives.cnn.com/2001/WORLD/asiapcf/central/10/07/ret.binladen.transcript/index.html.

92. Rubin and Rubin, eds., *Anti-American Terrorism*, esp. 137–42. For essays written by al-Zawahiri after 9/11, see Federation of American Scientists, web site at www.fas.org.

93. Al-Issawi, "Tape Urges Young People to Strike U.S.," Associated Press, October 2, 2004.

States were it not for his own dire financial situation. In fact, he had been battling for years elements inside his own terrorist group, al-Jihad, who opposed his relationship with Bin Laden.[94] Input from insiders close to al-Zawahiri and documents show that al-Zawahiri's money from Persian Gulf benefactors dried up after the Soviet War in Afghanistan ended and that he was facing serious difficulty funding himself and his men. Enter Bin Laden. He had the money to transform this dire situation but, in this version of the story, would only do so if al-Zawahiri agreed to attack the United States and also to divert attention away from Egypt and local struggles.[95] Such money may well have been a major consideration in al-Zawahiri's decision to unite with Bin Laden's International Islamic Front for Jihad against Jews and Crusaders in 1998 after a period of separation.[96]

Disagreement exists about where Bin Laden's funds came from at this time. It is clear, however, that previous American intelligence estimates are mistaken that he had received a $300 million inheritance from his family. A closer examination, based on access to various records and discussions with Bin Laden family members, reveals that the actual amount was far smaller. It is quite possible that he received some funding through various banks from two religious half-sisters, Nur and Iman, who tapped into this family fortune; however, a far larger amount of Bin Laden's funds prior to September 11 came not from his family fortune but from wealthy donors and Islamic charities.[97] Much of this wealth was tied to oil. Likewise, whatever funds can be traced to his family's fortune were derived mainly from the family's construction business, which flourished due to Saudi Arabia's oil wealth.[98]

The Non-Oil Motivations

Oil-related issues, viewed largely through a distorted religious prism, constitute an important set of motivations for September 11, but they tell only part of the story. A number of non-oil factors are important to a better view of the range of factors that enabled and motivated 9/11.

---

94. Wright, *Looming Tower*, 336–37.

95. Attacking America could also serve to attack Saudi Arabia, since Washington supported the Al Saud. Such thinking may have also been in play later on regarding Iraq. In September 2003, an Al-Qaeda planning document published on the internet asserted that the way to compel the United States and its allies to leave Iraq was to attack America's European allies. That would push them to withdraw from Iraq and put more pressure on the United States to withdraw as well. Subsequent attacks on Spain did push it to withdraw from Iraq. Pape, *Dying to Win*, 55–57.

96. This paragraph is based on Gerges, *Far Enemy*, 121–23. See also Springer et al., *Islamic Radicalism*, 64–65.

97. On this money trail, see Coll, *Bin Ladens*, 412–13, 483–95.

98. Even though some construction business, such as in the role of the official builders and renovators of the Muslim holy sites of Mecca and Medina, was not about oil infrastructure.

The multiple factors that are not related to oil or only indirectly related to oil include the desire to create Taliban-like states, angst over Muslim world decline, ineffective states in the Muslim world, the impact of failed states, global poverty, globalization, Western culture and democracy, Israel and the Palestinian issue, and personal factors related to the Al-Qaeda rank and file. All are often ignored in assessing terrorism.

Creating Taliban-like States

The American presence in the region is largely—though not solely—oil-driven, but an American withdrawal from the Gulf would not eliminate terrorism, although it would likely decrease it. As Bin Laden asserted in May 1998, the "jihad against the U.S. does not stop with its withdrawal from the Arabian Peninsula, but rather it must desist from aggressive intervention against Muslims in the whole world."[99] We can safely conjecture that U.S. foreign policy can be only part of what motivates Al-Qaeda. This is because its goals are maximalist. It is not a negotiating organization. And ultimately, it seeks to create Islamic states on the model of the Taliban in Afghanistan and to produce a global caliphate. Al-Qaeda sees itself as the representative of all Muslims, who, in its view, comprise one entity (the Islamic ummah) that crosses borders and regions. Consider this representative statement in 2009 by its general official in Afghanistan, Mustafa abu al-Yazid. He asserts that even if the United States were to meet Al-Qaeda's stringent requests to change its behavior, Al-Qaeda would still demand much more:

> We invite them from now to enter Islam, so if they entered Islam, the fighting stops between us and them forever, but if they do not enter we will, Allah-willing, seek to establish the state of Islam and the Islamic Caliphate, then we will again invite them to enter Islam, so if they did, then thanks to Allah, and if not then we will enforce upon them the Islamic governance.[100]

Once again the views of dominating figures such as Qutb were likely at play. He called for a fundamental transformation of the government of man in all of its forms, to be replaced by affairs run by *sharia* following an Islamic revolution.[101]

---

99. In an interview with John Miller of ABC News, www.pbs.org/wgbh/pages/frontline/shows/binladen/who/miller.html.

100. Mustafa abu al-Yazid, the general official of the Al-Qaeda Organization in Afghanistan, June 22, 2009, Al Jazeera.

101. Murawiec, *Mind of Jihad*, esp. 258–59.

Muslim World Decline

In referring to the 9/11 attacks in his first public statement about 9/11, Bin Laden asserted that, "What America is facing today is something very little of what we have tasted for decades. Our nation, since nearly 80 years is tasting this humility."[102] As suggested earlier in this book, he appears to have been referring to the abolition of the Turkish caliphate—a major signpost of decline.

For a good part of the past thousand years, the world looked to Muslims for solutions to its problems, for leadership in science, medicine, and literature. However, as Bernard Lewis puts it, in the "course of the nineteenth and twentieth centuries, the dominance of the West was clear for all to see, invading the Muslim in every aspect of his public and—more painfully—even his private life."[103] By the middle of the nineteenth century, the loss of power and sense of threat from outside states provoked violent movements directed against the West.[104] Some observers see radical Islamists as imperial in their own right, seeking to recapture the dominant position that Muslims once enjoyed.[105]

The September 11 attacks, then, could have been motivated by the humiliation of Muslim world decline as well as by a desire to reestablish that glory in the form of a global caliphate. Attacking the United States could be viewed as serving both goals. A powerful, Western hegemon of a different civilization would not allow such grandiose plans to be hatched, not in the oil-rich Persian Gulf and certainly not in such a poor country as Afghanistan.

While this explanation may hold some water, it is not sufficient. Otherwise, we would see terrorists all over the world decrying the fall of empire. This motivation for 9/11 is also problematic in part because it cannot explain the timing of the attacks. After all, the Muslim world has been in decline for several hundred years.

Ineffective States

The trajectory of Muslim world decline, accentuated by the abolition of the caliphate, continued throughout the twentieth century. Many states proved ineffective at providing for their citizens, especially in comparison to their capitalist Western counterparts.

---

102. See CNN archives at http://archives.cnn.com/2001/WORLD/asiapcf/central/10/07/ret.binladen.transcript/index.html.

103. Lewis, *What Went Wrong?* 151.

104. Hourani, *History of the Arab Peoples*, 277.

105. Karsh, *Imperial Islam.*

The United States in particular combined free market economics, democracy, and immense resources to rise to global economic primacy and to provide its people with a high standard of living. Meanwhile, many dictatorial and monarchical Arab rulers failed to provide their peoples with adequate prospects for employment, advanced education, civil liberties, and even a coherent sense of identity. These failures are well known and have been documented by a panel of Arab intellectuals, which found that the world's 280 million Arabs are falling further behind the rest of the world due to poor education and a lack of freedom and economic opportunity. The combined GDP of the twenty-two countries of the Arab League stands at less than that of California. Far more than half of the women are illiterate, thus depriving society of an engine of growth. Very few people have access to the internet, and their access is sometimes blocked by the government, while the number of books translated into Arabic from other languages is shockingly small, leaving Arab readers at a great disadvantage in learning from others and enhancing their life prospects.[106] It appears that these poor conditions contributed to the collective frustration that fueled revolts and revolution in the Middle East beginning in January 2011.

Depending on the context, the disaffection engendered by these failures has expressed itself in different ways, including anti-Americanism. Blaming the United States for Arab world failures is easy and psychologically satisfying. For the Al-Qaeda leadership, it has also facilitated recruitment and enabled intense indoctrination. Without an enemy, turning normal human beings into suicidal mass murderers would be far harder.

Moreover, frustration with such failed regimes has created an identity vacuum that transnational groups such as Al-Qaeda can exploit and fill. Instead of identifying with failed states, Al-Qaeda followers and sympathizers could identify with Islam and with a transnational religious community. In place of corrupt regimes, they can fancy themselves followers of God, of a pure form of Islam, and of the correct path to eternal bliss. In turn, in identifying and internalizing the Islamic identity fashioned by Al-Qaeda, these recruits become fertile soil for manipulation.

The inefficacy of states also creates pressures for reform and the political divisions that accompany it. Some observers even ascribe the most important cause of September 11 to the violent and enduring clash in the Muslim world between reformers who seek to secularize government and those who want to keep, advance, or impose various versions of Islamic fundamentalism or radicalism.[107] Al-Qaeda represents the most extreme form of the latter. But beyond

---

106. Arab Human Development Reports (yearly).
107. Halliday, *Two Hours That Shook the World,* esp. 46.

the failures of states to perform their duties, nation-states themselves are suspect as entities, even if they perform well. What Bin Laden emphasized is that the ummah is blessed by God, whereas the nation-state is not. Many Muslims can be loyal to both the ummah and the nation-state, even if that generates some tensions between the two. But Bin Laden saw states, and certainly the Saudi state, as illegitimate partly because they seek to command loyalty from individuals whose loyalty should be to God and the ummah.

Failed and Failing States

Ineffective states are not the same as failed and failing states that have trouble governing their territories. Many scholars and policymakers see a connection between these states and transnational terrorism. They believe that both failed and failing states are more likely to contain terrorist groups, to face terrorist attacks, to have citizens that participate in terrorist acts, and to have terrorists build bases on their territory.[108] One reason offered for this outcome is that in failed states terrorist groups can operate outside governmental control. Al-Qaeda under the Taliban in Afghanistan prior to the September 11 attacks is a good example. To what extent it was enmeshed with the Taliban regime is unclear, but it surely had its own agenda as well. It could operate freely in Afghanistan, which allowed it to prepare for September 11 in ways that would not have been possible if it had to evade the scrutiny of a state government. Groups that seek to launch transnational attacks, in particular, have more extensive logistical and training needs and therefore benefit from autonomous space without the costs of evading law enforcement.[109]

Global Poverty

A common view is that terrorism stems from poverty, as reflected in policy proposals such as a "Middle East Marshall Plan" that could help build the economies of the Middle East in the hope of decreasing poverty in the region. According to the 2009 Arab Human Development Report produced by Arab intellectuals and analysts, Arab countries are generally regarded as having a relatively low incidence of income poverty, compared to other developing areas in the world.

---

108. On this literature, see Piazza, "Incubators of Terror," 469–88. Piazza finds that states plagued by chronic state failures are statistically more likely to host terrorist groups that commit transnational attacks, have their nationals commit transnational attacks, and to be targeted by transnational terrorists themselves.

109. Ibid., 471–72.

In 2005, about 20.3 percent of the Arab population was living below the international poverty line ($2 per day).[110]

But the Middle East is poor compared to the industrialized world, generating speculation that terrorist activity may be linked to poverty. Some evidence suggests that poverty generates feelings of military and economic inferiority, which push people to express their discontent violently.[111] One experienced Yemeni official may have captured the general sentiment when he stated, "Osama Bin Laden does not appeal to people because he is defending Palestine. He appeals to them because of the issues and problems they have."[112]

The academic literature on the link between poverty and terrorism is still developing, with some studies finding little correlation between economic factors such as GDP per capita or GDP growth and the incidence of terrorism.[113] As one study argues, any connection linking poverty, education, and terrorism is indirect, complicated, and probably quite weak. Instead of viewing terrorism as a direct response to poverty, it is probably much more a response to political conditions and longstanding feelings of indignity and frustration that have little to do with economics.[114]

The poverty argument seems to make sense on the surface, but we must also consider the fact, now well known, that the September 11 attackers, as well as Bin Laden and his senior assistants, were neither poor nor uneducated. Bin Laden's father had amassed a fortune that exceeded $10 billion, and Osama was raised in an elite and powerful context due largely to his father's business and friendship with the royal family. His top aide, Ayman al-Zawahiri, is a former surgeon and member of an affluent, even elite family. Even the lower-level 9/11 terrorists were mostly from middle-class families and hardly uneducated. Beyond Bin Laden, studies have shown that a large percentage of Egyptians who belonged to groups affiliated to Al-Qaeda came from stable middle-class homes and were college educated. The same studies show that the connection between terrorism and poverty is quite weak.[115] The leaders of the Islamic Salvation Front in Algeria, for example, were much better educated than the public at large. Some evidence

---

110. United Nations Development Programme, *Arab Human Development Report 2009*, 11.

111. Li and Schaub, "Poverty Causes Terrorism"; and Munoz, ed., *At Issue: Is Poverty a Serious Threat?*

112. Abu-Nasr, "Yemen Tries."

113. On this literature, see Krueger and Laitin, "Kto Kogo," esp. 149. Krueger and Laitin's study also concludes that neither country GDP nor illiteracy is a good predictor of terrorist national origins. See also Arena and Arrigo, *Terrorist Identity.*

114. Krueger and Malečková, "Education, Poverty, and Terrorism," 119–44.

115. Von Hippel, "Roots of Terrorism," 26–28.

even suggests that suicide terrorists have educational levels exceeding the societal mean and are less likely to live in poverty than the average person.[116]

Poverty might seem to contribute to terrorism, but people, even the deprived and the angry, do not wake up in the morning and become terrorists. If that were true, every rich neighborhood near a ghetto would face suicide bombings every day. But we do not see that, so we know that deprivation and anger cannot be enough to cause people to act savagely. If poverty fundamentally begat terrorism, there are plenty of people who would be standing ahead of the 9/11 crew—or Middle Easterners in general—as terrorists.

Globalization

The factor of globalization is discussed in detail later, but a glimpse of its role can be provided here. The eclipse of Muslim civilization and the failure of many modern Arab states were especially problematic against the backdrop of the rise of America as the preeminent state. Jealousy and hatred may well stem as much from American prowess and wealth as from American foreign policy. Globalization, driven and dominated by the United States, adds fear and confusion, important elements that feed jealousy of America. The United States represents the epitome of capitalist success and excess. The September 11 hijackers aimed their fury at the heart of American and world economic prowess. They could at once cause great economic harm and assuage their own collective and historical feelings of inadequacy. As one Saudi insider put it, they want to go back to the seventh century as a reaction against modernization.[117]

Western Culture and Democracy

Some might argue that Al-Qaeda is threatened by the American way of life. For instance, in his address to Congress shortly after September 11, President George W. Bush asserted that "these terrorists kill not merely to end lives, but to disrupt and end a way of life."[118] This may be true. Bin Laden, unlike local terrorists, had a global view. In this cosmic struggle, Islamic fundamentalism and Western democracy cannot coexist on one planet. But we still must ask: if Western democracy and culture disturb Al-Qaeda so much, then why has its rhetoric been directed

---

116. Fair, *Madrassah Challenge*, 67–68.

117. Chris Matthews, CNBC interview of Saudi Ambassador to the United States, Prince Bandar, April 25, 2004.

118. See CNN.com, Transcript of President Bush's address to a joint session of Congress, www.cnn.com/2001/US/09/20/gen.bush.transcript/.

almost solely at Washington? Why didn't it attack the United States earlier? And why does it refer to this explanation in its justifications very little, compared to other issues? This explanation, abstract as it is, can only tell us so much.

Israel and the Palestinians

Bin Laden sought to portray himself as the savior of the Palestinian people. Al-Qaeda promotes a global Zionist-American conspiracy. He refers to Crusaders and Jews quite commonly and sees America's policy in the Middle East as aiming to "serve the Jews' petty state and divert attention from its occupation of Jerusalem and murder of Muslims there."[119] For Bin Laden, Israel was at once a Western outpost in the Middle East, an embodiment of all that is bad about the West and a prime reason that the United States seeks to weaken Muslim states in the region, including Iraq. In February 1998, Bin Laden issued a fatwa for the "World Islamic Front for Jihad against Jews and Crusaders." This fatwa stated ominously that all Muslims have a religious duty "to kill Americans and their allies, both civilian and military."[120]

By this time, however, Bin Laden had already identified the United States for attack, based on a long list of grievances tied to various events discussed earlier in this chapter. Israel, of course, is always a useful scapegoat in the Middle East. Palestinians want to be on the global agenda. Arab autocrats want to divert attention from their own economic failures. States that sponsor terrorism want to avoid overdue scrutiny. And some who seek to burnish radical credentials must be anti-Israel—the more virulently so, the better. Al-Qaeda knows that bashing Israel is a good recruiting tactic, because the Palestinian cause is widely viewed in the Muslim Street as important. It is no surprise that Al-Qaeda's recruitment video features Israel much more than its other videos, statements, and proclamations.[121]

But there are problems with the Israel explanation as a motivation for 9/11. Like al-Zawahiri, whose focus was initially on the government of his native Egypt, Bin Laden's initial fixation was his native land, Saudi Arabia. Israel came into the picture later. It was only in June 2001 that Bin Laden first publicly appealed to Muslims to join their brethren fighting in Palestine, and little of Al-Qaeda's terrorism was aimed at Israel; in fact, despite carrying out many attacks, it was not

---

119. "Jihad against Jews and Crusaders," World Islamic Front Statement, February 23, 1998, available at www.pbs.wgbh/pages/frontline/shows/binladen/who/family.html.

120. "Written Statement for the Record," 5.

121. For the transcript from the video, see Rubin and Rubin, eds., *Anti-American Terrorism*, 174–77.

until 2000—a time during which Bin Laden was criticized for neglecting the Palestinian struggle in favor of a broader battle against the United States—that Al-Qaeda directly attacked Israeli or Jewish targets. Al-Qaeda's bombings in Yemen, Bali, Spain, Saudi Arabia, Africa, and so forth were not about Israel. Nor does Al-Qaeda appear to coordinate with various Palestinian factions. Rather, it has focused far more on the U.S. role in the Persian Gulf and the global effort to undermine American power, with Israel apparently being partly a tactical concern and partly one of Al-Qaeda's larger set of issues with the United States and the West.

Personal Factors: The Al-Qaeda Leaders

The jury is out on the role of psychology in Al-Qaeda terrorism. Obviously, this variable is not so easy to assess. Some scholars believe that even the September 11 suicide bombers exhibited normal psychologies.[122] But even if we accept this notion, which challenges intuition, that still leaves a more critical question: what about the Al-Qaeda leadership that made the key decisions?

Bin Laden appeared deluded in thinking that he had a great mission as the savior of Muslims. His behavior may have reflected what Steven Diamond calls "a classic case of inflation: a pathological over-identification with the Messiah archetype, the universally innate image of an embodied savior or chosen one."[123] Bin Laden and his coterie seek to destroy the United States and its global presence rather than to achieve particular political goals in one issue area or region. This explains why Al-Qaeda, rather than other terrorist groups, would attack New York and Washington.

To be sure, Bin Laden's grandiose view was stoked by the success of the mujaheddin, which helped Bin Laden kick the Soviets out of Afghanistan in the 1980s. But to believe that he could fell another superpower of a different sort suggests megalomania, something psychological and not just political or religious. This megalomania may have been accentuated by a distorted view of Islam to produce a noxious brew of aggression, hatred, determination, and entitlement, an entitlement to greater influence in world affairs and divinely inspired victory over the infidels. Interestingly, Prince Turki viewed Bin Laden's offer to protect the kingdom against Saddam as the "first signs of a disturbed mind."[124]

For being increasingly vocal against the regime, the Saudis stripped him of citizenship in 1994, and he left the kingdom for Sudan, on the invitation of Islamist

---

122. Cronin, "Sources of Contemporary Terrorism," 24.
123. Diamond, "Messiahs of Evil."
124. Quoted in Coll, Ghost Wars, 601.

theoretician Hassan al-Turabi after an Islamist coup d'état. During this time, Bin Laden assisted the Sudanese government, bought or set up various business enterprises, and established training camps where insurgents trained. He was forced to leave Sudan, due to American and Egyptian pressure on the Sudan government sparked by his involvement in terrorist training in Sudan in general and particularly by his role in the attempted assassination of Egyptian president Hosni Mubarak in Ethiopia in 1995. Bin Laden then established himself in Afghanistan in 1996 as a guest of the Taliban regime. These factors, along with the American missile attacks on his compounds in 1998, generated what appear to be personal vendettas against Washington and Riyadh.

We cannot underestimate that Bin Laden held the United States responsible for having him evicted from Sudan in May 1996. Washington had pressured the Sudanese government to take this action, and Khartoum, feeling that its international legitimacy was at stake, complied Bin Laden did not like civil-war–stricken Afghanistan in his first months there, as compared to the more comfortable Sudan. Shortly after his arrival, he began to compose a long, angry declaration of war against the United States. It was the first document that he ever published which formally and publicly called for a violent campaign against the West.[125] Clearly, he now saw Washington as a primary enemy. He had already been agitated by the American presence in the Gulf and by other grievances, and he had already been nurturing a plan to bomb American embassies in Africa, which would be carried out in 1998.

However, these combustible views appear to have been at least partially caused by his eviction from Sudan. He would not have faced this plight had he not been kicked out of Saudi Arabia, which had also frozen his divested shareholdings, and then, two months later, stripped him of his citizenship. After his arrival in Sudan from Saudi Arabia, he became increasingly vocal against the Al Saud, writing dramatic and angry critiques of their rule.[126] Of course, several weeks after the East Africa bombings, President William J. Clinton fired cruise missiles aimed at killing Bin Laden, which may have added further to his interest in targeting America. Overall, then, personal factors placed both America and Saudi Arabia as prime targets.

Beyond psychology, other personal factors may have been in play. For instance, one motivation about which we hear little is that Bin Laden reportedly believed that an attack on the United States would be good for business. It could benefit Al-Qaeda by attracting more suicide operatives, drumming up more donations

---

125. Ibid., 417, 461–63.
126. Ibid., 408–12.

from the faithful or hateful, and increasing the numbers of sympathizers, all of which could facilitate its future operations and embolden him as a leader.[127]

The September 11 attacks, like other major events in world politics, will be studied for many decades; as more documents on the attacks are released, our view of what contributed to them will improve. It appears that Middle Eastern oil was an important factor in the 9/11 attacks because it helped to motivate the attacks, enabled them in various ways such as contributing to the development of Al-Qaeda and the Taliban, and contributed to a chain of events that contributed to setting up the attacks in the first place. The design of this chapter also shows the importance of non-oil factors as well and the distorted religious lens through which Al-Qaeda's leaders saw the world.

---

127. *9/11 Commission Report*, 251.

3

RISING ANTI-AMERICANISM IN THE GLOBAL AUDIENCE

The September 11 attacks were motivated in part by issues related to Middle Eastern oil, but such issues have been germane beyond their impact on Al-Qaeda. These issues are followed by a global audience, partly due to their emotive importance but also because globalization has allowed world politics to become a mass spectator event. The response of the audience of Muslims and non-Muslims matters to the broader question of transnational terrorism. We cannot understand it well if we treat it as a phenomenon in isolation from the larger context in which it gains meaning and which affects its nature and direction.

U.S. foreign policy has generated a variety of outcomes, but regardless of what one thinks of it, the U.S. role in oil-related issues tends to play into a not uncommon historical perspective in the Middle East and beyond: that the United States is a power-hungry imperialist actor seeking control over oil, a state bent on advancing its interests at the expense of local Muslims. Al-Qaeda has attempted to capitalize on this perspective in order to advance a conflict of ideas, to generate anti-Americanism even among those who would never adopt Al-Qaeda's ways, and to recruit followers to its side. Polling data from the Muslim world, which, given the difficulty of accurate polling in authoritarian societies, are not definitive, strongly suggest that aspects of Al-Qaeda's message did strike a broader chord, though its message lost traction over time. Al-Qaeda has been more effective at generating anti-Americanism than in making its own ideas attractive to others. It has sought to generate a clash of civilizations but so far appears to have failed in this effort. However, this does not mean that it has not gained adherents and sympathy beyond its small numbers.

Cognitive Lenses and Belief Systems

How human beings make decisions is an area of great interest and importance. We do know that in making decisions, we sometimes delve into the relevant past knowledge and experience stored in our long-term memory, such as that reflected in analogies.[1] Much of cognitive psychology revolves around schemas, scripts, and analogies.[2] Knowledge structures such as analogies help human beings process and evaluate information, in part by assisting them in matching new pieces of information against their stored memories.[3] Beliefs derived from analogies or other sources feed into decisionmaking by helping us decide what information matters, analyze new situations, and explore key questions about human behavior and the world in which they live.[4] Some scholars believe that "operational codes" represent an aspect of an individual's beliefs—those that deal with politics. They can be highly influential in affecting how individuals interpret information, perceive the broader environment, and make decisions in the political world.[5]

All of us draw lessons from the past to deal with current issues, either consciously or subconsciously. In the Middle East, perhaps more than in other regions, it is common to interpret the present through the lens of the past. This can illuminate events and the actions of others or distort them. While we must be careful not to indulge in gross generalizations, it is fair to say that some Westerners view some Middle Easterners partly through a lens that shapes what they see in the first place, what they consider important, what they fear, and what they mistrust. A *Washington Post*–ABC News poll released in March 2006 found that nearly half of Americans—46 percent—had a negative view of Islam, seven percentage points higher than in the tense months after the September 11, 2001, attacks on the World Trade Center and the Pentagon, when Muslims were often targeted for violence.[6] In a poll conducted in August 2010 by the Pew Research Center for the

---

1. For a good overview and formulation of cognitive process theory, see Taber, "Interpretation of Foreign Policy Events," 29–52.

2. Ibid., 25.

3. Nisbett and Ross, *Human Inference*, 17–42, 28–42; and Abelson and Black, "Introduction," 1–20.

4. Rosati, *Power of Human Cognition.*

5. On this literature, see Renshon, *Stability and Change in Belief Systems*, 820.

6. Deane and Fears, *Negative Perception.*

People and the Press and the Pew Forum on Religion and Public Life, 30 percent of those polled said that they had a favorable opinion of Islam, while slightly more (38%) had an unfavorable view; nearly a third (32%) offered no opinion. In 2005, slightly more expressed a favorable opinion of Islam than an unfavorable opinion (41% to 36%).[7]

At the same time, stereotyping appears to occur in the other direction even more prominently, a product of what I call "the historical perspective." It is a perspective through which I believe many Muslims, in varying degrees, view the United States. This book tries to recognize the complexity and varied views of Middle Easterners and the pitfalls of generalization, but it does aim to highlight strains of thought within this complexity.

The views that shape the historical perspective do contain a kernel of truth, but they are problematic insofar as they lead people to miss what they do not expect to see. Such beliefs can undermine a clear view of others if they introduce significant biases, exclude or restrict the search for novel information, or push actors to ignore the facts and options that clash with the message encoded in the analogy.[8] Studies of human behavior have shown that people can miss what they do not expect to see. The famous invisible gorilla experiment revealed as much.[9] Christopher Chabris and Daniel Simons asked people to watch a short video in which six people—three in white shirts and three in black shirts—pass basketballs around. Those watching were asked to count the number of passes made by the people in white shirts. During the video, a person in a gorilla suit strolls into the middle of the action, faces the camera, thumps its chest, and leaves, spending nine seconds on screen (out of twenty-four seconds). Half of the people who watched the video and counted the passes never saw the gorilla at all. It was as though the gorilla was invisible.

Ingrained perspectives can also focus attention on particular outcomes. Humans may well miss what they do not expect to see, but they also may see too much. Experiments have repeatedly found that people tend to search for evidence that will confirm their hypothesis. They have a hypothesis in search of facts and are biased toward confirming their own conscious and unconscious expectations and view of the world. Psychologists refer to this as confirmation bias.[10] They may do so in a variety of ways as they search for evidence, interpret evidence, recall memories, or selectively gather evidence.[11]

---

7. See The Pew Forum, "Religion and Politics," at http://features.pewforum.org/politics

8. On this literature, see Wallace et al., "Political Rhetoric of Leaders under Stress in the Gulf Crisis," 95–96. On the impact of stress, see Janis and Mann, *Decision Making*; and Brecher, "State Behavior in a Crisis," 446–80.

9. Chabris and Simons, *Invisible Gorilla*.

10. Baron, *Thinking and Deciding*, 162–65; and Kida, *Don't Believe Everything You Think*, 62–65.

11. Risen and Gilovich, "Informal Logical Fallacies," 110–30.

Playing into the Historical Perspective

The historical perspective has several key components.[12] First, the West has been viewed as composed of powerful, sometimes colonialist countries dominating weaker actors in the Middle East. And this refers not just to Western powers but also to the Ottoman Empire, which spanned much of the Middle East, and the many great powers that have sought to exploit the region much farther back in history. In more recent times, between the two world wars, Arab nationalism took root and was driven partly by anticolonialism.[13]

The colonial perspective is prominent enough that major leaders use it to sway Arab world opinion. For example, President Saddam Hussein, in trying to win support during the 1990–91 Persian Gulf crisis, appealed to it repeatedly, attempting to construct himself as the victim who would defeat a great power that he referred to as "Satan," the "Grand Satan," "Unholy," "Criminal Bush," "Loathsome Criminal," "Evil Butcher," and "Satan of the Era."[14] Saddam invoked al-Qadisiyah, where Arab armies defeated the Sassanid Empire of Persia during the early years of Islam, a battle to which he referred in his speeches during the Iran-Iraq and Gulf Wars.[15] Thus, Saddam's attempts to construct the 1990–91 crisis were part of a broader propaganda war directed at his domestic audience, at the Arab world, and at the West.[16] Certainly, the theme of colonialism is also prominent in Al-Qaeda's worldview. One of its most prominent documents asserts that "Muslim countries today are colonized" either in a "direct or veiled" manner.... The real ruler is the Crusader United States."[17]

The notion of a West seeking to dominate locals especially involves exploitation of the region's land and resources. This notion animates Al-Qaeda but also resonates more broadly. For instance, Saddam Hussein argued in a September 19, 2002, letter to the United Nations General Assembly that the United States wanted "to destroy Iraq in order to control the Middle Eastern oil, and consequently control the politics as well as the oil and economic policies of the whole world."[18]

---

12. For an analysis that supports aspects of this perspective, see Lynch, "Anti-Americanisms in the Arab World."

13. Barnett, *Dialogues in Arab Politics*, 61.

14. Bengio, *Saddam Speaks*.

15. Baghdad Domestic Service, in FBIS: NES, September 6, 1990, p. 27. See also Saddam's speech on Baghdad Radio, "Acts of Treachery against Iraq's Struggling Forces," February 24, 1991, translated by Reuters; and Bengio, *Saddam's Word*, 172–75, 205–6.

16. For an excellent work on symbolism and construction in inter-Arab politics, see Barnett, *Dialogues in Arab Politics*.

17. Pape, *Dying to Win*, 117–19.

18. *New York Times*, September 20, 2002, p. A12.

Beyond Al-Qaeda and Arab dictators, perceptions of resource-stealing Americans animate broader views, as we shall see in this chapter. Public opinion polls in authoritarian societies can be problematic for a variety of well-known reasons, first and foremost the reluctance of individuals to express their views candidly. Still, they help to piece together a picture that suggests that mainstream Muslims share some of the notions embedded in the historical perspective sketched out in this chapter: Muslims polled over the 2001–8 period in the Pew Global Attitudes Project have an aggrieved view of the West. Majorities in many Muslim nations— and in some Western European ones, for that matter—believe America's war on terrorism is really an effort to control Mideast oil or to dominate the world.[19] According to a Pew Research Center opinion poll, 76 percent of Russians, 75 percent of French citizens, 54 percent of Germans, and 44 percent of British believed that the U.S.-led invasion of Iraq in 2003 was driven by a desire to control Iraq's oil.[20] Most Iraqis, it is fair to say, held this view, which has been prominent among moderate and radical Islamists around the world.

One survey conducted in six Arab states in late February 2003 showed that more than 80 percent believed that dominating oil was an important motivation for America's invasion of Iraq; 70 percent thought that support for Israel was important; and virtually no respondents thought that the United States was seeking to promote democracy.[21] Such a view may help explain why polling data in a survey of seventeen nations conducted by the Pew Foundation showed that Muslim publics were somewhat more inclined to support suicide bombings when carried out against Americans and other Westerners in Iraq than in other places.[22] Concern about American regional domination may also explain why Arab publics fear the United States and Israel more than they do Iran. A poll by Zogby International and the University of Maryland released in August 2010 found that Arabs in Egypt, Jordan, Morocco, Saudi Arabia, and the United Arab Emirates were discouraged by American policies and had little confidence in President Barack Obama after having supported him in his first year. In addition, for the first time, a majority of respondents supported a nuclear-armed Iran.[23] Such polling results may stem from frustration with Washington and from an interest in seeing a Muslim state counterbalance America and Israel with nuclear weapons.

---

19. See Pew Global Attitudes Project, "Global Public Opinion in the Bush Years (2001-2008)" on http://pewglobal.org/reports/display.php?ReportID=263.

20. Cited in ibid., 280.

21. Lynch, "Anti-Americanisms in the Arab World," 211.

22. "Testimony of Andrew Kohut."

23. For an interview with Shibley Telhami, who conducted the poll with Zogby International, see www.npr.org/templates/story/story.php?storyId=129047080.

Global elites may share such views of American and Western interest in oil domination. For instance, in an interview on May 27, 2009, the OPEC Secretary General Abdullah al-Badri was asked if OPEC is still powerful, and he responded that OPEC has never sought power, that it was created "to protect the wealth and resources" of the locals and not to exert control over others.[24] For his part, Iraq's prime minister Nouri al-Maliki made various references to American domination of Iraq as American forces were withdrawing from Iraqi cities in June 2009, even suggesting a "heroic repulsion of the foreign occupiers." He felt it necessary or politically useful to make such comments. This may well be because he is playing up to an ingrained narrative, one that is widespread and sees the United States in unflattering terms, especially with the rise of American power globally and in the Middle East.[25] Consider that while 35 percent of Jordanians considered the 9/11 attacks to be terrorism, 86 percent viewed the U.S.-led invasion of Iraq as terrorism.[26]

For more moderate Muslims who were polled regarding U.S. foreign policy, their concerns extend well beyond oil, but oil is at once a real concern and a metaphor for imperialist impulses, a metaphor that reflects fears over the asymmetry of power and mistrust over the intentions of a dominating West. Many tend to believe that American hegemony has come at the expense of Muslims, that America is a unilateralist, arrogant power, that it supports corrupt governments, and that corrupt Western ways threaten the Muslim world.

As underscored throughout this book, the oil factor is prominent in Al-Qaeda's thinking. The view of oil-stealing Americans has permeated Al-Qaeda statements.[27] Whether or not one views America in these terms, the picture of an imperialistic America has bedeviled the United States. One common theme in editorials and official statements across the Middle East is that America is bent on hegemony, sometimes in collaboration with the Zionists.[28] As one scholar put it, America's powerful reaction to the September 11 attacks piqued and "reinstated Arab fears of the other who is out to get them," fears which have been formed in the crucible of history and are "deep down in the transitional memory, undetectable with simple methods and techniques."[29]

---

24. Interview by Melissa Francis on CNBC, May 27, 2009.
25. For an excellent analysis, see Lynch, "Anti-Americanisms in the Arab World," esp. 199–223.
26. Ibid., 211.
27. See, for instance, Whitlock, "Commandos Free Hostages."
28. A rough reflection of these views appears in Cairo Al-Akhbar in FBIS: NES, April 29, 2004 (WNC# 0hwzjsq02huz10); and Tehran Voice of the Islamic Republic of Iran Radio in FBIS: NES, May 1, 2004 (WNC# 0hx54gd03nosvi).
29. Nehme, *Fear and Anxiety in the Arab World,* 7.

That Washington did consider taking over Saudi oil fields during the 1973 oil embargo in order to prevent possible strangulation of the global economy is well remembered in the kingdom and elsewhere in the Arab world, and the memory has only added to suspicions of American motives.[30] Polling information to which I referred earlier strongly suggests profound distrust of American motives. Perceptions that Washington wants the region's oil may well inflame anti-Americanism, but that the Arabs control so much oil also spurs resentments in the West. Any time oil prices rise to a level that the West considers too high, resentment rises. Of course, Western dependence on oil puts a brake on how far the West is willing to break with oil-rich states. But globalization does not put a brake on global citizens. They are not restrained by the diktat of globalization.

The oil explanation is an important part of the perspective, but it can only take us so far. Polling shows that the United States was least popular and Bin Laden most popular in countries such as Pakistan, Jordan, and Morocco, which have no oil. We might expect them to be most negative toward the United States if fears about oil domination and oil-stealing were preeminent. Muslims may be concerned about the fate of Middle Eastern oil in general, even if their governments do not own it, but one would guess that other factors are at work in driving their positions.[31]

Third, religion is sometimes wrapped in these notions of domination and oil. Western powers are seen as seeking to undermine Islam, partly to control oil and to elevate Western and Israeli power in the region. Such views have deep antecedents. Bin Laden, for instance, was not the only one who viewed the Western presence in the holy land as problematic. According to the Hanbali school of Islamic law to which many Saudis subscribe, this is a major transgression, leaving many Muslims with serious doubts about American and Saudi regime behavior.

Most of Saddam's efforts in the 1990–91 Persian Gulf crisis, a bit like those of Bin Laden, were intended to make him appear to be a devout Muslim staring down the imperial Christian West and the Zionist-American conspirators, one who would deal a blow to the returning crusaders as a modern-day Saladin, protecting the integrity and power of Muslims. Frequently quoting the Qur'an, Saddam at one point referred to the famous battle of Badr in 624 A.D. in which a small band of Muslims defeated a far larger group of infidels. He reminded

---

30. Jedda Arab News, in FBIS: NES, 3, January 2004 (WNC# 0hr0vb000npw7x).

31. One explanation is that support for terrorism may be declining in part because Arab and Muslim publics see Islamic extremism as a threat to their own countries. This is especially true in Morocco, Pakistan, and Turkey as well as among Lebanese Christians. In contrast, relatively few Jordanians are concerned about domestic extremism. See "Testimony of Andrew Kohut."

Arabs how Muhammad had blinded his enemies by throwing sand in their eyes and suggested that the battle against the U.S.-led coalition could be similar: "You did not slay them, but God slew them."[32] In his famous "Mother of All Battles" speech, Saddam asserted typically that after Iraq won the war with the "infidels, the Zionists, and the treacherous, shameful rulers, such as the traitor Fahd," the door will then be "wide open" for the liberation of Jerusalem for all Muslims.[33]

The notion that Islam is a threat to the West has never really gone away, and its examination has become a cottage industry in academia.[34] But many in the Muslim world also see the "global war on terrorism" as a U.S.-led war on Islam.[35] In fact, in a 2004 poll in Egypt, Jordan, Saudi Arabia, Morocco, Lebanon, and the United Arab Emirates, political scientist Shibley Telhami along with Zogby International discovered that more than three-fourths of the respondents believe that American aims in Iraq are intended in part "to weaken the Muslim world," with dominating oil as one vehicle for this goal, and to defile Muslim holy places in order to spread Christianity.[36]

The United States at times fanned such notions of religious war. The whole concept of a "global war on terror," involving those who are "with us" and "against us," painted the conflict in such Manichean terms that it accorded well with Bin Laden's own descriptions of a cosmic war between good and evil, and almost seemed to elevate Al-Qaeda to the level of fighting one of history's greatest powers.[37]

President Bush also invoked religious imagery. This may have accentuated the struggle with Al-Qaeda as a truly grand fight.[38] From the day following 9/11, when he asserted that he was in the "Lord's hands," to his rhetoric about good and evil. Bush was prone to a religious interpretation of events.[39] He infused his rhetoric with a higher dose of religious imagery than any president in recent memory. His reference to the war on terrorism as a crusade meant to underscore an unrelenting effort to fight terrorism, but Muslims and others around the world were disturbed by this term, which refers to the slaughters and encroachments of Christian invasions during the Middle Ages and a form of collective emasculation.

---

32. Bengio, *Saddam's Word,* 182.

33. "The Mother of All Battles" speech on Baghdad Radio (translated by Reuters), January 20, 1991.

34. For instance, see Esposito, *Islamic Threat.*

35. Karam, *Transnational Political Islam.*

36. See Anwar Sadat, Chair for Peace and Development, Arab Public Opinion Surveys on www.sadat.umd.edu/new%20surveys/surveys.htm. Haddad, "Islamist Perceptions," 467–72.

37. On how Bush played into Bin Laden's hands, see Aslan, *How to Win a Cosmic War.*

38. Mahajan, *New Crusade.*

39. Bacevich and Prodromou, "God Is Not Neutral," 49. See also Juergensmeyer, "Religious Terror and Global War."

Bush's statement was interpreted as either a deliberate ploy or a reflection of true feelings; either way, his use of religious rhetoric seemed indifferent to the perspectives of many Muslims.[40] Crusader-era imagery was threaded through the Muslim narrative, and the Crusader's brutality had been captured and transmitted through the generations through poems, literature, and the oral tradition. In a critical philosophical treatise, Al-Qaeda lashed out against Bush's "crusade" gaffe, seeking to portray it as an indication of the true feelings and goals of the United States.[41]

Bush referred several times in the spring of 2004 to the notion that a higher source was driving his behavior. One might surmise that Bush would be criticized for copious religious imagery, and to some extent he was, but he may have struck a broader chord with many Americans. Even during the presidential election, the campaign of Senator John Kerry shied away from open criticism. Bush's religious imagery may have been resonant not only among Christian conservatives and evangelicals who interpreted world events partly through a religious lens, but also among those Americans who viewed Muslims negatively even prior to September 11.[42]

The Global Audience

Perspectives are critical because they are vehicles by which the global audience can be drawn into the conflict through framing and other techniques.[43] The audience for conflicts is rarely partial and unmoved, especially when it comes to a charged conflict between radical terrorists and the United States. Such conflicts tend to become socialized or, in other words, to involve and affect a range of actors who are not initially involved in the conflict. Actors drawn into conflict are significant because the nature and extent of their involvement may determine the direction and outcome of conflict. As political scientist E. E. Schattschneider put it, it is "extremely unlikely that both sides will be reinforced equally."[44]

The socialization of conflict and the role of the audience have become more prominent in world politics, partly due to rising globalization. The interests of actors caught in conflict are more likely to be intertwined with that of third parties. This is because globalization increases the probability that conflict between

40. Peters, "Firanj Are Coming—Again," 3–19.
41. Ibrahim, *Al-Qaeda Reader*, 25.
42. Gerges, *America and Political Islam*, esp. ch. 3.
43. On framing in general, see Tarrow, *New Transnational Activism;* and Keck and Sikkink, *Activists beyond Borders.*
44. Schattschneider, *Semisovereign People*, 3.

two actors will affect a range of other actors. If globalization is defined in part by interconnectedness, it stands to reason that countries and individuals will be less likely to engage each other in isolation of others than has been the case in eras of less globalization. The media, which represent a key element of globalization, also play an important role in socializing conflict. Thus, aspects of the historical perspective are well on display on Al Jazeera, with its fifty million viewers, as one complex analysis of the programming on this channel reveals.[45] And while Al Jazeera may well reflect the attitudes of its viewers, it also shapes those attitudes in turn. The effect of this interaction is hard to know, but intuition suggests that the one reinforces and strengthens the other.

Al-Qaeda's terrorist acts triggered a war on terrorism, which has a global audience that to some extent may have come to see world politics through the prism of Western liberalism against Islam. The front line in the war on terrorism is Al-Qaeda versus the United States, but individuals in the broader global audience will, at varying levels, side with one party or the other. They may sympathize with part of Al-Qaeda's message or have their own grievances against the United States, and they may take actions now or in the future to help one side or the other. The broader audience consists of Muslims of various stripes, including global radical jihadis, religious nationalists, secular Muslims, and also non-Muslims who may share antipathy toward the United States.

As one of the core principles of Al-Qaeda's strategic vision, Bin Laden certainly wanted to draw in the audience and to be an example to Muslims worldwide. One can argue that over time Al-Qaeda has sought to draw in the audience in two key ways, which, in effect, have included exploiting the historical perspective discussed above. It has directly or indirectly aimed to provoke a clash of transnational ideas, pitting its radical and distorted brand of Islam against Western liberalism.

Trying to Spread Transnational Ideas

Terrorism can be violent, but it is more than mere violence. The power of terrorism does not really come from blowing things up. It comes from the changes it brings to the discursive environment in which we think about world affairs and in which global opinion and policy is shaped. However, power cannot be destruction—it is the ability to change minds or instill fear in them, a process that the communications revolution under global globalization has greatly facilitated.[46]

---

45. Ibid., 216–23.
46. Hoffman, *Inside Terrorism*, 14–15.

Transnationalism is sometimes manifested in common ideas shared across borders, including religious ideas, perhaps especially in distorted religious ideas.[47] Such transnational ideas are not new to world politics. As Stephen Krasner and others have argued, they have been around in different forms for a long time.[48] The Catholic Church, especially prior to the Treaty of Westphalia in 1648, which signaled the start of its significant decline, represented a significant transnational organization that spread religious ideas across borders.

However, globalization, and especially the communications revolution, has created more potential for such ideas to take root at greater distances. Bin Laden inadvertently sought to confirm Samuel Huntington's controversial notion of the "clash of civilizations," of conflicts between nations and groups of different civilizations, and especially of Islam versus the West.[49] Bin Laden affirms Huntington in the sense that he saw elements of a war between Islam and the Jewish-Crusader alliance and wanted to widen the divide between civilizations. Like Huntington, who saw civilization as the "highest cultural grouping of people, and the broadest level of cultural identity people have short of that which distinguishes humans from others,"[50] the jihadists see a profound incompatibility between the Islamic and Western worlds and anticipate—and want to bring about—a confrontation between Islamic and Western civilizations.[51]

Al-Qaeda's actions indicate that it has sought to strike up this clash of civilizations, to agitate the audience to its cause, and to win the hearts and minds of the Muslim Street, a battle for the Street that some thought it was winning.[52] Following the 9/11 attacks, Bin Laden noted in a mid-November video that "the number of people who accepted Islam in the days that followed the operations were more than the people who accepted Islam in the last eleven years."[53] Perhaps Bin Laden was influenced by Qutb in thinking about a clash of civilizations. Qutb certainly sought to spur civilizational conflict, as reflected, for instance, in one chapter in his famous book *Milestones,* "Islam Is the Real Civilization," in his repeated reference to the superiority of Islam and to the depravity of Western civilization and to the need for jihad against the West.[54]

One of Al-Qaeda's key strategies has been to paint the war on terrorism as a war on Islam, so it seized on any available gaffes to illuminate this point, such as Bush's reference to the war on terrorism as a "crusade." For his part, Bush became

---

47. Rudolph and Piscatori, eds., *Transnational Religion.*
48. Krasner, *Organized Hypocrisy.*
49. Huntington, *Clash of Civilizations.* For a pre-9/11 critique of Huntington, see Mottahedeh, "Clash of Civilizations."
50. Huntington, *Clash of Civilizations.*
51. Schweitzer and Shay, *Globalization of Terror,* 3–7, 25–28.
52. Benjamin and Simon, *Age of Sacred Terror,* 157–58; see also Mazarr, *Unmodern Men,* preface.
53. For a transcript, see *Inside 9-11,* 316.
54. Qutb, *Milestones,* esp. ch. 7.

increasingly sensitized to the notion of transnational conflict but seemed to dismiss its gravity or importance. As he pointed out in his September 22, 2004, address to the United Nations General Assembly, "When it comes to the desire for liberty and justice, there is no clash of civilizations."[55] As suggested earlier, some polling data suggest that many Americans harbor distrust of things Muslim in the post-9/11 world and that this sentiment even affects how they view their own president. One poll conducted by *Newsweek* in August 2010 asked respondents the following question: "Some people have alleged that Barack Obama sympathizes with the goals of Islamic fundamentalists who want to impose Islamic law around the world. From what you know about Obama, what is your opinion of these allegations?" Surprisingly, 7 percent said this was definitely true; 24 percent responded that it was probably true; 36 percent said it was probably not true; and only 25 percent said it was definitely not true. Unsurprisingly, among Republicans, the figures were even more stark, it was definitely true 14 percent, probably true 38 percent, probably not true 33 percent, and definitely not true 7 percent.[56]

To some extent, the United States also saw the war on terrorism partly as a "war of ideas."[57] The September 11 Commission, drawing on hundreds of interviews, recommended in the summer of 2004 that the United States dedicate more energy to winning the hearts and minds of those in the audience who can be swayed.[58] Washington adopted these notions when it changed its Iraq policy in 2007 toward what would became known as the "surge" strategy. It not only increased the number of forces but also focused more attention on changing the minds of tribal leaders and others in the Sunni-led insurgency.

The conflict with Al-Qaeda would be a conflict of ideas only inasmuch as elements of its message about how to conduct political and religious affairs resonate more broadly. One anonymous CIA analyst identified many Saudis who considered Al-Qaeda and Bin Laden to be powerful forces in Saudi Arabia. He went as far as to describe Bin Laden as "a poster boy" of Saudi society—a kingdom that is "loaded with Bin Laden types."[59]

This view suggests that transnational liberalism may be confronted with a primordial brew of political and religious ideas under the terrorist banner that resonate beyond the fringe. If Al-Qaeda were able to socialize its conflict with the

---

55. A complete transcript is available at nytimes.com/international.

56. See TPMDC Newsweek Poll: "Republicans Think Obama 'Probably' Wants to Impose Islamic Law" available at http://tpmdc.talkingpointsmemo.com/2010/08/newsweek-poll-republicans-think-obama-probably-wants-to-impose-islamic-law.php.

57. For instance, see speech by Deputy Secretary of Defense Paul Wolfowitz, available at www.defense.gov/transcripts/transcript.aspx?transcriptid=3080.

58. *9/11 Commission Report.*

59. Scheuer, *Imperial Hubris,* 71–74.

United States to the broader Muslim world to the point that it did become an ideological war, a conflict played out in the ether of ideas and emotions on a stage that crosses borders and has no real bounds, that would be an decidedly different era. So far, however, the evidence does not support such an outcome. As polling data show, as I discuss later, confidence in Bin Laden decreased over time.

Few Muslims say that they would want to live under a Taliban-like regime, no matter how much they hate the United States. In this sense, the war of ideas or clash of civilizations is a misnomer. It suggests two competing models for how we should live our lives. In fact, Al-Qaeda's violent ideology does not in the least threaten to supplant Western liberalism, as Soviet communism did during the Cold War. Al-Qaeda has a palpable lack of soft power, a notion developed by political scientist Joseph Nye.[60] Nye asserted that in contrast to the "hard power" of economic and military might, soft power refers to the ability to shape the preferences of others, which involves "leading by example and attracting others to do what you want" by virtue of such things as attractiveness of political institutions, culture, and values and policies that exude moral authority.[61]

Anti-Americanism as a Phenomenon

We cannot draw a simple link between anti-Americanism and acts aimed at hurting the United States and its people, but the historical perspective is fed in part by oil-related issues, which generate anti-Americanism.[62] Those who see American actions through this perspective are much more likely to be anti-American. Anti-Americanism may generate sympathy for terrorists. As Giacomo Chiozza suggests, investigating anti-Americanism sheds light on the fringes of sympathizers with whom the actions of extremists may resonate.[63] Anti-Americanism could provide a breeding ground for terrorism by drawing supporters and facilitating recruitment.[64] Indifference to the types of behavior and rhetoric that bring about the conditions for terrorist thinking and behavior probably derive from anti-Americanism in some way. This would be different from anti-Americanism translating into terrorism, but it would become part of the problem of terrorism. This is especially the case because part of the challenge of addressing terrorism is to encourage Islamic moderates to try to deal with the radicals within their own

---

60. Nye, *Soft Power,* 5–11.
61. Ibid.
62. Bueno de Mesquita, "Quality of Terror."
63. Chiozza, *Anti-Americanism,* 40.
64. Katzenstein and Keohane, "Political Consequences of Anti-Americanism," 274.

religion. This is not to say that their challenge is to try to change Al-Qaeda. That is beyond the scope of sensible outcomes. However, they can challenge radicals that engage in actions that polarize their publics or encourage actions that counter negative images of non-Muslims.

As Chiozza indicates, most definitions hold that anti-Americanism is "some sort of opposition to America," but agreement does "not extend much further."[65] For present purposes, this book adopts the definition of anti-Americanism put forth by Peter Katzenstein and Robert Keohane, who view it as a "psychological tendency to hold negative views of the United States and of American society in general"; importantly, they distinguish anti-Americanism from opposition to U.S. policy.[66] One can oppose U.S. policy, as many Americans do, without being anti-American.

Katzenstein and Keohane stress that broad general explanations of anti-Americanism are inadequate. Rather, they identify four different types of anti-Americanism: liberal anti-Americanism, social anti-Americanism, sovereign-nationalist anti-Americanism, and radical anti-Americanism.[67] Each type differs in its orientation, but it is this last type that is most salient for this book. It emphasizes an extremist view of America and, unlike the other anti-Americanisms, sometimes involves a call to violence. Katzenstein and Keohane distinguish between explanations of anti-Americanism based on power imbalances, a globalization backlash, and conflicting identities. By power imbalances, they refer to anti-American reactions to American power. U.S. hegemony is not a necessary condition for anti-Americanism—anti-Americanism in Europe dates back further than the American Revolution in the late eighteenth century—but it is probably conducive to it. A second argument is that globalization generates anti-Americanism. Those adversely affected by globalization can be expected to resist such change. Rapid economic change and the uncertainty deriving from dependence on distant markets and sources of capital would generate resentment at the United States, the epicenter of pressures for such changes. The third manner by which anti-Americanism is generated is when American cultural and religious identities clash with those of other cultures.[68] Under this explanation, America's secular and sexualized culture penetrates the homes of patriarchal and authoritarian communities, Muslim and otherwise, with images of sexual freedom and decadence, female emancipation, and equality between the sexes.[69] This book emphasizes the globalization dimension far more than the power or religious explanations, although they all seem to be related. For instance, power

---

65. Chiozza, *Anti-Americanism,* 34.
66. Katzenstein and Keohane, "Varieties of Anti-Americanism," 12.
67. Ibid., 28–33.
68. Lieven, *America Right or Wrong;* Nau, *At Home Abroad;* and Huntington, *Who Are We?*
69. This paragraph is based on Katzenstein and Keohane, "Varieties of Anti-Americanism."

would enable American-led globalization which would facilitate the spread of cultural and religious ideas.

In addition to the typology offered above, we can also distinguish between, on the one hand, anti-Americanism as a syndrome and, on the other, what Chiozza refers to as anti-Americanism in terms of the "dimensions of America theory." The first is a rigid, negative and undifferentiated view of America; this type of hatred is not easily shaken or changed. By contrast, the second view accepts America as a multitude of characteristics. In this version, differing publics see America through differing lenses, and positive and negative opinions coexist in an ambiguous state. The end result is that what America does is more problematic than what it is.[70]

The historical perspective that I lay out here reflects aspects of the three dimensions of anti-Americanism noted above and, inasmuch as it is distinct, globalization in particular. However, the historical perspective highlights one aspect that deserves its own category: anti-Americanism caused by perceptions of imperial and colonial behavior. This moves beyond globalization in that it is derived more from historical remembrances than from present actions, even though present actions are seen through this lens. In addition, it involves a perception of resources being dominated or stolen, whereas globalization presents less of a territorial and direct threat than an abstract, global, capitalist, political, and cultural threat. This approach also resonates with Chiozza's distinction about an anti-American syndrome versus an ambiguous, fluctuating anti-Americanism, but it falls somewhere in between the extremes. That is, I see a limited anti-American syndrome in play that is fed by some past American and Western actions and is also quite exaggerated. The limited syndrome and these actions reinforce and reify each other.

In the next section, I explore anti-Americanism in light of the historical perspective that I have sketched herein. I then examine polling data and examine Al-Qaeda's efforts to exploit the American-led invasion and subsequent occupation of Iraq.

Generating Anti-Americanism

Al-Qaeda has sought to widen its conflict and seduce the broader audience by generating hatred of the United States. Hating the United States is not the same as trying to supplant its ideas with another set of notions about governance. One is a building project, aimed at offering an alternative mode of existence; the other is demolition, aimed at tearing down the existing civilization with no pretense toward replacing it. Al-Qaeda is hampered by a lack of soft power, but it is far less

---

70. Chiozza, *Anti-Americanism*, 41–50.

restricted in generating anti-Americanism. Most of the audience will not emulate Al-Qaeda, but Al-Qaeda still can stir anti-Americanism.

It would be a larger problem for the United States and the West if Al-Qaeda had gained strength due to a desire of others to follow its way of life than due to anti-Americanism. This is because it is easier to alter anti-American views than to alter more strongly rooted ideological views.

Anti-Americanism, of course, is also a problem, and it is certainly not limited to Muslims. While many non-Muslims saw Bin Laden as a fanatic with little common sense, aspects of his message do resonate among some sectors of the non-Muslim world where traditionalists bemoan the West and want to see its demise.[71] Of course, their motivations and views diverge significantly from those of Al-Qaeda, and they largely reject terrorism, but they are motivated by some similar anti-American views.

The global audience is structured as a series of concentric circles of people who could be affected by the war on terrorism. The hard-core center consists of Al-Qaeda supporters, but as the circles spread out they reach various anti-Americanisms.

The notion that Al-Qaeda can be unpopular as an organization but can still gain some sympathy or generate anti-Americanism is perhaps best illustrated in a tough case—Pakistan—which has been a hotbed of radicalism. In a July 1, 2009, Program on International Policy Attitudes (PIPA) poll of Pakistanis, a majority opposed Al-Qaeda's 9/11 attacks on Americans and saw the group as a rising and critical threat to Pakistan. That represented a twofold increase from 41 percent in late July 2007 to 82 percent in 2009. However, a majority also shared many of Al-Qaeda's attitudes toward America. In the same poll, 90 percent thought that President Obama holds the goal of weakening and dividing the Islamic world; 93 percent that he wanted to impose American culture on Muslim society; 92 percent that he has the goal of maintaining control over all the Middle East's oil resources; and only 25 percent that he favors the creation of a Palestinian state.[72]

Enthusiasm for Muslim Extremism Wears Off

To what extent has Al-Qaeda succeeded with the broader audience? It is not easy to answer with confidence, but polling data may offer some insights. Al-Qaeda succeeded in the years following September 11, retaining a significant number of

---

71. Sedgwick, *Against the Modern World.*

72. See World Public Opinion web site, "Pakistani Public Opinion on the Swat Conflict, Afghanistan, and the US" available at www.worldpublicopinion.org/pipa/pdf/jul09/WPO_Pakistan_Jul09_rpt.pdf.

potential supporters. However, the Pew Foundation surveys suggested encouraging trends in Muslim public opinion. They reveal a sharp decline in support for suicide bombing as well as in confidence in Bin Laden–type views.

The year 2006 was a turning point. For example, in Jordan, 24 percent expressed at least some confidence in Bin Laden, compared with 60 percent in 2005. A sizable number of Pakistanis (38%) said in 2006 that they have at least some confidence in the Al-Qaeda leader to do the right thing regarding world affairs, but that number had been 51 percent in May 2005. However, Nigeria's Muslims resisted this trend; 61 percent of Nigeria's Muslims said in 2006 that they had at least some confidence in Bin Laden, up from 44 percent in 2003. The belief that terrorism is justifiable in the defense of Islam, while less extensive than in previous surveys, still had a sizable number of adherents in 2006.[73]

The results improve even more when analyzed through 2008. Bin Laden inspired substantial confidence in a few predominantly Muslim countries in 2003, but his popularity has plummeted in recent years. Confidence among Jordanian Muslims dropped from 56 percent in 2003 to 19 percent in 2008; a mere 2 percent of Muslims in Lebanon and 3 percent in Turkey said in 2008 that they were confident Bin Laden would do the right thing in world affairs.[74] The share of Muslims who regarded suicide bombing as a justified means of defending Islam fell throughout the period from 2002 to 2008. In Lebanon, 74 percent of Muslims considered suicide bombing to be justified in 2002, but that percentage tumbled to 32 percent in 2008. Pakistani support for suicide bombing plunged from 33 percent to 5 percent.

Al-Qaeda, the Iraq War, and the Polls

No analysis of the historical perspective drawn here, and Al-Qaeda's efforts to exploit elements of it, would be complete without discussion of the Iraq War. To some extent, the Iraq War probably fed into the historical perspective. Whether or not one thinks that the U.S.-led invasion of Iraq made sense, the United States did irk a great many people worldwide when it invaded without clear UN authorization. But the pivotal event may have been the failure to find weapons of mass destruction. That failure suggested to the conspiracy-minded that the "real" reasons for the invasion were to seize Iraqi oil, to dominate the region, and perhaps to deal Islam a blow. That the United States also talked about Iran and Syria as possible targets added to this perception, in the context of Bush's

---

73. "Great Divide."

74. See Pew Global Attitudes Project, "Global Public Opinion in the Bush Years (2001–2008)" on http://pewglobal.org/reports/display.php?ReportID=263.

famous designation of Iran, Iraq, and North Korea as constituting an "axis of evil." While such threats may have been mainly at the theoretical stage in the White House, they were taken seriously in the Middle East.

Bin Laden appeared to have seen the invasion of Iraq partly as an effort to dominate and steal the region's oil. To him it may have been the first step in a broader effort to control the world's oil flow. As he put it, after Iraq, the crusader alliance will move to occupy the "rest of the Gulf states to set the stage for controlling and dominating the world. For the big powers believe the Gulf and the Gulf States are the key to controlling the world due to the presence of the largest oil reserves there."[75] In his "Message to the American People," Bin Laden asserted that George W. Bush had invaded Iraq because he was "blinded" by the "black gold," elevating "private interests over the interests of America" and leaving himself "stained with the blood of all those killed on both sides, all for the sake of oil and the benefit of private corporations."[76]

Bin Laden's view of Iraq was captured in part in an exchange with Abu Musab al-Zarqawi, whom the international media identified as the senior representative of global jihad in Iraq. In February 2004, he sent Bin Laden a letter, which American forces later obtained. In it, Zarqawi suggested that Iraq could replace Afghanistan as the new "land of jihad." He called for a civil war in Iraq in order to sabotage American interests in the region and suggested a deal in which Bin Laden would recognize Iraq as the principal land of jihad and, it is implied, Zarqawi would pledge his loyalty to Bin Laden. Evidently, Bin Laden agreed. On December 27, 2004, he released a tape in which he declared the unification of his own group and "the prince, the warrior, and the respected friend, Abu Mu'sab al-Zarqawi and the groups that have joined him, who are the best of the sect fighting for the word of Allah....We in Al-Qaeda very much welcome your unification with us."[77]

The opportunities in Iraq for audience manipulation were not lost on Al-Qaeda. It found the Iraq War and the U.S. role in postwar Iraq to be a prime opportunity to malign the superpower. Al-Qaeda constantly depicted the overthrow of the Baathist regime and the occupation of Iraq as an attack on Islam and used the war to recruit jihadists to its cause.[78]

The war on terrorism and the invasion of Iraq increased anti-Americanism. In particular, polls from the Pew Research Center for the People and the Press showed growing anti-Americanism in the period shortly after September 11, between 2002 and 2003. For instance, in the summer of 2002, 30 percent of Turks and 25 percent of Jordanians held a positive view of the United States; those

---

75. For the translated transcript of an audiotape, see http://news.bbc.co.uk/2/hi/3368957.stm.
76. Translated and analyzed in Kepel and Milelli, eds., *Al-Qaeda in Its Own World.*
77. On the Iraq war, Schweitzer and Ferber, "Al-Qaeda," esp. 80–81.
78. Springer et al., *Islamic Radicalism,* 146–48.

figures dropped to 15 percent and 1 percent, respectively. Moreover, more than half of those surveyed in Indonesia, Jordan, and the Palestinian Authority and nearly half in Morocco and Pakistan viewed Bin Laden as one of the three leaders in which they had the greatest confidence to "do the right thing."[79] *USA Today* discovered that during the summer of 2002, nearly four out of five hits on a secret Al-Qaeda website were made from within Saudi Arabia.[80]

A nine-nation poll of Muslim countries released on February 27, 2002, showed that only 16 percent of Saudis had a positive view of the United States; 64 percent viewed it negatively and 3 percent saw it as trustworthy.[81] Nawaf Obaid, a Saudi security analyst and advisor to the royal family, found in a poll of fifteen thousand Saudis conducted between August and November 2003 that while 95 percent were against Bin Laden ruling the Arabian Peninsula, many of them approved of some of his political views, with a minority 41 percent approving of close relations with the United States.[82]

Polling indicates that the subsequent occupation of Iraq worsened distrust of the United States and anti-Americanism in the broader Arab world as well as in Iraq, where 90 percent of those polled said that they distrusted the U.S.-led coalition.[83] The Saudi English newspaper *Jedda News,* noting the widespread view that America had invaded Iraq to take its oil, called on Washington to assure Arabs of its good intentions in Iraq.[84] We can also note that, according to the U.S. Department of State, in 2001 approximately 63 percent of all terrorist incidents worldwide were committed against U.S. citizens or property, compared to only 23 percent in 1995.[85]

Meanwhile, one poll found that in 2000 more than 60 percent of Saudi citizens expressed confidence in the United States, whereas by 2004 less than 4 percent had a favorable view.[86] That result is supported by other polls, such as in Indonesia, where favorable ratings of the United States dropped from 61 to 15 percent and in Nigeria where they fell from 71 to 38 percent in the same time frame.[87] In the 2004 Pew Global Attitudes survey, more than half of Jordanians and Pakistanis, as well as 40 percent or more of French and Germans, said that the war on terrorism was a smokescreen for a campaign against unfriendly Muslim governments.[88]

---

79. See Pew Global Attitudes Project, "Global Public Opinion in the Bush Years (2001-2008)" on http://pewglobal.org/reports/display.php?ReportID=263.

80. Baer, *Sleeping with the Devil,* xxvii.

81. See www.usatoday.com/news/attack/2002/02/27/usat-pollside.htm. Also, for opinion polls of the Arab world in 2002 and 2003, see Abdallah, "Causes of Anti-Americanism In the Arab World," 70–71.

82. "A Rare Saudi Public Opinion Poll Results Made Public," *PakTribune,* June 10, 2004.

83. Abdallah, "Causes of Anti-Americanism," 70–71; and Kassman, "U.S. Prepares."

84. Jedda Arab News, in FBIS: NES, 3, January 2004 (WNC# 0hr0vb000npw7x).

85. Perl, *Terrorism.*

86. See www.sadat.umd.edu/new%20surveys/surveys.htm.

87. *9/11 Commission Report,* 375.

88. See Pew Global Attitudes Project, "Global Public Opinion in the Bush Years (2001–2008)" on http://pewglobal.org/reports/display.php?ReportID=263.

The Iraq War fed into the historical perspective, and, as polling data reveal, the war on terrorism and the Iraq War generated anti-Americanism. The probable reasons for America's invasion,[89] and the reasons inferred by radical Islamists and many in the Muslim world, were quite different. This divergence in views can be viewed as part of the problem that Washington faces in its foreign policy toward the Middle East.

Middle Eastern oil generated a range of issues, which, seen through the distorted prism of radical Islam, contributed to terrorism on September 11 and have continued to feed it. But oil issues played another role beyond Al-Qaeda's motivations. At times, they expanded audience support for a terrorist group that had difficulty connecting with most elements in the Muslim world. Oil issues have not enabled Al-Qaeda to compete in a clash of ideas, as it has sought, but they have generated anti-Americanism, from which it sometimes benefited.

The historical perspective laid out here need not capture American motivations fairly in order to be powerful. Some perspectives have been extremely powerful in history, in part because they have been distorted or have been riveted with multiple half-truths. After all, the evidence strongly suggests that Washington did not seek to steal the region's oil. Nor has it had a colonial past in the Middle East or sought to subjugate Muslims for imperial purposes. As an example, after the United States evicted Iraqi forces from Kuwait in 1991, it could have seized Iraq's oil fields. Its military was unopposed and had routed Iraq's army in one of history's most lopsided military victories. However, Washington decided strongly against invading Iraq for various reasons, and did not contemplate dominating it for its oil resources.[90] For that matter, the 2003 war was not primarily about oil, unlike the 1990–91 Persian Gulf crisis. That said, the United States has misplayed its cards in the Middle East at times, but one could argue that there is a fairly sizable gulf between how it is viewed in the historical perspective, on the one hand, and the basic thrust of its regional policy and actions, on the other.

If we accept the notion that the historical perspective is in play and distorts U.S. intentions, we can see how it can shape how actors view the United States. Arguably, it has contributed to the complex mosaic of motivations that drives terrorists and that has brought them some support or sympathy in the broader global audience. It is impossible to measure the impact of the historical perspective, but it appears to play a role in this region where history is vital in shaping modern views, and in a world of interconnections and real-time media coverage that feed the perspective and that are fed by it.

---

89. See Yetiv, *Explaining Foreign Policy.*
90. Ibid.

4

OIL MONEY, TERRORIST FINANCING, AND WEAPONS OF MASS DESTRUCTION

The September 11 attacks cost roughly half a million dollars, but that is a small fraction of what it costs to run the entire infrastructure of terrorism.[1] This infrastructure includes recruitment, ideological indoctrination, salaries, housing, arms, support for various cells and like-minded terrorist organizations, payoffs to local governments and warlords, public promotion, communications, and enforcing discipline.

The terrorist infrastructure also consists of adaptation against dogged counterterrorism efforts. Just as countries fighting terrorism have developed new capabilities and techniques against Al-Qaeda, so too must the organization adapt in order to develop, to continue its operations, or just to survive.[2] Counterterrorism, especially the financial war on terrorism, has forced Al-Qaeda to move to expensive alternative approaches.[3]

Disagreement exists on how much money Al-Qaeda has needed to operate. Thomas Biersteker and Sue Eckert have concluded that the metrics most commonly associated with terrorist financing initiatives—the total number of designations and the amount of money frozen—are inadequate and can be misleading.[4] Al-Qaeda has changed over time, so estimates also vary in any time period and

---

1. Aufhauser interview; and Biersteker and Eckert, eds., *Countering the Financing of Terrorism*, 6.
2. Tucker, "What Is New?," 1–14.
3. Glaser interview.
4. Biersteker and Eckert, *Countering the Financing*.

over time. For his part, Rohan Gunaratna has argued that Al-Qaeda operated a significant financial network, approximating $300 million in value and dispersing between $30 and $40 million per year.[5] The 9/11 Commission Report estimated that Al-Qaeda needed $30 million a year to run operations and that it relied almost entirely on a fundraising network developed over time, on a "core group of financial facilitators who raised money from a variety of donors and other fundraisers, primarily in the Gulf countries and particularly in Saudi Arabia."[6] This chapter certainly supports this interpretation.

It is also hard to figure out exactly how much of Al-Qaeda's monies come from oil-related funds, but can venture an educated guess. If we accept that Saudi Arabia is an important direct and indirect source, consider that oil accounts for around 90 percent of total Saudi export earnings and state revenues and above 40 percent of the country's GDP.[7] Of course, there is a vast infrastructure associated with the production of oil; if we add oil-related business to the mix, those numbers rise.

Private wealth in states such as Saudi Arabia also comes from investment in the American stock market and in European real estate. But these monies are dwarfed by those that are oil-related, and, in any case, the Saudis would not have much money to invest in the West were it not for oil or oil-connected business. Without oil, Saudi Arabia might look something like cash-strapped Yemen or Egypt with a higher dose of Islamism.

This chapter offers a rough sketch of likely oil-related sources of income and their salience in the development and role of Al-Qaeda. The level of importance of various sources of income will vary over time, but this chapter examines the central bases of financing across a broad period of Al-Qaeda's existence.

As one high-level official pointed out, terrorists are involved in "shadow warfare and the primary source of the stealth and mobility necessary to wage it is money. It is the fuel of terror's enterprise."[8] Oil money has not been important to single or even multiple terrorist acts, nor to any particular element of the infrastructure of terror.[9] However, it is vital in helping create, maintain, and expand this entire infrastructure. Al-Qaeda's most important financial support has come from charities, nongovernmental organizations (NGOs), mosques, intermediaries, and wealthy individuals. This chapter argues that a large amount

---

5. Gunartna, *Inside Al-Qaeda*, 54.
6. Ibid., 170.
7. U.S. Energy Information Administration, "Saudi Arabia" available at www.eia.doe.gov/cabs/Saudi_Arabia/Background.html.
8. Aufhauser, "Keynote Address."
9. Ibid.

of these monies have been oil-related.[10] Oil money may well have decreased in importance compared to other sources of income over time, and that trend may continue, or else it may reverse, as the world becomes more dependent on Middle Eastern oil and other factors come into play.

As discussed in chapter 2, oil money may have played a key role in enticing Ayman al-Zawahiri to join Bin Laden in focusing attention on the United States, while American oil interests in Afghanistan and the Middle East may have made the United States less zealous against Al-Qaeda prior to 9/11. But beyond those issues, this chapter identifies multiple direct and indirect connections between oil and terrorism.

States Funding Terror Directly

State support for terrorism by oil-rich states helped in Al-Qaeda's development. Indeed, David Aufhauser, the Treasury Department's former general counsel who also led the Bush administration's interagency process on terrorist financing, declared in June 2003 that Saudi Arabia was the "epicenter" for the financing of Al-Qaeda and that the United States put enormous pressure on the Saudis to deal with any potential connections to terrorist financing emanating from the kingdom.[11] In mid-June 2004, the September 11 Commission reported "no evidence" that the Saudi government or senior officials financed Al-Qaeda.[12] But there remain key aspects of the indirect Saudi connection to terrorist financing to explore.

The Importance of Ideology

Ideology is a key reason for why it is difficult to delink Saudi Arabia from terrorism. Wahhabism draws inspiration from the teachings of Muhammad bin Abd al-Wahhab, who spread his message throughout the eighteenth century until his death in 1787. Modern Saudi Arabia not only draws religious inspiration from al-Wahhab, but it is also politically forged partly on an alliance that he made in 1744 with Muhammad ibn Saud. The founder of the kingdom, a local ruler of

---

10. Gunaratna, *Inside Al-Qaeda;* and Coll, *Ghost Wars.*

11. For an overview of diplomatic pressure on the Middle East regarding terrorist financing, see Wayne, "Testimony."

12. *Update on the Global Campaign against Terrorist Financing.*

a small Arabian oasis town, received al-Wahhab and gave him protection.[13] The brutal fundamentalist Wahhabi tribesmen known as the Ikhwan proved central to Ibn Saud's military conquests, including the capture of Islam's two holiest sites at Mecca and Medina and to the formation, contrary to what most might have predicted, of the Saudi nation. The alliance between Ibn Saud and al-Wahhab, cemented through generations of intermarriage, would offer the royal family religious legitimacy for its rule.[14]

Descendants of the royal family and those of Abdul Wahhab have set the governmental and religious dimensions of rule, respectively. Even in more recent times, when Iraq invaded Kuwait, King Fahd turned to and gained reluctant support from the Wahhabi clerics, as he had done several times in the past, for his considered decision to allow non-Muslim troops on Saudi soil. The clerics, meanwhile, have benefited from largely free rein in religious practices—an arrangement that was shaken by the effects of 9/11.

Saudi Education and Religious Leaders

Saudi oil money has funded a large educational and religious establishment that has been blamed for creating an anti-American context and for providing places for terrorists to recruit, train, and become indoctrinated in a virulent, anti-Western ethos. Saudi textbooks have included negative references to the inferiority of non-Muslims and to the need to vanquish them and denunciations of teachings that do not mesh with strict Wahhabist beliefs.[15] Some Muslim leaders around the world deplore such educational materials. For instance, Adnan Khalil Basha, secretary general of the International Islamic Relief Organization, asserted that such books are used to "exploit some of the half-educated people and uneducated people" and to give them the "illusion that this is the real Islam."[16]

In the fall of 2003, the U.S. Congress introduced legislation that connected Saudi teachings with global terrorism, alleging that they inspire it, and called more broadly on Saudi Arabia to end all funding to institutions that incite or encourage global terrorism.[17] The regime showed some recognition after September 11 that changes are needed in its religious schools. In response to criticism, and following a review of Saudi textbooks in 2002, the Saudi foreign minister claimed that 5 percent of the material in textbooks was "horrible," 10 percent was questionable,

---

13. Al-Rasheed, *History of Saudi Arabia*, 15–20.

14. Helms, *Cohesion of Saudi Arabia*; and Safran, *Saudi Arabia*.

15. Prokop, "Saudi Arabia," 77–89; and Front Line Archives on Saudi Arabia available at www.pbs.org/wgbh/pages/frontline/shows/saudi/etc/textbooks.html.

16. Quoted in MacFarquhar, "Anti-Western and Extremist Views," B1.

17. Armanios, *Islamic Traditions of Wahhabism and Salafiyya*, CRS-6.

while 85 percent called for understanding with other religious faiths.[18] Explicit terror aimed at the regime in 2003 further motivated it to take some action, but while some steps have been taken, it has not gotten very far.[19] The Education Ministry was slow to start but moved in 2004 with plans to develop the national education school syllabus for 2005 in a way that puts greater emphasis on lessons of tolerance, and the evils of extremism and violence.[20]

The House of Saud remained somewhat in self-denial about the extent of its homegrown problem. In a series of articles in the Saudi English daily *Arab News*, journalist Ra'id Qusti described the regime as an ostrich with its head in the sand and underscored the critical importance of reevaluating an education system that does not teach tolerance of other cultures.[21] This problem has been recognized within Saudi Arabia. Other columnists such as Suleiman al-Hattlan underscored that not enough is done to attack the ideology of extremists, pointing out that Saudis used soft language about Al-Qaeda in Saudi Arabia; Abdullah Bjad al-Qtaibi, a radical-turned-reformer, observed that the "problem is that the official religious establishment does not admit that there is a problem inside Wahhabism itself."[22] Even Prince Bandar started to take a public and more trenchant approach in boldly asserting that Saudi Arabia's problems with extremists is homegrown and has "nothing to do with America or Israel or the Christians or Jews," none of whom were not involved during the long history of violent opposition to mainstream Islam extending back to the prophet Muhammad.[23]

For his part, then Crown Prince Abdullah, who succeeded to the throne and became king upon the death of his half-brother, King Fahd, on August 1, 2005, supported some of the demands by a rising group of so-called Islamo-liberals. They have sought a compromise between democracy and Islam and want to move Saudi Arabia beyond Wahhabism. They evidently were successful in pushing Abdullah to organize a national dialogue on the subject. But Abdallah's influential brothers have been critical of such pressures and movements.[24]

Saudi Foreign Minister al-Faisal and other Saudi leaders blamed Zionists for a string of Al-Qaeda attacks on domestic targets in the summer of 2004—a charge made by others in the Middle Eastern media.[25] This charge served the domestic

---

18. Armanios, *Islamic Religious Schools*, CRS-4.
19. For extensive evidence, see "Testimony of Steven Emerson," 1.
20. FBI National Press Releases. FBIS: NES, February 18, 2004 (WNC# 0hteaw1024hiqb).
21. See, for instance, Arab News (Saudi Arabia), May 5, 2004.
22. Quoted in MacFarquhar, "Anti-Western and Extremist Views," B1.
23. Quoted in ibid.
24. Lacroix, "Between Islamists and Liberals."
25. See his news conference on Dubai Al-Arabiyah Television in FBIS: NES, May 4, 2004 (WNC# 0hx8szx02t2gi5). Crown Prince Abullah asserted as much on tape as translated on NBC news on June 15, 2004. See the comments of a former Egyptian official in Al-Ahram in FBIS: NES, June 6, 2004 (WNC# Ohzln88037o6ff).

purposes of describing Al-Qaeda and the Zionists as having a similar interest in toppling the Saudi regime. Moreover, it may have been meant to counter Al-Qaeda's repeated characterization of the Saudi family as allied with the Zionist-Crusader alliance. But it also underscored the failure of the regime to educate its public in a manner that would allow sensible reform. Blaming Israel skirted the problem of homegrown Saudi extremism. Bin Laden gained admirers among the many teenagers who attend radical mosques that teach an anti-Semitic and anti-American curriculum. Many of them lack skills and are unemployed, leaving time for them to pay homage to the Bin Ladens of the world.

For its part, the royal family created the broad system of mosques, bureaucracies, and schools run by religious leaders, and they sustain, finance, appoint, govern, and sometimes even sanction or fire them. Over time, in fact, the regime has gained more influence over religious leaders and their activities and has bureaucratized the religious establishment.[26] High-level members of the royal family controlled and funded key elements of the establishment, which were tied to Al-Qaeda, including, perhaps most notoriously, the Al-Haramain Islamic Foundation.[27] Al-Haramain, a Mecca-based charity headed by Sheikh bin Abdul Aziz al-Ashaikh, the minister of Islamic affairs no less, had clear links in supporting Al-Qaeda. Although the royal family took measures to control that foundation in the summer of 2004, it is unclear to what extent that action will have a serious and lasting effect, because the forces that gave rise to the group are not casual or short-lived.[28]

Spreading Islam Internationally

While Wahhabism is taught in Saudi schools, a primary aim of Saudi foreign policy has been to fund conservative Sunni movements around the world. The indirect connections to terrorism stem from the spread of ideology that in its virulent form can breed hatred.

In 1962, Riyadh established the Muslim World League in Mecca with the goal of spreading Wahhabism internationally, which it did by funding institutions all over the world; from then through 2004, Saudi support for these institutions has been estimated to be over $75 billion.[29] Riyadh significantly enhanced its role in

---

26. Gause, *Oil Monarchies,* 12–16; Kechichian, *Succession in Saudi Arabia,* ch. 3; and Al-Yassini, *Religion and State,* 70–76.

27. "Testimony of Steven Emerson."

28. "Prince Salman Patronizes Charity Ceremony," Saudi Press Agency, November 12, 2002.

29. Comras, "Al-Qaeda Finances and Funding to Affiliated Groups," 119.

funding Sunni Islamic movements in the 1970s. This effort was partly spearheaded by rising oil prices during the 1973 oil embargo. Saudi oil revenue increased from $4.3 to $34.5 billion between 1973 and 1978.[30] As analyst James Adams put it, countries that "benefited from the oil bonanza found they had more money than they could possibly absorb internally...which contributed to the establishment of terrorism as a permanent feature of international politics."[31]

By the early 1970s, Islamists who were fueled by Saudi largesse gained influence on university campuses in places such as Egypt, Pakistan, and Malaysia and began to spread their word throughout the Muslim world—especially to young urbanites, who were receptive to Islamist ideology over nationalist rhetoric. Prior to 1973, Islamism was much less transnational in nature, reflecting local or national traditions, and Saudi Wahhabism was held in suspicion; after 1973, Saudi petrodollars spearheaded a vast effort to win converts across national borders and develop Islamic unity.[32] Just as oil money was allowing Saudi Arabia to become a stronger national actor on the global stage, it was also helping spread Wahhabism. The two were not necessarily at odds at the time. Leadership in the Muslim world strengthened Saudi Arabia as a state, and the stronger it was as a state, the more it could advance transnational Islam. Little did the Saudis know that radical Islamists would later emphasize transnational Islam over nation-state power, making it hard for Riyadh to bridge the two. Eventually, the Saudi regime became a target as an exemplar of state power.

The 1970s also saw a decrease in state services, thus allowing Islamists to fill the void. In doing so, they presented a quasi-alternative to state power while criticizing state failures.[33] The Saudis also had to fight off Nasser's pan-Arabism, which threatened their political position in the Arab world and their security. Promoting Wahhabist Islam and Islam in general as an ideological competitor to pan-Arabism served that goal, and rising oil monies helped push this agenda.

At the global level, the Saudis have also exported Wahhabism by offering money to governments on the condition that they Islamize. For instance, evidence suggests that the Saudis offered Egypt money only if it would encourage such a move, and they subsequently have had success in infiltrating Egyptian cultural, economic, and social life.[34] They also spread Wahhabist thought through international organizations such as the Jeddah-based Organization of the Islamic Conference, created in 1969 to promote Islamic solidarity, or through a complex

---

30. Brisard and Dasquie, *Forbidden Truth,* esp. 80.
31. Adams, *Financing of Terror,* 53.
32. Kepel, *Jihad,* 66–74.
33. On the rise of political Islam, see Yamani, *Changed Identities;* Al-Naqeeb, *Society and State;* and Henry and Springborg, *Globalization.*
34. Napoleoni, *Modern Jihad,* 119.

banking system controlled by high-level Saudi princes.[35] In the 1970s, Riyadh created the Islamic Development Bank, which was intended to help finance development in Muslim countries but also became a primary vehicle for exporting Wahhabism. Petrodollars were vital to this broader internationalizing effort.[36]

By the 1980s, Saudi Arabia's export of Wahhabism was funded by its banking system. To do this, it used core institutions including the Dar al-Maal al-Islami Trust; its subsidiary in Sudan was the Al-Shamal Islamic Bank of Sudan. Osama Bin Laden, according to the U.S. State Department, controlled that bank, although it is more likely, given the trial testimony of one of his former business associates, that he was only a large shareholder who used the bank to channel money to his followers around the world.[37]

Whatever the exact connections linking Saudi Arabia, Wahhabism, and September 11, we do know that the 9/11 attacks put the spotlight on Wahhabism. That ideology could not spread too far without oil money. The number of devout Wahhabis is small in comparison to other religions.

The connection between the Saudi spread of Wahhabism and terrorism is not just indirect but also direct. It is indirect in that it supports radical indoctrination and breeds anti-Americanism. The Muslim World League was not simply connected to terrorism by virtue of spreading Wahhabism. It continued to fund major Islamic movements around the world from the 1960s onward, and major Saudi elite figures were connected to it. U.S. investigators, law enforcement for the FBI, and intelligence investigators at the CIA have collected abundant material showing Muslim World League connections to Al-Qaeda.[38]

The International Islamic Relief Organization, formed in 1978 as an arm of the Muslim World League, was another institution funded by oil-rich Saudi patrons as well by as the Saudi regime; it has branch offices around the world. The CIA has reported that funds raised by this organization were used to finance at least six Al-Qaeda training camps prior to the attacks of 9/11 and to support Al-Qaeda thereafter; in 2006, the U.S. Department of the Treasury charged the organization with providing such support to terrorists, as it had done with a number of other Saudi-supported organizations.[39] Evidence suggests that in 1994, Mohammed Jamal Khalifa, Osama Bin Laden's 37-year-old brother-in-law, was arrested in California coming from the Philippines, holding documents that connected Islamic terrorist manuals to the International Islamic Relief

---

35. Ibid., 87.
36. Esposito, *Islamic Threat*, 107.
37. Napoleoni, *Terror Incorporated*, 123–24.
38. "Terrorism Financing," 194.
39. Comras, "Al-Qaeda Finances and Funding to Affiliated Groups," 117–21.

Organization, the group that he had headed in the Philippines. In addition, the Canadian government has stated in testimony in Canadian courts that, from 2001 to 2003 at least, this organization secretly funded terrorism.[40]

The Madrassas

Madrassas range from small schools to colleges to academies where a large array of classical Islamic disciplines are taught, often with additional instruction in philosophy, mathematics, Arabic, and literature. They may have developed from the outset of the rise of Islam but can be formally traced back to Baghdad in the eleventh century. Their prominence was eclipsed by the advent of Western secular practices, but they saw a resurgence in the 1970s, partly due to the rise of political Islam and also of petrodollars. They spread dramatically by the end of the twentieth century.

Madrassas, of which there are over ten thousand in Pakistan alone, were conduits for Islamic radicalism in the 1980s in the war against the Soviet occupation of Afghanistan. The Taliban, who later controlled Afghanistan and harbored Bin Laden in the face of American military threats after 9/11, was a product of madrassas in Pakistan. So were the thousands of demonstrators who protested the American-led effort to oust the Taliban by burning American flags, desecrating images of President Bush, and proudly carrying portraits of Mullah Omar and Osama Bin Laden.

Most madrassas are supported by charitable donations from Muslim believers. The vast majority of madrassas play a positive role in preserving Islamic tradition and teaching humanistic values embedded in Islam and have no connection to hatred and violence.[41] It is important not to exaggerate their connection to militancy. Some studies suggest that they have only provided a minor number of terrorists. For example, Christine Fair finds that of 141 mujaheddin that she studied, only 19 were recruited at a madrassas; by contrast, 50 militants were recruited through friends.[42] However, most problematic are politically charged madrassas, in particular the Deobandi madrassas, controlled by radical *mullahs* whose message is not tempered by a diversity of views or a broad curriculum. The fifteen Saudi members of the 9/11 terrorist squad were not trained in madrassas, but these schools have been fertile ground for shaping the minds

---

40. Ibid.
41. Winthrop and Graff, "Beyond Madrasas."
42. Fair, *Madrassah Challenge*, 68–70.

of terrorists and for maintaining a cottage industry of terror sympathizers.[43] As Director of Central Intelligence George Tenet asserted, "Madrassas provide the foot soldiers for many of the Islamic militant groups that operate throughout the Muslim world."[44]

Madrassas are not expensive to run, since the students and teachers live an austere life, but the sheer numbers of madrassas and other schools mean that costs add up. In March 2002, *Ain al Yaqeen,* an official Saudi magazine, asserted that the royal family has partly or wholly funded 210 Islamic centers, 1,500 mosques, 202 colleges, and 2,000 schools in countries, such as Cambodia, without Muslim majorities.[45] One can only imagine the broader extent of Saudi financing.

Following the Iranian Revolution in 1979, Shia Iran also played a major role in funding madrassas and exporting its view of the need for clerical rule. One might argue that it used non-oil monies to do so. However, in Iran, oil exports have generated approximately half of government revenues, while crude oil and its derivatives account for nearly 80 percent of Iran's total exports.[46] Of course, if we add natural gas to the mix, these numbers go up significantly, as would be the case if we add oil-related business to the mix. Iran's role in funding madrassas further pushed the Saudis and other Sunnis to fund their own madrassas, which rejected the Shiite model and view that they were illegitimate monarchies. The Soviet War in Afghanistan increased funding for madrassas with the blessing of the West, which saw these zealous recruits from madrassas as anti-Soviet fighters rather than future would-be terrorists. Whereas Pakistan had approximately 244 madrassas in 1956, that number grew to ten thousand by 2001, indoctrinating one million students compared to 1.9 million for primary-school enrollment.[47]

Elusive Elites

Oil monies also reach terrorists unwittingly, through government and elite channels. Governing Saudi elites and citizens is no easy task. Can the House of Saud persuade the thousands of princes and mullahs? Can the mullahs sway the many Saudis who either sympathize with or outright support Al-Qaeda? Can the Saudi citizens control the few among them who want to subvert the kingdom in cahoots

---

43. Richards, "At War."

44. Tenet, "Converging Dangers in a Post 9/11 World."

45. Cited in Beyer, "Inside the Kingdom."

46. U.S. Energy Information Administration, "Iran," available at www.eia.doe.gov/emeu/cabs/Iran/Oil.html.

47. On the evolution of madrassas, see Haqqani, "Islam's Medieval Outposts."

with Al-Qaeda? The leadership may be officially against supporting any terrorist group, but this need not stop elites from taking individual action.

Al-Qaeda also has had supporters in the Saudi elite, outside of government, such as in the business world. For instance, one well-publicized magnate, Yasin al-Qadi, has supported both Hamas and Al-Qaeda, according to American intelligence, through a number of front companies and charities. His assets were frozen after 9/11, but those of countless other individuals have not been.[48] The Saudi government itself audited the kingdom's National Commercial Bank in 1999 and discovered that five of Saudi Arabia's top businessman had transferred million of dollars to the accounts of Islamic charities that served as fronts for Bin Laden, while other financial support came from other elite Saudis, including princes of the royal family who were seeking to depose the king.[49] Some of this aid may have been given to pay off Bin Laden not to attack particular businesses in Saudi Arabia, but according to some estimates, Islamic organizations linked to armed groups can draw on giant sums of money, as the Saudi government alone donates perhaps $10 billion via the Ministry of Religious Works every year.[50] Naturally, individuals contribute on their own account as well.

Abu Zubaydah, a top operative, identified Prince Ahmed, nephew of King Fahd and several other princes, as his contact when he was interrogated after being captured in March 2002. Whether he was telling the truth or simply trying to set up the royal family is not clear. But American agents in Bosnia discovered computer files in 2002 that included Bin Laden's early financial supporters. Reportedly, three billionaire Saudi tycoons and several industrial magnates were among the twenty names on the list. As one indicator of Saudi financial exports, at least 50 percent of the Hamas operating budget has come from Saudi individuals, according to estimates by the United States and Israel, even though the Saudis assert that their support of $80–100 million per year goes directly to the Palestinian Authority and does not support terrorism.[51] Here we see part of the problem of terrorist financing. As one former high-level official put it, "Until the Saudis entertain the idea that giving Hamas money is an act of shame, you will never get to the bottom of terrorist financing."[52] That is far less a problem with Al-Qaeda, which is viewed as a threat to the regime, but it may be an aspect of the problem on a smaller scale.

---

48. Brisard and Dasquie, *Forbidden Truth,* 128–30; Emerson, "Testimony of Steven Emerson"; and Gerth and Miller, "Nation Challenged."
49. Scheuer, *Through Our Enemies' Eyes,* 28–29.
50. Napoleoni, *Terror Incorporated,* 125–27.
51. Richards, "At War."
52. Aufhauser interview.

The Role of Charities

Al-Qaeda has benefited from a network of wealthy supporters, a number of legitimate and illegitimate businesses, and Islamic charities.[53] Similar to Amnesty International, Al-Qaeda has made humanitarian appeals, collecting funds through Islamic charities.[54] In addition to diverting money, radicals have subverted local branches of some of these charities. NGOs offer terrorist operatives a legitimate job and identity as well as access to local communities. The CIA found that one-third of the Muslim charities in the Balkans were helping various Islamic terrorist groups.[55] Many endorsed the value of violent jihad, a hostile view of U.S. policy, and a sentiment that Arab regimes are not legitimate. Such proselytizing has enabled Al-Qaeda to appeal to recruits already sympathetic to its worldview. Juan Zarate, a Treasury Department official, noted that Al-Qaeda has taken advantage of state-supported proselytizing around the world.[56]

Al-Qaeda has targeted many Saudi charities partly because the oil-rich Saudi state has traditionally lacked adequate enforcement mechanisms. Canadian intelligence has estimated that Saudi-based charities have channeled between one and two million dollars to Al-Qaeda per month, and the Council on Foreign Relations has cited Saudi Arabia as the most important source of Al-Qaeda funds.[57]

In a memo dated December 30, 2009, Secretary of State Hillary Rodham Clinton asserted that cutting off the flow of funds to terrorist organizations and achieving stability in Afghanistan and Pakistan are top U.S. priorities. The memo highlighted fundraising in the Persian Gulf chiefly by Al-Qaeda but also by the Taliban, and other associated violent extremist groups. In talking points sent to American embassies, Clinton noted that long term success in combating terrorist financing required comprehensive, strategic measures. They included aggressive action to identify, disrupt, and deter terrorist donors, fundraisers, and facilitators; appropriate legal measures, including effective prosecution, to hold terrorist financiers and facilitators publicly accountable; strong oversight of charities, including their overseas branches, to ensure that these organizations are not supporting terrorist and extremist elements; strict enforcement of UN sanctions; and full compliance with standards for international anti-money laundering and combating the financing of terrorism, including vigorous enforcement.[58]

---

53. For a good overview, see Basile, "Going to the Source."

54. Comras, "Al-Qaeda Finances and Funding to Affiliated Groups."

55. National Commission on Terrorist Attacks upon the United States, "Monograph on Terrorist Financing."

56. As quoted in Schmidt, "Spreading," A1.

57. "Terrorism Financing." Gunaratna estimates that the Saudis donate $1.6 million a day to Islamic causes in general. Gunaratna, *Inside Al-Qaeda*, 144.

58. See "A Selection From the Cache of Diplomatic Dispatches."

Nearly all donors of charity aim to help charities, but some of those monies also are diverted to terrorist causes. Part of the problem is sheer volume. Muslims are expected to donate 2.5 percent of their wealth each year to charity in a process of alms-giving called *zakat,* which generates significant unregulated funds. As one of the five pillars of Islam, zakat is heavily ingrained in Muslim culture, so ingrained that the Saudis, for instance, have a department of finance that collects it for the whole country. Donations from Saudi Islamic banks, drawn from charity, reached $267 million in 2001, driven by a wish to bolster various Muslim causes abroad. Indonesian intelligence officials, for instance, estimate that 15 to 20 percent of Islamic charity funds are diverted to politically motivated groups and terrorists.[59]

The Saudis are hardly the only ones that have supported charities with direct or more often unwitting ties to terror. All of the Gulf States do so to some extent. For instance, the Qatar Charitable Society, a humanitarian organization in Qatar, has been actively involved in financing Al-Qaeda.[60] Kuwait, for its part, has tried to crack down on its extremists, but several Kuwaitis played prominent roles in Al-Qaeda. Moreover, questions arose about the extent to which Kuwait was supporting the war on terrorism. Sheikh Saud Nasser Al Sabah, Kuwait's Ambassador to the United States during the 1991 Gulf War, criticized Kuwait in mid-October 2001 for being "hesitant and timid" in the U.S.-led campaign against Osama Bin Laden and Al-Qaeda, blaming Kuwait's Islamists and their charities for the tepid response.[61] At the same time, by mid-October, Kuwait claimed that it had shut down 127 unlicensed charities as well as the cash flow to potential terrorist organizations, and by January 2002, U.S.-Kuwaiti cooperation to prevent the criminal misuse of Kuwait's financial system and charities appeared to gain some initial traction.[62]

Yet, Secretary Clinton's memo of December 2009 noted ongoing problems with Kuwait. In particular it asserted that Kuwait's "law prohibits efforts to undermine or attack Arab neighbors, a basis for the prosecution of al-Qa'ida facilitators. Kuwait remains the sole Gulf Cooperation Council (GCC) country that has not criminalized terrorist financing." Moreover, it noted that Kuwait's lack of parliamentary support makes obtaining good cooperation in Kuwait an "uphill battle," and that the regime itself was slow to support anti-terrorist efforts. The memo noted that a "particular point of difference" between the U.S. and Kuwait concerns the Revival of Islamic Heritage Society (RIHS). Washington

---

59. Ibid.
60. For extensive evidence, see "Testimony of Steven Emerson," 1.
61. "Shaikh Saud Hits Govt's Support for U.S. War on Terrorism."
62. *Kuwait Times,* January 27, 2002, p. 5.

had evidence that it provided financial and material support to Al-Qaeda and its affiliates, including Lashkar e-Tayyiba, Jemaah Islamiyah, and Al-Itihaad al-Islamiya, and pushed that case in summer 2008. However, in part because the RIHS enjoys broad public support in Kuwait as a charitable entity, Kuwait "has not taken significant action to address or shut down RIHS's headquarters or its branches."[63]

The sheer volume adds to problems of accountability. Most of the charitable monies are intended for causes that have nothing to do with terrorism. However, Zakat transfers are not accounted for in the books and therefore are hard to track. Saddled with the difficult task of changing American public opinion, Saudi spokesman Adel al-Jubeir asserted that since Saudis do not pay taxes, the regime does not receive tax returns and do audits, so it is not a question of "laxness in the system, it was just that we didn't have a mechanism that requires nonprofit organizations to perform audits. Now, we do."[64] But both Saudis and Americans alike have remained beset by the challenge of tracking charities. In the view of Secretary of the Treasury Paul O'Neill, who oversaw American efforts through 2002, "We know there's a lot more money out there that we just can't seem to get to"; the problem is that "we don't know where it is until long after it has been allocated and spent. By then, it's too late."[65]

Another element of the problem is that cracking down on charities can lead to problems elsewhere. While terrorists know the cracks in the financial system, the goal, as two key Treasury Department officials point out, has been to impede terrorist financing—while keeping banks, economies, and legitimate charities running normally.[66] Cracking down on charities is unpopular domestically. In the two-year period following 9/11, it appears that restrictions on Islamic charities had only a temporary impact on the flow of money, partly because regimes are reluctant to crack down charities and give Al-Qaeda or homegrown Islamic radicals fodder for criticism. Moreover, charities are not conveniently located next to the neighborhood McDonald's in just one country. They are scattered all over the world and are sometimes virtual, housed in non-brick reality, or so small that they could pass for a shoe repair side-shop. Al-Qaeda relies on charities that operate in regions such as Southeast Asia, where antiterrorist efforts are far harder to conduct and the shadowy realities of these social polities provide refuge for seedy activities.[67]

---

63. See "A Selection From the Cache of Diplomatic Dispatches."

64. For the transcript, see SUSRIS, Saudi U.S. Relations Information Service on www.saudi-us-relations.org/defense/saudi-counter-terrorism.html.

65. Suskind, *Price of Loyalty*, 199.

66. Author interview with U.S. Department of Treasury officials.

67. Abuza, "Funding Terrorism."

The Hawala Banking System

Charitable giving is problematic in and of itself, but it becomes especially hard to regulate and track when combined with the well-known *hawala* banking system. Hawala, which is sometimes referred to as underground banking, can be traced as far back as 5800 B.C. in the Indian subcontinent as a means of settling accounts within villages but was first developed in more recent times in India in the eighteenth century.[68] At its core is the practice of "transferring" money without actually transferring any money at all. A client deposits cash in one country and is given a code, and when that code is delivered to a hawala agent in the target country, the money is returned, with no accounting of the transactions. The business is conducted on the basis of honor. The hawala dealer who is part of a broader network of dealers called hawaldars assures that the cash reaches its target in exchange for a 1 percent commission. The hawala system, which regularly interacts with Islamic banks and commodity trading and which is often regulated by religious precepts under the sharia or Islamic law, is viewed as entirely legitimate in the Muslim world.

After September 11, efforts have been made to develop the first regional organization in the Middle East to track terrorist money that exploits the hawala system. It has been a major challenge. As a central official in these efforts points out, "New regulatory regimes have hampered the use of hawalas, but changing the reporting, documentation, and regulation of hawalas is a decades-long endeavor."[69]

Part of the problem is the sheer volume of money that passes through this system. While it is difficult to measure, officials in Pakistan estimate that more than $7 billion flows into Pakistan alone via this route.[70] Although Pakistan is a hotbed of hawala trading, we can still extrapolate that massive amounts are transferred via hawala in the Muslim world. Even if Al-Qaeda accounts for a small portion of that money, that is still a small fortune.

Whatever the exact amount, Al-Qaeda has used this system to its benefit to elude global financial scrutiny.[71] Much has been done to dismantle terrorist use of the hawala system. Al-Qaeda has been effective because it has, if not loyal supporters in the hawala system, then at least many sympathetic ones who, dealing in cash, are not likely to reveal their business partners. As a political matter, at least some involved and perhaps many would not want to help the "Great Satan" track down Al-Qaeda operatives anyway. In this context, being a sleuth is no easy task because there are no witnesses, at least none that will talk much.

---

68. Tripathi and Misra, *Towards a New Frontier.*
69. Aufhauser interview.
70. "Contributions," 15.
71. On the Islamic monetary system, see Napoleoni, *Modern Jihad,* ch. 10.

Cutting off the flow of money is also complicated by the ingenuity of funding organizations and cash nature of most transactions. As Robert Jordan, U.S. Ambassador to Saudi Arabia, put it, it is "sort of like trying to stamp out crabgrass. As soon as you stamp one of them out, something springs up somewhere else under a different name."[72] Hiding money is not especially difficult. As one U.S. Treasury Department official put it, referring to Bin Laden: "We don't know where his money is. That is why the Treasury Department has never frozen any of Bin Laden's accounts. Not a single dime."[73] Underscoring the difficulty of tracking money, Prince Bandar noted that that the "money leaves Saudi Arabia, goes to Europe, and we can follow it; goes to the United States, America, and we lose contact with it."[74] At the same time, the Treasury Department has innovated significantly in how to cut off terrorist funding through global banks, putting Al-Qaeda under some financial stress.[75]

Oil Money: Bringing WMDs and Terrorists Together

Oil funds also can help Al-Qaeda's efforts to obtain WMD. One month after September 11, a CIA source code named Dragonfire reported that Al-Qaeda had obtained a ten-kiloton nuclear weapon that had been stolen from Russia. The CIA, which informed President Bush, found the report plausible, and some evasive actions were taken to protect the chain of command in the event that an attack was being planned for Washington, D.C.[76]

The WMD threat is of paramount concern in Washington. Presidents George W. Bush and Barack Obama have described it as "single most serious threat to American national security," with Secretary of Defense Robert Gates, who has served both presidents, describing it as one of the few things that keeps him up at night.[77] Weapons of mass destruction are the bogeyman of modern world politics. After a respite at the end of the Cold War, when it seemed as though they were losing their luster as threats against humanity, they have returned. The September 11 Commission recommended that we devote a "maximum" effort to countering the proliferation of weapons of mass destruction in the broader

---

72. Quoted in Beyer, "Inside the Kingdom."
73. Quoted in Kaplan and Kurlantzick, "How a Terror Network Funds Attacks."
74. Quoted in Baer, *Sleeping with the Devil*, 69.
75. Off-the-record interview with a high-level official.
76. This is documented in Allison, *Nuclear Terrorism*.
77. See foreword by Graham Allison in Mowatt-Larssen, "Al Qaeda Weapons of Mass Destruction Threat."

war on terrorism, before it is too late.[78] Terrorists could wreak physical havoc with such weapons, change how we govern ourselves, and alter the course of global politics as well. As Michael Ignatieff argues, a grand challenge would be to fight terror without losing our democracy in the process. That may well prove an uphill climb.[79]

September 11 heightened the fear of terrorism, but that concern has been around since the 1970s.[80] The danger is that we live in a world of WMD with terrorists who want to use it at their earliest convenience. WMD is challenging to obtain and to use, but Al-Qaeda's radical ideology provides an immense motivation, while its distorted lens sees a variety of deserving targets. There are many terrorist groups, but religious terrorists, as Audrey Cronin points out, are special because they see "apocalyptic images of destruction" as a necessity, which "makes them uniquely dangerous, as we learned painfully on September 11."[81] Such destruction would certainly be facilitated by weapons of mass destruction.

To be sure, it is very hard for terrorists to use even nonnuclear WMD effectively. Only in a very few cases have groups been able to amass the skills, access, knowledge, material, connections, financing, and tools to perpetrate WMD attacks. However, the intent of terrorists should certainly not be underestimated. Al-Qaeda has tried to acquire nuclear weapons.[82] The CIA reported that terrorist interest in obtaining WMD grew in the years prior to 9/11.[83] According to the February 7, 2001, court testimony of Al-Qaeda operative Jamal al-Fadl, Al-Qaeda sought to buy uranium in the Sudan in the early 1990s. Al-Fadl stated that he was directly involved in this attempt on behalf of Bin Laden at the end of 1993 or the beginning of 1994. Al-Fadl was telephoned by a senior Al-Qaeda official with information to meet a contact in Khartoum, Sudan, who allegedly possessed uranium. Al-Fadl met with several individuals, who finally led him to a man named Basheer, and the two met in an office on Jambouria Street in Khartoum. When questioned by Basheer as to whether Al-Qaeda was serious about acquiring uranium, Al-Fadl claimed, "I know people, they [are] very serious, and they want to buy it." He noted that Al-Qaeda was concerned primarily with the quality

---

78. See summary of the final report, The National Commission on Terrorist Attacks Upon the United States (also known as the 9-11 Commission) available at http://govinfo.library.unt.edu/911/report/index.htm.

79. Ignatieff, *Lesser Evil.*

80. Jenkins, *Countering Al-Qaeda,* 12.

81. Cronin, "Behind the Curve," esp. 41–42.

82. *Global Reach of Al-Qaeda,* 32. See also Jenkins, *Will Terrorists Go Nuclear?*

83. Combating Terrorism. See also Leader, "Usama Bin Laden."

of the material and the country of origin and only secondarily with the cost. The arranged price was around $1.5 million.[84]

Bin Laden declared in 1998 that it was a "religious duty" to acquire WMD.[85] In fact, he claimed on November 10, 2001, that Al-Qaeda had nuclear and chemical weapons and that he would use them in retaliation if the United States were to use WMD in its war in Afghanistan.[86] Numerous documents were recovered by American forces in Al-Qaeda houses in Kabul soon after it fell in November 2001 to the Northern Alliance forces allied with Washington. They demonstrated that it was pursuing a sophisticated biological weapons program and was certainly seeking to build and deploy a low-grade "dirty" nuclear device; the evidence suggests that it has also sought to develop or acquire a nuclear device.[87] This goal was confirmed by captured Al-Qaeda leader Abu Zubaydah, who, among other things, told American interrogators in April 2002 that Al-Qaeda had been working aggressively to build a dirty bomb.[88]

Not only has Al-Qaeda sought WMD, but it appears that it would be quite willing to use it in massive attacks. Richard Myers, chairman of the U.S. Joint Chiefs of Staff from 2001 to 2005, who had access to secret intelligence on Al-Qaeda's WMD plans, described Al-Qaeda as ruthless, relentless, and bent on using nuclear and biological weapons to do away with America's way of life.[89] That is certainly confirmed by jihadis who discuss obtaining and using nuclear weapons and other weapons of mass destruction almost casually on online forums, with some prominent Al-Qaeda regional leaders even claiming online that Al-Qaeda already possesses nuclear weapons—wishful thinking about a key terrorist goal. In 2002, Al-Qaeda spokesman Sulaiman Abu Geith posted on the internet that Al-Qaeda has the right to punish America for its oppression of Muslims by killing "four million Americans—two million of them children."[90] This notion was backed by a fatwa from a fugitive Saudi cleric who was later arrested by Saudi authorities; the notion of how many Western infidels should be killed became a normal issue to discuss and consider in radical circles.[91] That was not the case until around May 2003. That was when Al-Qaeda received some Islamic grounding to justify such attacks, in the form of a treatise issued by a Saudi cleric named Sheikh Nasir bin Hamid al-Fahd. He noted that some thinkers put the

---

84. For his testimony, see http://fl1.findlaw.com/news.findlaw.com/cnn/docs/binladen/binladen20701tt.pdf.
85. Tenet, "Converging Dangers in a Post 9/11 World."
86. CNN, November 10–11, 2001.
87. Tenet, "Converging Dangers in a Post 9/11 World."
88. Perl, *Terrorism,* CRS-7.
89. For an extensive discussion, see Myers, *Eyes on the Horizon.*
90. Jenkins, *Will Terrorists Go Nuclear?* 255.
91. Ibid., 256–58.

number of Muslims killed directly or indirectly by America at nearly 10 million and that it is permissible to treat others as we have been treated.[92]

In an interview with Al Jazeera, Mustafa Abu al-Yazid, the general official of the Al-Qaeda organization in Afghanistan, asserted in June 2009 that if the fighting in the tribal areas of Swat, Bajar, and elsewhere went out of control and Pakistan disintegrated into chaos, he hoped that "the nuclear weapons will not fall in the hand of the Americans, and the Muslims take them [weapons] and use them against the Americans."[93]

At times, Al-Qaeda describes nuclear weapons as offensive; at other times, they are described as being intended for defensive purposes, although it is not exactly clear if this is a real distinction or a rationalization. Thus, in April 2009, Al-Qaeda's leader in Iraq, Abu Hamza Al-Muhajir, emphasized in an audio tape posted on the jihadi online forums, that it was important to acquire biological, chemical, and even nuclear weapons in order to compensate for the superiority of the enemies with conventional weapons. He said that the Muslim scientists should try hard to develop weapons of mass destruction for deterrence purposes, triggering a broader discussion in online forums on how this could be done.

The connections between oil and WMD are manifold. As an Arab Human Development report pointed out, "Arab oil exporting countries have been in a position to direct large streams of revenue towards their military and security forces."[94] Oil-rich states have greater resources with which to produce WMD. In turn, they may help non-oil states obtain WMD. States that develop WMD may well prevent it from reaching terrorists in one form or another, but it is fair to say that the greater the number of states with WMD programs, the harder WMD will be to control. It is expensive to develop some types of WMD, especially nuclear weapons. High oil revenues allow for greater state spending on WMD, as does the accumulation of wealth over time, irrespective of the level of oil revenues in any year. Saddam, for instance, spent billions to develop nuclear weapons, an effort that failed partly because Israel destroyed Iraq's nuclear reactor at Osirak in 1981, but Saddam's ill-advised wars were an even bigger factor. As a result, Iraq's many billions did not even produce a crude nuclear weapon.[95] Iraq's case demonstrates that oil money is important to having even a chance to accomplish this difficult task.

The states in the Middle East that have mounted a serious nuclear weapons program have all been oil-rich: Iraq, Iran, and Algeria. No oil-poor country in

92. For an extensive discussion, see Scheuer, *Imperial Hubris,* esp. 155–58.
93. See The NEFA Foundation, "Mustafa Abu al Yazid's Interview on Al Jazeera, June 22, 2009" available at www.nefafoundation.org/miscellaneous/FeaturedDocs/nefa_yazidqa0609.pdf.
94. *Arab Human Development Report 2009,* 106.
95. Kamp, "WMD Terrorism: An Exchange."

the Middle East has done so. Iraq and Iran are well-known cases, but oil wealth has also allowed Algeria to develop elements of a nuclear program. Algeria lacks nuclear weapons, but it has had two nuclear research reactors capable of generating several kilograms of plutonium each year. While it cannot reprocess or separate this plutonium from spent fuel, it is considered a state of active proliferation.[96] By contrast, Libya pursued WMD not by trying to develop its own capabilities, as have Algeria, Iran, and Iraq, but rather by drawing on oil monies to buy the technology and materials required to do so. Libya appears to have given up its dreams of obtaining WMD, but that does not detract from the notion that oil money allowed it to aspire in that direction and that it could do so in the future as well.

Some states, of course, will be fairly insensitive to the costs of building nuclear weapons either because it is a priority, often of the leader or a few elites or because they feel they must match a perceived or real threat. Israel is an exception as an oil-poor state with a major nuclear program in the Middle East. However, Israel is sui generis inasmuch as it has consistently faced existential threats, against which nuclear deterrence is an outright survival mechanism. Moreover, the United States has been helpful to Israel, albeit not directly on its nuclear program. Israel also has a much larger intellectual infrastructure of trained scientists for conducting WMD development than do the oil-rich states and a far stronger non-oil based economy. It can support its nuclear program by virtue of its non-oil-based GDP.

Absent significant oil money, the tradeoff between guns and butter would be much more painful, and some states would be more inclined to eschew the pursuit of nuclear weapons. Consider the case of Iran. The United States has a policy of regime change in Iran using economic sanctions. It may also use military force to destroy Iran's nuclear facilities, if sanctions and diplomacy fail. Whether or not a U.S. or Israeli military attack ever succeeds, Iran may rebuild these facilities and is likely to continue to build its conventional forces for greater power and influence in the Persian Gulf. This requires oil money.

As touched on earlier, Iran relies overwhelmingly on oil exports. In March 2006, the International Monetary Fund noted the "vulnerability of [Iran's] economy to a potential decline in oil prices."[97] It would be far more difficult for Iran to fund a costly nuclear program (or a major conventional military buildup) with oil prices at $50 per barrel than at $80 or more per barrel. In the event of one or

---

96. Cirincione, *Deadly Arsenals,* ch. 17.
97. IMF, Public Information Notice, March 5, 2007 "IMF Executive Board Concludes 2006 Article IV Consultation with the Islamic Republic of Iran" available at www.imf.org/external/np/sec/pn/2007/pn0729.htm.

more military confrontations with the United States or Israel, it would be much harder for Tehran to rebuild its damaged nuclear facilities. Funding the country's nuclear aspirations would require deeply unpopular cuts in domestic programs.

Matching Israel, in any event, will involve more than the construction of nuclear weapons alone. It will require an effective delivery system, the ability to avert Israel's anti-missile capabilities, and constant efforts to match Israel in a high-tech race. The latter race alone will be very expensive, especially given the likelihood that Israel sabotaged Iran's nuclear centrifuges with the Stuxnet virus in 2010 and could probably attempt similar efforts in the future, given its substantial high-tech edge over Iran. The less oil revenue Iran expects over a period of a decade or more, the less likely it will be to countenance these costs of building and protecting nuclear assets, even if the military or political elites support it.

Oil is also related to the chances of whether terrorists will acquire and detonate a nuclear bomb. The threat is often exaggerated because it is hard for terrorists to go nuclear. Weapons-grade uranium and plutonium are highly guarded and difficult to access, as are nuclear warheads. But the threat is real and must be considered.[98] Terrorists may obtain fissionable material, as Graham Allison elaborates, by stealing it or obtaining it from a state that has produced it. If they do so, then they may well be able to produce a crude nuclear weapon. The disintegration of the Soviet Union has created opportunities that did not exist before. Yuri Vishnevsky, the head of Russia's nuclear regulatory agency, asserted in November 2002 that "instances of the loss of nuclear materials have been recorded, but estimating the quantity is another question."[99] The Russian-American Nuclear Security Advisory Council reported in 2002 that "roughly half of the nuclear weapons-grade material in Russia remains inadequately secure."[100] One captured internal Al-Qaeda document, probably written in 1994, revealed that jihadists "look forward to Russian gangs selling nuclear weapons."[101] Even if a modest portion of fissionable material were stolen or bought, which is not impossible, it could be enough to turn the terrorist threat into a nightmare.[102]

Sensitive fissile material needed for a nuclear bomb is fairly well protected, although the International Atomic Energy Agency (IAEA) did warn in May 2004 that more measures were needed to guard stockpiles of highly enriched uranium in atomic power reactors and other sources throughout the world and sought to take measures with Washington toward that goal.[103] The number of states with

98. On why this is so, see Jenkins, *Will Terrorists Go Nuclear?*
99. Cirincione, *Deadly Arsenals*, ch. 17.
100. "Reshaping U.S.-Russian Threat Reduction."
101. Quoted in Jenkins, *Will Terrorists Go Nuclear?* 87.
102. Allison, *Nuclear Terrorism*, esp. 68–74.
103. Miller, "Nuclear Monitor," A5.

nuclear weapons technology also has expanded and is likely to expand more in the future. The proliferation of knowledge and technical knowhow has made it easier to obtain these materials. Nuclear explosive material is expensive and its price, as Michael Levi puts it, "is a big barrier to all but the richest terrorist groups."[104] Oil money might help in bribing elements within states to provide fissionable material—such as radical politicians, paramilitary forces, clerics, or avaricious businessmen with high-level contacts. Witness the damaging work of A. Q. Khan, the founder of Pakistan's nuclear-weapons program, who for a decade or more sold nuclear technology and knowhow on the global black market, including sensitive uranium enriching equipment to Iran.[105]

Terrorists could also use oil money to buy nuclear materials from existing states, such as North Korea and Russia. The greater threat from North Korea perhaps is not that it will use nuclear weapons but will sell nuclear expertise and technology. In the case of Iran, its opaque and fragmented government is made up of competing factions. Extremist factions could conceivably sell a nuclear weapon to terrorists, thus making some money while striking at America. Research scientists or even sympathizers with Al-Qaeda in the military might do so as well.

While it is very hard to obtain nuclear materials and while building a bomb faces numerous barriers, it is not inconceivable that, under the right circumstances and with the right funding, Al-Qaeda could assemble a broad group of actors that could help it make a nuclear weapon.[106] This team could include Pakistani nuclear scientists who may be sympathetic to Al-Qaeda; their counterparts in Pakistan's intelligence services, many of whom were sympathetic to the Taliban and Al-Qaeda in Afghanistan; and knowledgeable experts from other countries, including Russia or Iran. They might produce a crude nuclear weapon that may still cause much damage.[107]

The connection between oil money and nuclear proliferation has another side as well. Oil monies have contributed to the development of nuclear weapons in non-oil-exporting countries. Pakistan is a case in point. Saudi Arabia has probably funded Pakistan's nuclear program. In turn, Pakistan has supported other states, not necessarily officially, through the activities of its scientists and businessmen. In this case, Saudi oil monies are potentially related to terrorism in several ways. They help produce Pakistani nuclear components and weapons

---

104. Levi, *On Nuclear Terrorism,* 28; on the cost of obtaining such materials, 28–35.
105. Ferguson and Potter, *Four Faces of Nuclear Terrorism,* 8–9.
106. Levi, *On Nuclear Terrorism,* esp. 38–49.
107. Ferguson and Potter, *Four Faces of Nuclear Terrorism,* 8, 116. On how terrorists can obtain less-than-ideal nuclear materials, see Levi, *On Nuclear Terrorism,* 66–87.

and may do the same for Saudi Arabia, and these components or weapons can be bought or stolen by terrorist groups.

The connection between oil and nuclear capability need not be direct. For instance, if Pakistan fell to Islamic militants, they could then sell nuclear components to others or others could steal them. This is not an entirely wild scenario. While the evidence is not ironclad, a 2004 IAEA study found that Pakistan, through A. Q. Khan, aided Iran's nuclear efforts by providing such things as designs for centrifuges capable of making bomb-grade nuclear fuel.[108] The oil connection here is a bit submerged, but it is still there. Iran is an important ally of Pakistan partly because it is oil-rich. That makes Pakistan more likely to cooperate with Iran, even at the risk of angering the United States, not to mention Saudi Arabia, as does Iran's significant reserve of petrodollars.

Pakistan appears to be even more strongly connected to Saudi Arabia. Prime Minister Benazir Bhutto's press adviser, Khalid Hasan, asserted that much of the funding for Pakistan's nuclear program under Khan, which can produce several nuclear bombs per year, came from Saudi Arabia.[109] Khan asserted that, more than any other state, Saudi Arabia had supported Pakistan whenever it needed financial assistance and that without this support, Pakistan could "never have conducted nuclear tests."[110]

Some additional information to consider comes from Mohammed Abdalla Al Khilewi, who was first secretary at the Saudi Arabian mission to the United Nations in New York. In May 1994, he issued a statement on embassy letterhead declaring King Fahd a despot and demanding a redistribution of the country's wealth and power. The House of Saud, not unexpectedly, was not pleased. Khilewi defected to the United States, where he was granted political asylum in August 1994. He asserted that he had made copies of thirteen thousand official Saudi documents that had passed through his office that show that from 1975 to 1990, the Saudi Arabian government provided some $5 billion to help fund Saddam Hussein's nuclear efforts and that it tried to acquire nuclear weapons from Pakistan and the Soviet Union.[111] But as Khilewi has not made this archive public, it is hard to confirm his claims.

In one interview, Khilewi estimated conservatively that the Saudi government has spent at least $7 billion on nuclear armaments since 1975, including millions of dollars to buy nuclear reactors for what it likes to call "scientific" and "peaceful" uses and for nuclear research and data collection. But most of the money

---

108. Sanger, "Pakistan Found to Aid Iran Nuclear Efforts," A7.
109. Cited in Allison, *Nuclear Terrorism,* 76–77.
110. "Pakistani Scientist Credits Saudi Arabia for N-Test Help."
111. *Sunday Times,* July 24, 1994.

went to support nuclear programs in other countries—Iraq and Pakistan, with most going to Iraq. In his view, Pakistan would transfer nuclear technology out of economic interest.[112] Numerous reports suggest that Riyadh agreed in 1998 to provide free oil to Pakistan. Arab diplomatic sources said that Crown Prince Abdullah approved the continuation of such an arrangement in late 2003. The sources stated that Saudi oil deliveries to Pakistan were part of a strategic relationship in which Islamabad provided weapons, technical help, and a nuclear umbrella over the Saudi kingdom.[113] Several reports suggest that Saudi Arabia bought the CSS-2 ballistic missile from China and that, in return, either China funded Pakistan's weapons programs or Pakistan profited from brokering the deal between China and Saudi Arabia.[114]

It appears that Saudi Arabia's oil monies helped Pakistan develop nuclear weapons and indirectly allowed for the Khans of the world to do their business. Riyadh might well be able to purchase nuclear components or a nuclear weapon in the future from Pakistan as a counterweight against a nuclear-armed Iran.[115] Khilewi asserted that the Saudis would "pay anything to acquire a nuclear capability as long as the cost is just money....They are willing to pay financial costs, not political costs. They don't like to forego power to the army or scientists. So long as the technicians stay out of politics, they don't give a damn if the scientists use nuclear fusion or fission or whether they get it from uranium 235 or plutonium 239."[116]

Notice the self-defeating nature of the transactions in this story. Saudi Arabia helps Pakistan with its nuclear program. Pakistani actors help Iran. Saudi Arabia feels threatened by Iran's nuclear program. This chain of events might lead to a nuclear arms race in the Middle East if Iran succeeds in developing nuclear weapons.

We know that terrorists also seek to influence certain states in world politics, sometimes with the highly ambitious and elusive goal of subverting or overthrowing their governments. Some of these states are oil-rich, creating the prospect that terrorists can benefit from these oil resources and WMD capability. Al-Qaeda clearly seeks to hijack a state in order not only to launch global jihad and serve as a base of operations but also to serve as a model of a caliphate. Al-Zawahiri

---

112. Al Khilewi, "Saudi Arabia Is Trying to Kill Me."

113. See Bristol Blog, Special to World Tribune.com, November 4, 2003 "Nuclear Deal: Pakistan gets free crude oil from Saudi Arabia" available at www.sullivan-county.com/id3/pause.htm. See also Borchgrave, "Pakistan."

114. Levy and Scott-Clark, *Nuclear Deception,* 173–74. See also the essay by former U.S. Defense Intelligence Agency analyst Thomas Woodrow, Jamestown Foundation, November 9, 2002.

115. See Kate Amlin, NTI Issue Brief "Will Saudi Arabia Acquire Nuclear Weapons?" available at www.nti.org/e_research/e3_40a.html.

116. Ibid.

has stated that only after taking over territory for a state can the "Muslim nation reinstate its fallen caliphate and regain its lost glory" and that victory against crusaders cannot be achieved without an Islamic base, a fundamentalist state to restore the fallen caliphate.[117] Recapturing lost glory, even if it means confronting the West politically, strikes a chord in the broader Muslim world.[118]

We need not even have the complete fall of an oil-rich state. Al-Qaeda did not overthrow the Taliban and still had enormous influence over Afghan politics. Were extremists to take over in Jordan, they could more easily affect Iraq and the tenor of regional politics. The worst-case scenario is for an oil-rich state or a state like Pakistan that has nuclear weapons, to fall to such extremists who exploit it for WMD purposes. This is very unlikely but far from impossible. An oil-rich state could now or in the future already have WMD in its possession or nuclear materials that could finish the puzzle of production for terrorists. Or the oil-rich state might not have WMD or WMD materials, but its wealth could be seized by terrorists and whisked away in various forms, to be used for the purchase or production of WMD. Terrorists might insinuate themselves into the national political life of the oil-rich state and support actors who tend to be more sympathetic to their causes. In turn, they could slowly support a WMD program and in this way generate a symbiotic relationship with a regime that is anti-American.

While nuclear weapons pose one threat, the far more likely threat is nonnuclear. In the view of former veteran CIA analyst Rolf Mowatt-Larssen, Al-Qaeda has doggedly sought from 1988 to at least 2003 to obtain biological and chemical weapons, including ricin and anthrax, as well as nuclear weapons. While other analysts disagree with his view of the Al-Qaeda threat, he has assembled convincing evidence that Al-Qaeda operatives would launch such attacks, killing tens or even hundreds of thousands of Americans, if they could do so.[119]

Biological, chemical, and nuclear weapons differ quite significantly. Chemical and biological weapons can be made, bought, and used more easily than nuclear weapons; they can be used in the air, in the water, or on various physical surfaces. Producing mass civilian casualties using these weapons is not easy, but it's much easier than using nuclear weapons.

It is costly to produce biological and chemical weapons indigenously, store them, and master delivery systems for them.[120] Bin Laden's group tried to

---

117. Quoted in Benjamin and Simon, *Age of Sacred Terror,* 134, 139–41; and Laqueur, ed., *Voices of Terror,* 426.

118. For instance, see Tehran Siyasat-e Ruz in FBIS: NES, 10, April 2004 (WNC# Ohxi36-c034le7e).

119. Mowatt-Larssen, "Al Qaeda Weapons of Mass Destruction Threat."

120. On the many obstacles to terrorist WMD, see Bowman, *Weapons of Mass Destruction,* CRS, 4–7.

accomplish this task in Afghanistan but failed due to the technical difficulties. A radiological bomb involves radioactive ingredients wrapped around a conventional explosive device that, when detonated, contaminates a large area with radiation. The effectiveness of the weapon would depend on a number of factors, including the damage potential of the isotopes used, the size of the explosive, and wind speed and strength. Massive casualties would not result, but it is possible that a major attack, if not decontaminated, could cause several city blocks or more to be uninhabitable for many years,[121] although some view even such an outcome as an exaggeration. At a minimum, though, the use of such a bomb, by heralding a possibly new era in terrorist tactics, would engender fear on a broad basis.

It is well known that Al-Qaeda has tried to develop such a weapon, which is far easier to assemble than a nuclear bomb.[122] But there are many sources of radioactive material, including those used in external beam radiation devices to treat cancer and equipment to monitor wells for oil. Such materials may be bought or stolen and are widespread enough to be of great concern.[123] A major book on the subject published by the Center for Nonproliferation Studies of California's Monterey Institute of International Studies found that terrorists are "all but certain" to set off a radiological weapon in the United States and that there are thousands and possibly tens of thousands of high-risk radioactive sources already in use worldwide.[124] Producing such a bomb may be inexpensive, but it is costly to engage in serious biological warfare, which involves obtaining and innovating with biological strains that can be delivered effectively and can elude Western defenses. It is also more expensive if actors want to be able to deliver their weapons via missiles.

Funding an Arms Race

Oil can contribute to a regional WMD arms race in two ways. It can fund arms, and arms are needed to protect a commodity as precious as oil. Even a small nuclear weapon could destroy major oil facilities, and threats of radiological, chemical, and biological weapons attacks cannot be discounted. Even if Iran or other states in the region never use WMD, they could enable brinkmanship or coercion because others would be aware of their existence. This could facilitate efforts by Iran to coerce other OPEC states such as Saudi Arabia into lowering

121. See, for instance, Levi and Kelly, "Weapons of Mass Disruption."
122. For good studies on radiological bombs, see Medalia, "Terrorist 'Dirty Bombs.'"
123. Ferguson et al., *Commercial Radioactive Sources*.
124. Ferguson and Potter, *Four Faces of Nuclear Terrorism*.

oil production to raise the price of oil or into launching an embargo for various political ends. Nuclear weapons could also make it harder for the United States to deploy regional forces, for the obvious reason that leaders would be less willing to take the risk of massive casualties.

Iran and Iraq had each other in mind, not to mention Israel, when they started to develop their programs. The Saudis, for their part, may join the race in the future, buying one or more nuclear weapons from Pakistan to deter perceived threats from Iran, Iraq, or Israel.

While defensive reasons may be at play, offensive ones are important as well. Oil itself usually increases the influence of states, and may whet their appetite for greater power or for maintaining the influence they have obtained. Rivalry in the Persian Gulf is unlikely to end, even if Iraq makes a smooth transition to democracy. Democratic states still seek power, especially in a neighborhood where that has been a requisite for influence and even survival.

Despite the embarrassing fact that Saddam had no WMD, the United States has played a central and indispensable role against the proliferation of WMD, especially since September 11.[125] The Cooperative Defense Initiative has been a central United States Central Command activity that seeks to enhance deterrence by reducing the vulnerability of Gulf Cooperation Council (GCC) states to "WMD coercion and to the effects of WMD use."[126] It enhances interoperability, active defenses, and medical countermeasures to protect soldiers and civilians against WMD.[127] GCC states have also sketched plans for a nuclear program that might counter Iran's,[128] and such an option, while inchoate, would depend fundamentally on American technology, support, and back-up.[129]

Gaining Cooperation

Gaining longer-run cooperation represents another great challenge in the fight with terrorism. As one high-level American official involved in these efforts observes, "Without international cooperation and coordination, an order to freeze assets borders on political theater."[130] Although the United States can take unilateral measures to fight terrorism, the *modus operandi* for stopping

---

125. *National Military Strategy to Combat Weapons of Mass Destruction.*
126. *Cooperative Defense.* The GCC was formed in May 1981 and is composed of Saudi Arabia, Kuwait, Oman, Qatar, the United Arab Emirates, and Bahrain.
127. Ibid.
128. Kechichian, "Can Conservative Arab Gulf Monarchies Endure," 297–99.
129. On GCC threat perceptions, see Mattair, "Mutual Threat Perceptions," 133–40.
130. Aufhauser, "Keynote Address."

terrorist financing also lies in international laws and action. That is represented by UN Resolutions 1267, 1333, and 1390, which jointly criminalize terrorist financing and require the implementation to investigate, deter and freeze terrorist funds.

On September 14, 2001, the Bush administration established a new Foreign Terrorist Asset Tracking Center to coordinate efforts by intelligence, diplomatic, and financial agencies in the effort to drain terrorist financing.[131] The Terrorist Financing Executive Order enacted by George W. Bush on September 24, 2001, made it legally possible to pursue financial supporters of terrorism as terrorists. It significantly expanded the U.S. government's powers to indict those providing funds and infrastructural support to alleged terrorists, and to freeze and block assets. The order also published a blacklist of terrorist organizations and individuals whose assets were to be frozen globally. And much has been accomplished in the financial war on terrorism.[132] Centrally, as one high-level official in partial charge of such affairs put it, we "decapitated the central banking system, which helped support terrorism, albeit private donors are still at play."[133]

The record of tracking money has also improved over time. On January 8, 2002, the United States had frozen well over $30 million in assets of more than 150 organizations and individuals. Yet, it still lacked good coordination with other nations on a global scale, despite the International Convention for the Suppression of the Financing of Terrorism, struck under UN auspices in December 1999. That coordination improved significantly in October 2001 when European officials agreed on tough measures against terrorist financing.

The Saudi Case: The Slow Path to Cooperation

The Saudis were slow to take action related to terrorism, but in order to understand their role, several qualifying points are necessary. We need to distinguish government and individual behavior. The behavior of Saudi citizens, of course, may not be condoned or promoted by the government. Moreover, charity givers may not intend to support terrorism, and we need to make the difference

---

131. On the financial war on terrorism and documents relevant to it, see U.S. Department of Treasury Web site, www.treas.gov/offices/eotffc/publications/index.html.

132. See U.S. Department of Treasury Press Releases on www.treas.gov/press/releases/reports/js721.pdf.

133. Aufhauser interview.

in our evaluations. Even the best sleuths, in government and outside, who have spent countless devoted hours to tracing down the Saudi connection to terrorism assert that it is hard to do. The Saudis may also cooperate more than we think behind the scenes because they do not want to telegraph their cooperation publicly. They must weigh American requests for greater action against a range of other interests. In particular, they do not want to offend important domestic constituencies. These include religious figures who want to preach as they see fit, princes in the royal family who may be interrogated or even ousted in a serious crackdown, citizens who are anti-American or see the royal family as lackeys of the United States, and those that sympathize with or support Al-Qaeda. The last thing the royals want is to be perceived as cracking down on Islam to appease the Christian West.

They also face a difficult task, because charity is crucial to Islam—one of its five pillars. Regulating charity too strongly then may appear un-Islamic, as would taking actions against the Palestinians whose actions are viewed differently in Riyadh and Washington.[134] Finally, Riyadh did hear a partial wakeup call after 9/11 and took some important actions to combat terrorism.[135] As discussed earlier, it showed some recognition that changes are needed in its religious schools and took increasing steps to curb its own radical Islamists.[136] At the financial level, the regime moved to freeze suspected terrorist holdings, to police local charities and financial institutions more vigorously,[137] and to provide some intelligence assistance to Washington.[138] It also developed a somewhat more sophisticated scheme to fight money laundering, moved to control cross-border money transfers, and developed a joint task force with the United States to execute the war on terrorism in the kingdom.[139]

These actions represent an improvement over the Saudi historical record on terrorism or even its immediate post-9/11 response when the Saudi Vice Minister of Finance, perhaps fearing internal dissent, told American officials on September 28 that "he did not think that they had any accounts that might help

---

134. This is clear, for instance, in U.S. Secretary of the Treasury, Paul O'Neill, Media Roundtable, Conference Palace, Jeddah, Saudi Arabia (Department of the Treasury, March 6, 2002).

135. For a list of post–September 11 Saudi actions against terrorism, see Cordesman, *Saudi Arabia Enters*, 214–21.

136. Saudi foreign minister Faisal indicated at least that the regime had taken measures to remove anti-American teachings from its madrassas. Interview on CBS, September 15, 2002.

137. "Riyadh Cracks Down on Terrorists Assets," *APS Diplomat Recorder*, October 27, 2001.

138. Lorenzetti, "U.S. Firms."

139. See comments by David Aufhauser, who was involved in these efforts, in Aufhauser et al., "Saudi Arabia, Enemy or Friend?" 3–4.

terrorism."[140] As one knowledgeable intelligence official put it, "Since September 11, not a single indictment or useful lead has come out of Saudi Arabia."[141]

Saudi officials admit, usually privately, that high-level Saudi agencies including the Ministry of the Interior failed to adequately monitor charities and that money from members of the royal family and senior Saudi business elites supported charities that disbursed monies carelessly and could have funded terrorism.[142] Saudi cooperation, according to Bush administration officials, was very slow and difficult in regulating some 300 charities that may dole out nearly $4 billion a year, perhaps because Saudi officials and state-paid religious leaders sat on the boards of charities that the United States suspected of supporting terrorism.[143] In the year following 9/11, U.S. federal officials sent hundreds of written requests for specific information to their Saudi counterparts and have expressed frustration that many of them have gone unanswered.[144] But cooperation slowly began to increase. The shift began in earnest with the May 12, 2003 Al-Qaeda bombings on Western residential compounds in Riyadh that killed thirty-five people, as well as by a plot to attack Mecca. Prior to the May 2003 crisis, threats to the kingdom were either external or could be viewed as aimed at foreign forces, and the sentiment, as encapsulated by Prince Nayef was that the Al-Qaeda presence in Saudi Arabia was "weak and almost nonexistent."[145]

Events in the kingdom made the regime more serious about confronting its own profound and, to some extent, self-inflicted problems of extremism, and cooperating with Washington.[146] It cracked down on militants, and more zealously sought a dozen prominent Saudis suspected of giving Al-Qaeda millions of dollars. For his part, FBI Director Robert Mueller praised Riyadh for a swift-moving investigation that resulted in over twenty arrests, calling it "exceptionally significant" in the fight against terrorism.[147] This may have reflected typical official efforts to downplay U.S.-Saudi tensions, but the crack down on terrorists continued in July and August. Sixteen Al-Qaeda-linked suspects were arrested; authorities uncovered a network of Islamic extremists so large that it surprised Saudi

---

140. Quoted in Suskind, *Price of Loyalty,* 197.
141. Baer, *Sleeping with the Devil,* 20.
142. Cordesman, *Saudi Arabia Enters the Twenty-First Century,* 166–67.
143. Gerth and Miller, "Saudi Arabia." The Saudi estimate is more modest, pointing to approximately $24 billion spent on charitable causes since 1970. See *Update on the Global Campaign against Terrorist Financing,* 21n12.
144. Sanger, "Bush Officials Praise."
145. Gause, "Saudi Arabia Challenged."
146. Glaser interview.
147. Quoted in Montgomery, "FBI Chief."

officials.[148] These efforts were further energized when investigations revealed that Al-Qaeda was effectively organized within Saudi Arabia, that it clearly sought to overthrow the regime, and that it even targeted senior Saudi officials, including Nayef.[149]

Despite improving cooperation, U.S. Senate hearings revealed that Riyadh had much work to do on its unregulated, seldom audited Islamic charities. A July 2003 congressional report asserted that senior officials in Saudi Arabia, under the guise of support for Islamic charities, funneled hundreds of millions of dollars to charitable groups and other organizations that may have helped finance the infrastructure for September 11. A twenty-eight page section of the report was classified, but according to some individuals, who saw it, provided some support for implicating the royals. While the report was not conclusive and the Al Saud denied it emphatically,[150] the classified status of part of the report reflected the administration's sensitivity about complicating relations. Saudi Foreign Minister Saud al-Faisal met with Bush and asked that Washington declassify the report so that Riyadh could purportedly defend itself. But President Bush refused, claiming that it would "help the enemy" by revealing intelligence sources and methods, a point that some on the House Intelligence Committee publicly doubted.[151]

After terrorists attacked residential compounds near major oil facilities in May 2004, Saudi officials announced that they were dissolving the Al-Haramain Islamic Foundation and folding its financial assets into a national commission that can be regulated by the government. The action was important because the Saudis had not cooperated fully on Al-Haramain, despite its support of Al-Qaeda elements. Al-Haramain in Somalia, for instance, disguised funds allegedly intended to be used for orphanage projects or the construction of Islamic schools and mosques.[152] In March 2002, the Saudis reluctantly agreed to curb donations from the Somali and Bosnian branches of Al-Haramain, but the effect appeared limited and temporary.[153]

As suggested earlier, the 9/11 Commission Report seemed to vindicate Saudi protests over the July 2003 congressional report, noting that it found "no evidence that the Saudi government as an institution or senior Saudi officials individually funded the organization"; it estimated that Al-Qaeda needs $30 million a year

148. Ambah, "Saudi Raids."
149. Ambah, "Saudis Hint Al-Qaeda Presence"; and "Bush Denies Saudi Request to Release 9/11 Information," Knight Ridder, July 30, 2003.
150. Johnston, "Classified Section," A1, 8.
151. CNBC, July 30, 2003.
152. *Contributions*, 13–14.
153. Ibid., 13–14.

to run operations, most of which came from rich donors in the Gulf countries and particularly Saudi Arabia.[154] Thus, the report contradicted the notion that Al-Qaeda received funding from Bin Laden's purported inheritance of $300 million when his father died or that it relied on the trade of drug or conflict diamonds, as had been touted; the commission did hold out the possibility that charities with significant government sponsorship were diverting funds to Al-Qaeda.[155] That is a fairly significant qualification. After all, we would expect support for Al-Qaeda, always controversial in the elite circles of the kingdom, to come through indirect venues.

While it is fair to say that Saudi cooperation improved throughout 2003 and 2004 and that the Saudis took additional actions to monitor charities and hawala activities, many problematic areas were not addressed. Despite all the rules and regulations, there were few, if any, publicly announced arrests, trials, or incarcerations relating to the financing of terrorism.[156] Such actions are hard to carry out, in part because, as terrorist expert Steven Emerson rightly points out, "it must be recognized that the centers of terrorist gravity within Saudi Arabia have assumed an independence of their own.[157] Yet, as David Aufhauser, former general counsel for the Treasury Department and chair of the NSC policy coordinating committee on terror financing, points out, "Systematic changes have been made which are significant, but the Saudis have not held people personally accountable. You never stop terrorism without holding people personally accountable."[158]

On the whole, the Saudis continued to make improvements after 2005. Riyadh ordered an end to the practice of collecting donations at mosques and instructed retail establishments to remove charity collection boxes from their premises; these actions may well have significantly reduced the flow of cash from Saudi Arabia to Al-Qaeda.[159] And some more improvements followed. In 2009, for example, the Saudis aggressively pursued Al-Qaeda and took actions at home to diminish its funding. Ensuring consistent Saudi cooperation, however, requires constant American attention and does not mean that Al-Qaeda facilitators would not enable monies from Saudi Arabia to reach Al-Qaeda.[160]

---

154. Ibid., 170–71.

155. Ibid.

156. On the improvements and remaining problems, see *Update on the Global Campaign against Terrorist Financing*.

157. "Testimony of Steven Emerson," 1.

158. Aufhauser interview.

159. Wayne, "Testimony."

160. Background interview, August 7, 2009.

Indeed, in the December 2009 memo to which I referred earlier, Clinton sent country-specific talking points to various embassies, including Saudi Arabia, Kuwait, Qatar, and the United Arab Emirates. The memo noted that despite Saudi efforts, "donors in Saudi Arabia constitute the most significant source of funding to Sunni terrorist groups worldwide," and that continued senior-level engagement is "needed to build on initial efforts and encourage the Saudi government to take more steps to stem the flow of funds from Saudi Arabia-based sources to terrorists and extremists worldwide."[161] Saudi cooperation appeared to come sometimes grudgingly and often only under much pressure, unless it had to do with Al-Qaeda, which threatened the Saudi regime directly.

An Economy of Terror?

Some have posited that a terror economy has evolved over time. Loretta Napoleoni, for instance, argues that we are facing a global clash between two economic systems, one dominant—Western capitalism—and the other insurgent, what she calls the "new economy of terror." Her account suggests a massive shadow economy of terror that involves trafficking in drugs, arms, precious stones, and humans and is loosely affiliated with Islamic states, networks of mosques, and Islamic finance institutions.[162]

The September 11 Commission reported that non-oil sources of terrorist financing such as drug trade are not prominent in Al-Qaeda's overall financing. But this has changed over time—a trend that may or may not reverse itself. The problem is thorny because Al-Qaeda and its leaders also own legitimate businesses, including real estate, large tracts of forest, shrimp farms, a construction firm, and import export companies. Al-Qaeda also quite likely speculates in the stock market, even in conjunction with its own terror attacks.[163] In addition, Al-Qaeda has collected funds through involvement in organized crime. This money has been covertly collected, distributed, and otherwise manipulated using international banks, precious commodities like diamonds and gold, and exploitation of the hawala system.[164]

---

161. See "A Selection From the Cache of Diplomatic Dispatches."
162. Napoleoni, *Modern Jihad*, 161–65.
163. Ibid.
164. Comras, "Al-Qaeda Finances and Funding to Affiliate Groups"; and Farah, "Al Qaeda's Road Paved with Gold."

Trade in heroin, honey, and conflict diamonds, among other things, also add to Al-Qaeda coffers. The extent of its involvement in diamonds is fairly significant and coordinated, and yields it some monies, albeit not always reliably.[165] Honey entrepreneurs have included some of Bin Laden's top aides, such as Abu Zubaydah, and U.S. intelligence claims that Bin Laden also owned a network of honey shops in the Middle East.

Rohan Gunaratna has argued that Al-Qaeda's funding has gone through four phases. Initially, it was built on the monies of wealthy Middle East benefactors (1984–91); it then received monies from business fronts and Bin Laden's personal fortune (1991–96); in phase 3, it was sustained by charity diversion, smuggling, and solicitations under the Taliban; and finally, after 9/11, it received monies from the self-financing of cells through petty crime.[166] His account suggests that oil money has decreased in relative importance. Gretchen Peters has also found that heroin is increasingly important in funding both the Taliban and Al-Qaeda. She argues that the Taliban insurgency reemerged in force in the spring of 2003 and then in 2007 just as opium cultivation sped up in southern Afghanistan and that the Taliban grows 70 percent of Afghanistan's poppy crop.[167] Of course, the Taliban and Al-Qaeda are not the same entity. While many argue that Al-Qaeda has refused to benefit from the drug trade because it is un-Islamic and would corrupt its movement, she dismisses this argument and suggests that while senior Al-Qaeda leaders are not much involved in the drug trade, low-level Al-Qaeda fighters are involved—a finding that she says is also confirmed by some American intelligence officials and intelligence reports indicating that Al-Qaeda was better organized and better funded in 2007 than at any time since 9/11.[168]

Whether or not this trend continues is unclear. It seems that oil money can reach Al-Qaeda in different ways, making it an important general source of money and, as evidence reported earlier suggests, a continuing source of funds. The Obama administration's special representative for Afghanistan and Pakistan, Richard Holbrooke, asserted in testimony to Congress in June 2009 that while drugs were an important source of funding for the Taliban, they "get a lot more money out of the gulf, according to our intelligence sources," referring to wealthy donors living in the Persian Gulf.[169] If the Taliban is connected to Gulf donors in this way, it is a safe bet that Al-Qaeda is too. In fact, according to interviews

165. Farah, *Blood from Stones.*
166. Gunaratna, "Evolution of Al-Qaeda," esp. 50–58.
167. Peters, *Seeds of Terror,* 3–4, 14–15.
168. Ibid., 14–17.
169. Donadio, "U.S. Plans," A12.

with jihadis, traders, security officials, and terrorism experts, Al-Qaeda may have used the hawala system to reestablish its money line, formerly a partial casualty of the global financial crackdown, by latching onto Taliban crime while making a modest comeback on illicit business and donations after the American-led invasion of Iraq.[170]

Oil sources, in any case, are different in nature than other sources of money and can be connected to terrorism even if Al-Qaeda's use of them decreases. Oil is largely controlled by states, and it allows them to use oil money to promote their political and religious goals. Saudi Arabia and Iran promote their goals in religious schools. Moreover, non-oil trade does not generate issues that can provoke jihadists and the global audience. It does not, for instance, push the United States into war in the Gulf, generating a media frenzy and other worldwide effects. Furthermore, oil is sold everywhere and legally. We neither can nor want to stop this trade. Being illegal, heroin, by contrast, offers better opportunities to cut it off from terrorists. For example, kicking Al-Qaeda out of Afghanistan, a heroin-growing area, helps disconnect it from heroin trade.

Beyond the potential for non-oil sources, another problem is that terrorists are not easily dissuaded from their sordid vocation. They are driven at least partly by God, by visions of religious deliverance, and by powerful human emotions. Such resolve is hard to check and counter. This argument would suggest that even if their funds are cut back, they will still be dangerous. This is surely true. But a resolved, even maniacal enemy is easier to face when it has fewer resources.

Determining to what extent oil money funds terrorism and in what measure terrorists rely on such money is a guessing game that even the most knowledgeable government operatives must play. Oil money facilitates terrorism not so much because terrorists cannot blow things up without oil money. Terrorist acts themselves are not very expensive. Rather, oil money has helped to fund an entire infrastructure of thought, ideology, and bias that sustains terrorism and its direct and indirect supporters. It makes a sustained terrorist confrontation with the West more likely, and that does require much money. Bin Laden, of course, understood that well, developing a thick Rolodex of contacts that helped fill Al-Qaeda's coffers. As one operative in the antiterrorism industry points out, "Impeding terrorist financing will not stop the suicide bomber, but it may help disrupt the broader operation of terrorism that allows such bombings to occur."[171]

Most estimates suggest that it has cost about $30 million per year to run Al-Qaeda, and that money has come mostly from donations. Those donations,

---

170. Gannon, "Taliban Gains Money."
171. Interview with Treasury Department counterterrorist financing officials.

meanwhile, come chiefly from charities or individual donors in Gulf countries whose monies are fundamentally tied to oil. Meanwhile, oil money allows for other crucial elements of the infrastructure, including the spread of extremist ideology. There is evidence that terrorists have increasingly drawn on non-oil sources of money, but it is unclear whether that change will be transient or enduring.

5

OIL MONEY AND HATED REGIMES

Fueling Terrorism

The administration of President George W. Bush shifted gears after the September 11 attacks, adopting a strategy that the United States had employed elsewhere for decades but had not previously promoted in the Middle East, much less by the use of massive force. The Bush team had entered office largely as foreign policy realists but, after September 11, it sought to democratize Iraq and, as a more distant goal, a region that was largely undemocratic and whose peoples, many decades after their states had achieved independence, remained dominated by a variety of autocrats. As Francis Fukuyama put it, "Realists by and large do not believe that liberal democracy is a potentially universal form of government or that the human values underlying it are necessarily superior to those underlying non-democratic societies."[1] Yet the Bush administration evidently assumed that liberal democracy was not simply a Western phenomenon. And its democratization move contrasted sharply with a hardcore realist approach to the Middle East and beyond, one that assumed that supporting autocrats made sense if they served American interests and that the use of force to change the ideology of states was not wise.

Past U.S. presidents had talked much about the value of democratization in the world, but they had been careful not to push the notion in a region where they needed autocratic allies to protect the free flow of oil to the global economy

---

1. Fukuyama, *America at the Crossroads*, 37.

at reasonable prices. The American failure to find WMD in Iraq and to establish connections between Al-Qaeda and Saddam Hussein—two of the threats that motivated the invasion—pushed the administration to focus even more on democratization as a justification for the war.

When the Bush administration hatched the idea of advancing democracy in the Middle East in an aggressive manner, it may not have considered or known how oil was related to problems of democratization; how the region that it hoped to change had the world's largest reserves of a commodity that could bedevil the administration's democratization effort. But to what extent has oil impeded democratization? In what measure did nondemocracy contribute to terrorism? If the Bush administration was really driven by democratization in invading Iraq, was the assumption correct that nondemocracy was linked to terrorism? These are challenging questions, but they are worth exploring in examining the broader issue of the links between oil and terror.

Evidence suggests a connection between oil and nondemocracy, but the link between nondemocracy and terrorism remains unclear. Scholars need to do more work on this subject in order to reach clearer conclusions. However, there is a difference between claiming that nondemocracy is linked to terrorism and asserting that the type of governance of a state is linked to terrorism. The latter argument is easier to make and is advanced in this chapter. The impact of oil on governance may well be linked to terrorism in that oil monies enable the survival of regimes that engage in actions that provoke terrorists.

U.S. Foreign Policy and Democratization

In contrast to his father, who was sometimes criticized for lacking vision, George W. Bush articulated a broad vision. On November 6, 2003, he outlined a strategy aimed at generating significant reforms in the region. It did not fixate on democratization initially as a motivation for war, but it would be a mistake to consider democratization as simply an afterthought.

Administration officials played up the goal of democratizing Iraq and the Middle East after no WMD was found in Iraq, but Bush asserted the need for democratization well before the United States ran into trouble in Iraq, claiming in an address to the nation on September 11, 2001, that the United States "would go forward to defend freedom and all that is good and just in our world."[2] And

---

2. "Statement by the President in His Address to the Nation," September 11, 2001.

he repeatedly stated that mantra in 2002 and 2003 before the invasion of Iraq.[3] The implication was that a democratic Iraq would not attack its neighbors and would be a model for the region and that, in a probable reference to Saudi Arabia, democratization could diminish terrorism amid those societies from which it gains recruits.[4]

Even the Clinton administration, which prided itself on respect for human rights abroad, did not launch a democratization drive in the Middle East. As Secretary of State Madeleine Albright wrote, "We have been afraid to push too hard for democracy, especially in Arab countries. We worry, perhaps with reason, that if radical Islamists obtain power through an election, there would be no more elections...and instability might be created."[5] A larger worry must have been that pro-American autocrats across the Persian Gulf could be threatened if democratic forces were unleashed upon them. By contrast, Secretary of State Condeleezza Rice asserted in June 2005 that for "60 years, my country, the United States, pursued stability at the expense of democracy in this region here in the Middle East—and we achieved neither. Now we are taking a different course. We are supporting the democratic aspirations of all people."[6]

Following a negative reaction to its first major democracy initiative, Washington advanced a toned-down version of its "Greater Middle East Initiative" in Summer 2004 called the "G-8 Plan of Support for Reform." Rather than calling for outright democratization, which made regional autocrats nervous, it envisioned a framework for ongoing engagement at the ministerial level of G-8 and Middle Eastern countries for political, economic, and social reform.[7] Summing up regional sentiment, Saudi Arabia's foreign minister asserted in a news conference that "reform must stem from the region itself and not from outside and under foreign conditions."[8]

Al-Qaeda sought to capitalize on America's apparent push for greater democracy in the Middle East. For his part, al-Zawahiri asserted in a taped video that the "so-called American reforms will not bring us our independence or our dignity" but rather seek to replace existing Arab governments.[9] Of course, Al-Qaeda

3. See White House News Releases available at www.whitehouse.gov/news/releases/2002/02/20020218. For instance, see the President's Address to the American Enterprise Institute, February 26, 2003.

4. Ibid.

5. Albright, *Madam Secretary,* 416.

6. Weisman, "Rice Urges Egyptians and Saudis to Democratize," A1.

7. C-SPAN2, May 24, 2004, courtesy of TV7, Tunisia.

8. See his news conference, Dubai Al-Arabiyah Television in FBIS: NES, May 4, 2004 (WNC# 0hx8szx02t2gi5).

9. Quoted in Michael, "Purported Al-Qaeda Tape."

sought to do the same thing but wanted the renovated political landscape to assume Taliban rather than Jeffersonian trappings.

Several proposed links are assumed to exist between nondemocracy and terrorism. Nondemocratic environments can allow for terrorist recruitment, because they shut off peaceful avenues for changing governments via elections. They also preclude channels for dissent and political discussion offered by legislatures, government, and nongovernment institutions, and the media. Such institutions can also investigate leaders and other institutions, including government-owned or -related businesses, and can offer more accurate information to the public without which radical elements can shape negative views of others. The Human Development Report, produced by the United Nations Development Program, repeatedly held that democracy is critical for human development, because it is more highly associated with economic success from which individuals benefit and because it is anchored in ideals of equality, tolerance, and equal status under law.[10] Such values can have an estimably positive effect on self-perception and development in a way that can diminish the lure of radical ideology. As asserted in the 2009 Arab Human Development Report, most Arab states "failed to introduce democratic governance and institutions of representation that ensure inclusion, the equal distribution of wealth among various groups, or respect for cultural diversity. Such failures of political and economic governance have led identity-based groups in some Arab countries to try to free themselves from the captivity of the nation-state in whose shadow they live."[11]

Oil and Nondemocracy

Democratic theorists have long struggled to explain what facilitates and sustains democratization. They have identified many variables, ranging from education, political culture, levels of hierarchical government, war, regime type, and elites.[12] Most explanations of democratic reforms in the Middle East link the process of

---

10. For example, see UNDP Human Development Report 2002 on http://hdr.undp.org/en/media/HDR_2002_EN_Complete.pdf.

11. *Arab Human Development Report 2009*, 54.

12. On the levels of government, see Huntington, "Will More Countries Become Democratic?"; Dahl, *Democracy and Its Critics;* Putnam, *Making Democracy Work,* esp. introduction; Yashar, *Demanding Democracy,* ch. 1; Diamond, ed., *Political Culture;* and Sorensen, *Democracy and Democratization,* ch. 1, esp. 13–16. On regime type, see Snyder, *From Voting to Violence.* For a classic argument on how war affects nation-building, see Tilly, "Reflections on the History of European State-Making." On the role of war in empire building, see Lustick, "Absence of Middle Eastern Great Powers," 653–83. On how the absence of inter-state war was a hindrance to state-building in Africa, see Herbst, "War and the State in Africa," 117–39. On various potential causes, see Mazo, "What Causes Democracy?"

political change to economic crises, but wealth is one of the general conditions viewed as favorable to democracy worldwide.[13] Yet the monarchies of the Middle East are oil-rich. Based on the variable of wealth, we would expect them to tend toward democracy, all other things being equal. How can we explain that they are oil-rich and democracy-poor?

The actual use of energy is believed by many to be correlated with greater freedom, a connection that may be spurious.[14] But a theory that seems more clear, although it is not without its detractors, is that oil is an impediment to democratization.[15] Much qualitative and some quantitative work supports the finding that the oil resource has impeded democratic progress in the Middle East. Terry Karl has argued that oil wealth in particular, and natural resource wealth more generally, leads almost inexorably to authoritarian or autocratic government or at least is negatively correlated with "democracy," "democratization," or more broadly political participation and accountability.[16] Using pooled time-series cross-national data from 113 states between 1971 and 1997, political scientist Michael Ross has supported this general finding via the use of regression analysis.[17] Meanwhile, economist Kevin K. Tsui, using a different methodology based on actual oil resources, has found that states that discover one hundred billion barrels of oil (approximately the initial endowment of Iraq) achieve a level of democracy that is almost 20 percentage points below trend after three decades. Tsui also varied the size of oil fields and the quality of the oil discovered to see if either affects democratization. He found that the estimated effect is larger for oil fields with higher-quality oil and lower exploration and extraction costs. However, he believes that the estimates are less precise when oil abundance is measured by oil discovery per capita, and he interprets this finding to mean that politicians may care about the raw level instead of the per capita value of oil wealth.[18]

---

13. Wiktorowicz, "Civil Society as Social Control," 47–48. Of the twenty-six variables that Huntington identifies as potentially associated with democratization, only two are even indirect international variables. Huntington, *The Third Wave*, 37–38. The focus on internal variables also applies to the study of full-fledged democracies. Barzilai, "War, Democracy, and Internal Conflict," 318; Brynen et al., eds., *Political Liberalization*, esp. 18–20; and Bunce, "Comparative Democratization," 703–34.

14. Smil, *Energy at the Crossroads*, 103.

15. One problem with the theory is that in some cases, such as in Malaysia, Norway, Chile, and Indonesia, natural resource wealth has not impeded democratization. The theory cannot account for these cases. Nor can it explain how natural resource endowment may aid democratic development in states such as Bahrain, Kuwait, and Indonesia. See Gurses, "State-Sponsored Development, Oil, and Democratization."

16. Karl, *Paradox of Plenty;* and Karl, "Oil-Led Development."

17. Ross, "Does Oil Hinder Democracy?" 325–61. Using different data and methods, Herb questions the extent of the oil-democracy connection. Herb, *No Representation without Taxation?* 297–316.

18. Tsui, "More Oil, Less Democracy."

The Arab world experienced a liberal phase in the nineteenth and early twentieth centuries, this in spite of colonialism, which was reversed, in part due to increasing oil discoveries, in the 1950s and 1960s.[19] The biggest oil producers in the region have the worst records on democracy. Freedom House, the nonpartisan American human rights group, ranks only Kuwait as partially free, while the United Arab Emirates, Iran, Iraq, and Saudi Arabia are ranked as not free or as absolute dictatorships.[20] Kuwait has the best record among these countries, but it ranks lower on the democratic rankings than a number of Muslim states that lack oil, including Turkey, Bosnia, Albania, and resource-poor Bangladesh.

Oil is not necessary for autocratic government in the Middle East or elsewhere for that matter. For instance, former Syrian president Hafez Assad and his son, Bashar, who succeeded him, would have gone to great lengths to have Kuwait's oil but had no problem dominating their people. The father was infamous for crushing a revolt in the city of Hama in 1982 where his soldiers wiped out an estimated ten to twenty thousand people in a few days.

While oil may be an important factor that bolsters autocracy, it is not so important as to be a sufficient factor. That leaves us with a central question here: how strong is the oil link to nondemocracy?

Why Oil Impedes Democracy

Several explanations for the oil connection to nondemocracy have been put forward in the literature. Dependency on oil export revenue has been identified as a potential "curse" rather than a blessing for development. Economists have pointed to the notion of "Dutch disease," whereby major revenue in a single sector of the economy can raise the exchange rate, which reduces the competitiveness of other sectors of the economy and impedes diversification. It has also been argued that dependency on a single commodity is an unsustainable route to development because of the likelihood of declining terms of trade.

Beyond economics, a common explanation for why Gulf states lack parliaments is encapsulated in rentier state theory. The theory, which predicts that oil states will not democratize, appears to be borne out by some important surveys and studies. The basic assumption is that wealth generated from rents, which can come from oil or any other good, produces a negative and different impact on democracy than wealth generated by a diversified economy.[21] Nathan

---

19. Ibrahim, "Open Door."
20. See www.freedomhouse.org.
21. Herb, "No Representation without Taxation," 300.

Jensen and Leonard Wantchekon point out that a rentier state is characterized by high dependence on external rents produced by a few economic resources, not from production (labor), investment (interest), or management of risk (profit).[22] Rentier economies obtain most of their monies from foreign sources based on one good, which they sell at a much higher price than it costs them to produce. A minority of their people generates the rent and also controls it, while the majority is involved only in its distribution and use.[23] Some democracies also benefit from external rents from energy and other exports, but these funds are treated differently. They are often managed professionally and are not used for political means. By contrast, in authoritarian regimes most of these rent monies are controlled by and bolster the elites.

A prominent version of the theory posits that these states lack parliaments because their enormous oil resources free them from having to tax their citizens and also allow them to provide major services to their citizens free of cost.[24] As a result they do not have to bargain with their citizens, which is the purpose of parliaments and which is one of the main reasons that they arise in the first place. They are not accountable to the citizenry, which cannot demand representation.[25] Without the need for accountability to the wider population, they solidify their autocratic control, with the state surviving on "rents" captured from the oil industry.

Oil rents can also be used by oil-rich regimes to placate dissent, thus stifling democratic impulses, as some scholars have found in earlier studies, for instance John Entelis's work on Saudi Arabia and Dirk Vandewalle's work on Libya.[26] In the view of one Saudi official, "Critics underestimate us. Unlike the Shah, we know how to modernize without excessively Westernizing, to handle relations with religious forces, to accommodate our critics, and to have evolution and not revolution."[27] Part of this ability is due to the leverage and opportunity afforded by oil largesse. Oil monies can help obtain allegiance from individuals and groups that otherwise would be much more unpredictable and even volatile. They may even block the formation of independent social groups that can become the bedrock of democratization.[28] For instance, facing rigid state control, organized labor

---

22. Jensen and Wantchekon, "Resource Wealth."

23. Beblawi and Luciani, eds., *Rentier State,* esp. 11–16.

24. On rentier theory and challenges to it, see ibid., esp. 298–99.

25. On how oil made Kuwait and Qatar less accountable to the merchant class, see Crystal, *Oil and Politics in the Gulf.*

26. See, for example, Vandewalle, *Libya since Independence.*

27. On how the regime can deal effectively with domestic instability, see Dunn, "Is the Sky Falling?" 36–39.

28. See, for instance, Shambayati, "Rentier State"; and Chaudhry, "Economic Liberalization," although in Chaudhry's later work she questions some of the earlier findings on rentier scholarship.

groups have been destroyed in the Persian Gulf due to the oil boom, whereas once they were the backbone of nationalist movements.[29]

Another explanation is that democratization requires cultural and social changes, and that these changes require economic development. If oil impedes economic growth, then it will indirectly impede this critical process of modernization.

Nondemocracy and Terrorism

Most of the literature supports the notion that oil impedes democratization, but how about the connection between nondemocracy and terrorism? Was the Bush administration correct in assuming this connection as one justification for invading Iraq in 2003? The answer is not clear-cut; the scholarly literature has not reached any consensus.

As suggested earlier, there are two general arguments in the literature. Democratic societies offer the potential for citizens to seek redress for grievances, while democratic rules enable nonviolent conflict resolution. Hence, groups in democratic societies are more likely to pursue nonviolent alternatives rather than costly terrorist activities to further their interests. In contrast, the second argument holds that democratic countries facilitate terrorism. This is because they provide relatively more freedom of speech, movement, and association, permitting organized dissent and lowering the costs of conducting terrorist activities.[30]

At present, some complex and important work does find that democracy decreases terrorism. Quan Li reports that democratic participation increases the satisfaction and political efficacy of citizens, reduces their grievances, thwarts terrorist recruitment, and raises public tolerance of counterterrorist policies.[31] Brock Bloomberg and Gregory Hess find that democracy, development, and openness decrease terrorist activity.[32] There is reason to believe that this connection is in play with regard to transnational terrorism. For instance, the International Crisis Group has suggested that the root of terrorism among militants in Saudi Arabia has been tied to intolerance and to the lack of pluralism and political participation in the kingdom.[33] Overwhelmingly, Al-Qaeda's recruits are not from industrialized states like the United States, Australia, and Germany but from states

---

29. Gause, *Oil Monarchies*, 70–75.
30. Li, "Does Democracy Promote."
31. Ibid.
32. Bloomberg and Hess, "Lexus and the Olive Branch," esp. 146.
33. See International Crisis Group web site available at www.icg.org/home/index.cfm?id= 2864&1=1.

with oppressive regimes. Al-Qaeda has also splintered into countries with weak governments, corruption, and questionable democratic practices. Mohammed al-Shayef, a member of Yemen's parliament, suggests a point that finds a significant number of adherents: "Power and money are concentrated in the hands of a few who have turned the country into a private company. If there's democracy and equality, terrorism will end."[34]

Mohammed Hafez makes a compelling case that the lack of democracy is linked to terrorism. Charting militant Islamist activism in Algeria and Egypt beginning from the mid-1970s to 1995, he finds that increases in extremism are linked to political exclusion. Moreover, where Islamist activists were afforded some political participation, such as in Tunisia, Islamist extremism was ameliorated. In Algeria, for instance, Islamists rebelled after the military cancelled elections, banned the most prominent Islamist party, and arrested thousands of its supporters. These acts were followed by a period of brutal repression. Muslims also rebelled in Kashmir, Chechnya, the southern Philippines, Tajikistan, and Egypt when "institutional channels for participation were blocked."[35] The effects extend beyond these groups because many of the members and affiliates of Al-Qaeda, including the Egyptian Islamic Jihad, have been motivated by a repressive and exclusionary political environment.[36]

Based on the notion that democracy decreases terrorism, some analysts argued that the United States must make an increase of democratic practices in the region a priority.[37] America's difficult experience in Iraq has tempered such enthusiasm, but it could reemerge if Iraq stabilizes in the future and has, in any case, been stoked by the uprisings and revolutions in the region that started in early 2011. Yet, while there is reason to think that democracy can stem terrorism, there are also good reasons to believe it would not do so. As chapter 2 explained, the September 11 attacks were enabled and motivated by numerous factors. Nondemocracy did not rank high on this list of factors, although it may have had a general effect. For instance, had Pakistan been a democracy, it may not have built so many madrassas; had Afghanistan been a democracy, the Taliban may not have gained power and had the ability to host Al-Qaeda. These are not unreasonable assumptions, speculative though they may be.

Al-Qaeda and its militant affiliates also are not likely to be swayed by greater democratization.[38] A democratic Saudi Arabia, for instance, might placate some

---

34. Abu-Nasr, "Yemen."
35. Hafez, *Why Muslims Rebel*, 200–201.
36. Ibid., 206–7.
37. For such an argument, see Windsor, "Promoting Democratization Can Combat Terrorism."
38. For a succinct challenge to the notion that democracy decreases terrorism, see Gause, "Can Democracy Stop Terrorism?"

dissenters in the kingdom by allowing them to express grievances. After all, in Saudi Arabia, the secret services are invasive, arbitrary arrests are common, and Miranda rights are a mirage. The media and most nongovernmental organizations that may challenge laws and norms are forbidden. No elections are held, and no political parties exist.[39] However, it is hard to see how a more democratic Saudi government would be less abhorrent to Al-Qaeda than the current regime. Some democracies might also empower peoples in the region who dislike the United States and the West more than the current regimes do. That could make it harder for Arab regimes to cooperate with the West in the fight against terrorism. In turn, that might lead to an increase in terrorism. Such concerns spurred a national debate about how the uprisings and revolutions in the Middle East would impact American national interests in the region. The answer was unclear because it remained to be seen how these movements would turn out over the longer run. President Hosni Mubarak of Egypt, for instance, had supported American efforts to check Islamic radicals, including Al-Qaeda. But would a future Egyptian government do the same or would it be influenced by the radical faction of the Muslim Brotherhood that might urge the government to distance itself from Washington and to renegotiate the peace treaty with Israel? Middle East democratization had its advantages for the United States, especially over the longer run, but it raised legitimate questions about its security interests in the nearer term.

Beyond the statistical analyses cited above, when we focus on the Middle East, it becomes clear that some repressive countries have not generated terrorist movements, while more democratic countries have done so. The Palestinians tend to rank higher on the democratic index but have produced Hamas-related terrorism. Meanwhile, Gulf states other than Saudi Arabia have been repressive without producing major terrorism.

Oil and Governance

If we accept that oil impedes democratization but that the impact of democratization on terror is unclear, where does this lead us?[40] Is it still the case that oil is connected to terrorism via its impact on nondemocracy? Even if oil is not connected to terrorism via its direct link to nondemocracy per se, oil does affect governance in a manner that is indirectly linked to terrorism: oil resources help develop and sustain governments that Al-Qaeda has rejected and reacted against.

---

39. On the state of Arab governance, see *Arab Human Development Report 2009*.
40. Note that further work is needed on this link in order to distinguish better the effects of oil from other variables that may be linked to nondemocratization.

Al-Qaeda rejects regimes that do not accept its radical version of Islam, that are secular, and that embrace the West or even merely have correct relations with Washington. Al-Qaeda leaders have repeatedly asserted that they want to get rid of the Saudi government, as well as other un-Islamic governments, in part due to such reasons. As Bin Laden put it at the end of the Soviet War in Afghanistan, Al-Qaeda's primary goal was to unite its fighters together around the world to overthrow Arab governments, "because there's no Muslim government."[41]

We cannot know for sure how well these governments would survive without oil money, but we can offer educated conjecture. Oil generates rents that become the property of an elite group of leaders. Many people have benefited from oil, but none more so than the royal families in the region.[42] Their longevity, despite the many detractors that they have, partly results from the absence of competitors for and challengers to governance, as well as other factors that scholars have examined.[43]

Resources allocated for enforcing state authority came from huge oil reserves, which created a region-wide oil economy in the 1970s that was boosted by the Arab oil embargo of 1973–74 and subsequent spikes in the price of oil.[44] These monies contributed to the expansion of security apparatuses as well as the bureaucracy, which provided the rulers with a stable platform, a control device, and a space for extending patronage.[45]

While funding an extensive internal security network in Saudi Arabia, oil wealth has also given the regimes the financial ability to appease their opponents. Since the 1960s at least, a large portion of the regime's oil benefits have been shared with commoners in exchange for their tacit understanding not to challenge the legitimacy of the regime.[46] What have oil-rich Arab states done with their money? A new database called AidData allows for new insights and suggests that Arab donors haven't been allocating their rising wealth to foreign aid. Rather, it appears that they have spent more of these funds at home, substantially increasing government expenditures on domestic matters. Why so? It is possible that they are concerned with the fate of their regimes during periods of growing opposition and may have decided that it is best to distribute national wealth at home for purposes of political viability and survival.[47]

---

41. "Court Testimony of Al-Qaeda Operative Jamal al-Fadl."

42. Herb, *All in the Family*, ch. 3.

43. On why authoritarianism persists in the Arab world compared to other developing regions where political transition did occur, see Albrecht and Schlumberger, "Waiting for Godot."

44. Mohapatra, *Democratization in the Arab World*.

45. Ayubi, *Over-stating the Arab State*, 308.

46. Seznec, "Stirrings in Saudi Arabia," 35.

47. On this database, see Shushan and Marcoux, "Arab Generosity."

For instance, Saudi religious leaders, who share power with the royal family, see Shiites as deviants from Sunni Islam. They are viewed as in need of being brought back to Saudi Arabia's brand of Sunni Islam, known as Wahhabism. These 2 million Saudi Shiites—out of a total population of perhaps 20 million Saudis—are discriminated against for jobs and government largesse. To keep them under control, the Al Saud have used secret police as a stick and sometimes monies and services as a carrot. Obviously, Al-Qaeda does not want a bill of rights for all Saudis or peoples in other Muslim states or indeed anything that empowers the people in a democratic sense. It is not against Saudi repression because it deprives Saudis of voting rights—it would do the same if it were in power. Rather, it wants freedom of maneuver for its own elements, so as to enhance its chance of radicalizing societies behind its broader agenda or at least against Arab regimes. The Al Saud's combination of carrots and sticks probably has made it harder for Al-Qaeda to operate in Saudi Arabia and to subvert antiregime elements. In turn, that may well add to the incentive to attack foreign targets.

The appeasement approach was in full display in February 2011 when Saudi King Abdullah announced a $37 billion aid package for Saudi citizens in the lower and middle classes. Following the uprisings in Tunisia, Egypt, and next-door Bahrain, the king may well have sought to preempt unrest among Shiite Muslims in Saudi Arabia, especially in its Eastern Hasa oil province. The prospect that Saudi Shiites would, like Shiites in Bahrain, revolt against the regime in order to seek greater democratic rights, certainly must have been viewed with great concern in Riyadh. It is, of course, hard to imagine that the king would have had such largesse were it not for Saudi Arabia's oil riches. Certainly, Egypt's Hosni Mubarak could not have deployed massive amounts of cash for the purposes of quieting the democratic impulses bubbling across his country, which eventually lead to his ouster in February 2011.

Even if oil money does not impede democratization, it does make the elites richer than they otherwise would be. After all, the oil-poor Egyptians, Syrians, and Jordanians, and other Arabs of the Middle East lack the wealth of the Gulf Arabs. And the Saudis do not have an economy diversified enough to have become rich on something other than oil, at least not for the foreseeable future. Of course, oil money does not necessarily corrupt elites, but it allows for corrupt behavior on a large scale and for the perception of it. Poor leaders cannot live in multiple palaces, drive expensive vehicles, own yachts, invest billions in stocks, and travel luxuriously around the world. The perception that the Al Saud are corrupt exists in the Middle East and strongly agitates and animates Al-Qaeda. It clashes fundamentally with Al-Qaeda's strict and radical interpretation of Islam and with the notion of an ascetic existence that Al-Qaeda leaders demand that others pursue. It also contrasts sharply with the sacrifice of the Afghan rebels against the Soviets and with Al-Qaeda's continued struggle with the West, which requires of it a modest existence.

At a global level, protecting oil has drawn the United States and oil-rich states together in an embrace that Al-Qaeda has bemoaned. Through its radical lens, the Saudi-American connection has made both Riyadh and Washington prime targets of Al-Qaeda terrorism. Bin Laden disliked Riyadh for its relations with Washington, and it dislikes Washington for its perceived cozy and domineering relationship with Riyadh. Bin Laden had a long history with the Saudi regime.

Personal factors probably worsened political and religious grievances. Bin Laden was rejected in his efforts to protect the Saudi kingdom against Iraq in 1990. Such treatment was related to, and possibly enabled by, major oil wealth. The Saudis would not have invited American troops into the kingdom were it not for their oil wealth and would not, therefore, have injected additional animus into their relations with Bin Laden. Nor would Washington have been so eager to reverse Iraq's invasion of Kuwait were the Persian Gulf region oil-poor.

In brief, Saudi oil wealth generates a host of effects on its regime that has made it anathema to Al-Qaeda. This does not mean that if the Saudis were oil-poor, they would have good relations with Al-Qaeda. The two actors have different religious views and historical orientations, but it is much less likely that Al-Qaeda would have become a radical and hyperviolent organization and identified the Al Saud family as one of its main targets for elimination, if not indeed the main target.

Of course, non-oil monies also help prop up these regimes. But regimes such as Iran and Saudi Arabia obtain the lion's share of their funds from oil and oil-related business, and from other energy sources such as natural gas. One might counter that the United States also supports the Saudi regime against internal and external threats and that oil monies are secondary to this security apparatus. However, the United States can only do so much to protect the regime, which sometimes likes to distance itself from Washington. It cannot dole out funds to run the cradle-to-grave society; it cannot placate those who are disappointed with the royals, such as the Shiites of the Hasa province; it cannot use money to manipulate economic and political outcomes and socially engineer the population. After all, what could it do to save Hosni Mubarak? If anything, the United States was largely a bystander to the Arab uprisings and revolutions, at times trying to spur them on and at other times appearing unsure about its position. In any case, the United States would not be protecting the Al Saud to the extent that it has been were it not for the vast oil wealth of the kingdom.

Oil may well impede democratization, although the impact may be related to many other variables such as the level of education per capita and the percentage of the oil industry that is privatized. For example, Russia, especially after the reversion back to greater authoritarian rule under President Vladimir Putin, is sometimes considered an example of the "resource curse"—in which its oil wealth undermines democracy. However, Daniel Treisman believes that Russia has escaped this effect because it has an industrialized economy, a highly educated and urbanized population, and an oil sector that remains mostly private-owned.[48] Mehmet Gurses argues that oil wealth can promote liberalization if it is used to eradicate poverty, to invest in human capital, and to sponsor industrialization from which new social actors can arise and push for participation.[49]

The notion of oil as an impediment to democracy is weightier if one is an optimist and believes that democratization is possible in the Middle East on a large scale. If democratization is possible or better yet probable, oil might play a spoiler role for what otherwise might be significant reform and progress. If one is a pessimist about democracy in the region, then it does not much matter if oil is an impediment. This is because nondemocracy would be overdetermined. In other words, it would be caused by so many factors as to make oil a less significant force.

Even if the link between oil and nondemocracy is not fully clear, what is clearer is that the impact of oil on governance is related to terrorism. Oil enables regimes to survive whose existence agitates terrorists and whose behaviors further make them and their allies, such as the United States, targets of terrorist action. Al-Qaeda may have found it easier and more interesting to attack the perceived patrons of local states. It may have found it easier to do so because American society is penetrable and lacks an oppressive state control, and more interesting to do so because America is a superpower that, if weakened, will elevate Al-Qaeda's reputation and weaken America's patrons in the Middle East, which Al-Qaeda has targeted.[50]

---

48. Treisman, *Oil and Democracy.*

49. Gurses, "State-Sponsored Development, Oil and Democratization," 509.

50. As Robert Pape argues, terrorists see democracies as "softer" targets than authoritarian regimes in that they have low thresholds of cost tolerance and that they will not retaliate as strongly as authoritarian regimes. Pape, *Dying to Win,* 44.

Part II

GLOBALIZATION AND TRANSNATIONAL TERRORISM

6

THE DEADLY NEXUS OF GLOBALIZATION, OIL, AND TERRORISM

The impact of Middle Eastern oil on transnational terrorism is only half of the story that this book seeks to tell. We also have to consider the global context, which produces its own important contributions. The other half of the story about terrorism concerns the role of globalization. Middle Eastern oil and globalization contributed individually to the threat of transnational terrorism, but they have also combined to enable its rise as a serious international security problem.

Globalization took off as the oil era was also gaining significant traction, after World War II. Our ancestors would probably be surprised by the rise of globalization in all its dimensions and by the emergence of oil as the dominant form of energy. When oil was discovered in 1859 in Pennsylvania, the big rush involved not oil but gold and silver. Nor could our ancestors have predicted that the Middle Eastern oil and globalization eras would roughly overlap, producing what I believe to be important combined effects.

Globalization and Oil Demand

I make three related arguments in this section. First, globalization has increased the demand for global oil; second, the increased demand for oil has made and will increasingly make the Persian Gulf important to the global economy; and third, this dynamic has linked and will continue to link Middle Eastern oil to some of the oil-terror connections that this book has explicated.

The rise of globalization, as discussed in the introduction, is important for the arguments of this book: there is a connection between globalization and economic growth and, in turn, oil demand. Not surprisingly, scholars have not reached consensus on this issue, largely because some disagree about how to measure globalization and about how to draw causal inferences about its effects.[1] However, we have strong theoretical and empirical reasons to believe that globalization matters, and most scholars support that view.

One of the fundamental features of international trade theory is that open economies achieve higher economic growth rates than closed economies do. The notion of comparative advantage, first put forth by David Ricardo, is key here: openness (to both trade and international capital) allows countries to specialize in (and then to export products derived from) their comparative advantage while importing products in which they are disadvantaged. Other arguments, such as the importance of openness to realizing economies of scale, have been added to the equation over time. But these only reinforce the mantra that openness is good.

A large literature confirms the trade-growth proposition in particular, although dissenting opinions certainly exist.[2] Many scholars reveal a strong relationship between economic performance and openness to trade, and between economic performance and trade flows.[3] Other analysts have shown that trade increases income significantly, as well as overall global growth, albeit not enough to offset serious global poverty.[4] Using panel data for 123 countries over the 1970–2000 period, one scholar found that globalization promotes growth—but not to an extent necessary to reduce poverty on a large scale—and that actual economic flows promoted growth most, information flows did so less robustly, and political integration had no effect.[5] While the type of globalization mattered, so did the strength of economies. Global trade may well benefit industrialized nations more than less-developed states.[6]

Marked by international trade, foreign direct investment, and porous borders for penetration, globalization creates prospects for economic interaction that require oil. Consider China's significant rise in world politics from the 1980s

---

1. On the literature, see Brune and Garrett, *Globalization Rorschach Test*.

2. On this literature, see Dani Rodrik and Francisco Rodriquez "Trade Policy and Economic Growth" (2000) available at www.hks.harvard.edu/fs/drodrik/Research%20papers/skepti1299.pdf, 1–3.

3. On this literature, see Dreher et al., *Measuring Globalisation*, 120–26.

4. See Jeffrey Frankel and David Romer, "Does Trade Cause Growth," available at www.econ.berkeley.edu/~dromer/papers/AER_June99.pdf. See Axel Dreher "Does Globalization Affect Growth? "(2003) available at http://129.3.20.41/eps/dev/papers/0210/0210004.pdf.

5. Dreher, "Does Globalization Affect Growth?" See also Dreher et al., *Measuring Globalisation*.

6. On this literature, see Brune and Garrett, *Globalization Rorschach Test*.

into the twenty-first century. It is a dramatic example of how oil is critical to economic growth and how economic growth increases oil use. Energy security has become vital to China and central in its foreign policy. China's 10th Five-Year Plan (2001–5) referred explicitly and for the first time publicly to energy security, which is defined as guaranteeing and securing oil supplies from abroad, since they are essential to China's continued economic growth and modernization. Beijing's intention is to increase its interest and position in the Persian Gulf gradually over the next three decades, in line with its goal of expanding its trade and economy.[7] China's oil imports are expected to grow fourfold from 2003 to 2030, with Persian Gulf oil feeding much of that increased oil demand.[8]

Like China, many other states in the world have used increasingly greater volumes of oil to run their economies, and this trend appears to be driven partly by globalization. Oil and globalization cannot be easily separated, nor can the problems that they spawn. As noted in the introduction of this book, the U.S. Department of Energy projects that the use of all energy sources, including oil, will increase through 2035, though oil use is not expected to grow faster than other energy sources.[9]

Globalization has contributed to economic growth and oil demand, but it has also altered the concept of space and interaction, chiefly by increasing our transportation needs and capabilities. As Saudi Oil Minister Ali Naimi asserted, the "world's demand for energy will grow because of globalization," and this may well be because globalization increases the demand for oil by virtue of its impact on transportation.[10] There are currently no viable large-scale substitutes for oil, particularly in the transportation sector, which consumes most of the world's oil. Even if we factor in the rise of alternatives, global oil demand is still projected to rise in the future.

The many far-flung connections that constitute globalization have increased and allowed for global travel and transportation usage. In a less globalized world, there would be less need and capability to travel on such a massive scale and so quickly. As Ken Button underscores and demonstrates, globalization can be defined as high demand for greater mobility and access and for the movement of people and goods between countries.[11] Globalization increases international air transportation. A clear correlation exists between world trade and the revenues of

---

7. This paragraph is based on Yetiv and Lu, "China, Global Energy, and the Middle East."

8. EIA, *International Energy Outlook 2006*, 25.

9. See EIA, International Energy Outlook 2010 available at www.eia.doe.gov/oiaf/ieo/pdf/0484(2010).pdf, fig. 2.

10. Naimi, "Globalization."

11. Button, *Impact of Globalization*, 37, available at www.oecd.org/dataoecd/51/53/41373470.pdf.

airlines; even within countries, we also see such a connection toward greater air transportation, because globalization increases economic activity, which makes domestic travel important as part of the enlarged value chain.[12]

In past centuries, we did not travel by the millions across states, oceans, and continents. Globalization has increased such travel significantly. This was indicated earlier in figure 4, which underscored tremendous increases in vehicle miles driven. It is also indicated by the fact that, according to the UN World Tourism organization, international tourist arrivals have increased dramatically from a few million in 1950 to over 700 million in 2000 and above 898 million by 2007.[13] Those dramatic increases underscore the rising connections among states and peoples and also the elevated pressures on global oil demand. Such major transportation was impossible prior to the rise of the requisite technologies. But even after they arose, there was not much reason to travel on such an expanded scale. Dependencies between states were more limited, and the number of existing states was smaller. Businesses did not have as many dealings abroad; countries were not engaged in as many joint projects; foreign direct investment was lower; and cultural interaction was more limited.

Moreover, as a result of the higher economic activity, globalization also leads to higher income and consumption in many countries, even if the affluence is not spread evenly. Air transportation facilitates some of this consumption. In larger countries, as incomes rise, people spend more on domestic vacations and make more frequent visits to family and friends.[14]

The wireless world has altered how and where people work, what they produce, and how they and the groups and organizations to which they belong interface within and across borders. And all of these changes have produced their own changes. We are no longer tied to land nearly as much as our forefathers were, nor are we necessarily tied to geography in general. We don't stay in the villages or small cities where we were born as much; we don't take vacations fairly close to home; we can work from afar; and we can migrate more easily. All of these changes increase transportation, be it by car, train, boat, or airplane.

Oil demand from the countries in the Organization of Economic Cooperation and Development (OECD), which represents 54 percent of world demand in 2009, could peak or may have already peaked due to changes in consumption

---

12. Ibid., 10, fig. 1; on the rising throughput of freight at major Chinese cargo hub airports, 10–15, 36, fig. 12.

13. For a graph broken down into regions, see UN World Tourism Organization Web site on *www.world-tourism.org/facts/eng/pdf/highlights/UNWTO_Highlights09_en_HR.pdf.* For a graph, see Capital Consult Realty, "World Tourist Arrivals 2007" available at http://hotels-ccr.com/article/analit ics/analytics/world.

14. Ibid., 15.

habits. This possible trend will help counteract oil demand growth in less-developed countries.[15] However, even so, the projected increases in the use of oil are significant and will likely put pressure on the supply of oil—a subject to which we now turn.

The demand for oil is expected to rise significantly. That has made and will likely continue to make the Middle East more vital, but it is also important to consider problems of oil production. Current trends suggest that they will further highlight the Middle East, thus bolstering some of the dynamics in the petroleum triangle.

Different estimates exist on when global oil production will peak, but whatever the case, the Middle East is projected to be the last region to peak. The oil peak refers to a turning point in which ever-growing production volumes will be followed by a period of shrinking volumes. The oil peak phase follows two phases of the life cycle of oil. The first phase is called "pre-peak" and refers to continual production increases. In the second phase, production is "at peak" and growth is stagnant. Some analysts believe that we are facing an impending peak, if oil production has not already peaked.[16] Analysts of the Association of the Study of Peak Oil believe that oil is peaking right now, in the 2006–11 period.[17] Some of them, as well as other scientists, draw inspiration from geologist M. King Hubbert, who correctly predicted the 1970 peak in U.S. oil production, contrary to conventional wisdom.[18]

Pessimists argue that oil reserves are exaggerated, partly because OPEC countries want higher output quotas. These quotas are pegged to the size of the oil reserves that they claim. Thus, they may be exaggerating the size of their reserves. The pessimists also question technological fixes and the human leadership needed to cause a major change in consumption habits. They believe that these pitfalls, combined with rising population and limited sources, spell trouble ahead.

The pessimists were given a boost in November 2008. The authoritative International Energy Agency (IEA), which is the global energy watchdog for consumers, radically changed its forecast on oil. Before that date it had predicted oil demand growing briskly to 2030 with abundant energy sources to meet demand, suggesting a peak farther down the road.[19] The 2008 study, based on actual studies of the world's eight hundred largest oil fields rather than on previously used

---

15. Brady, "Peak Oil Demand."

16. Deffeyes, *Hubbert's Peak*; Goodstein, *Out of Gas*; Roberts, *End of Oil*; and Simmons, *Twilight in the Desert.*

17. Leblond, "ASPO," 28.

18. Goodstein, *Out of Gas*, 17.

19. "IEA: World Energy Demand to Grow Briskly to 2030," *Oil and Gas Journal*, October 14, 2002, p. 16.

economic models, found that oil production rates are declining, which will put peak oil around 2020.[20]

The IEA's chief economist, Fatih Birol, explained that the IEA "always used assumptions to determine world oil production but then we moved toward actual field studies. We found serious problems from an investment and geological perspective. We found steep declines in non-OPEC areas especially. We are not spending enough to deal with declines and decisions are too affected by politics."[21] The problem of investment for oil discovery and production is more broadly recognized. Even analysts at the more optimistic Cambridge Energy Research Associates have found that the real problem is not likely to be a shortage of oil but rather sustained exploration and continued investment to find that existing oil, supported by sensible government decision making.[22] In particular security and politics could interrupt oil production potential,[23] as suggested, for instance, by the turmoil that gripped the Middle East beginning in early 2011 and disrupted oil production from Libya.

The U.S. Department of Energy has seen peak oil occurring closer to the middle of the twenty-first century than to its beginning.[24] Some oil industry leaders also assert that the world recovery rate or ability to exploit oil reserves has increased from 22 percent in 1980 to 35 percent in 2003.[25] That means that effective technology has extended the life of existing reserves.

The optimists think that changes in technology and in oil prices could delay peak oil.[26] Optimists also include many economists who believe that as oil prices increase, exploration into alternative energies will rise, bringing other forms of energy on the market.[27]

No one can predict an oil peak definitely or predict its exact effects. However, in addition to causing oil prices to rise, especially if production rates decline faster than expected, the oil peak will signal an era in which the Middle Eastern oil becomes even more critical.[28]

As figure 7 shows, the world's oil reserves are concentrated in the Middle East. The region holds about two-thirds of the one trillion barrels of global oil reserves

20. For the full report, including more easily accessed slide presentations and graphs, see Post Carbon Institute Energy Bulletin, November 12, 2008 available at www.energybulletin.net/node/47190.

21. Birol interview.

22. Jackson et al., "Pausing for Breath," 2, 23.

23. Jackson, "Why the Peak Oil Theory Falls Down," 5.

24. EIA, *International Energy Outlook 2004*, 15.

25. Maugeri, "Not in Oil's Name," 169.

26. On possible problems with this analysis, see *Hubbert's Pique*, Deutsche Bank, June 9, 2003. Goodstein, *Out of Gas*, ch. 1.

27. For thinkers representative of this school, see Simon, *Ultimate Resource*, 2; and Adelman, "My Education."

28. Cambridge Energy Research Associates, for instance, does not see endless abundance, but neither does it see a sharp drop after peak. Jackson, "Why the Peak Oil Theory Falls Down," 1, 9–10.

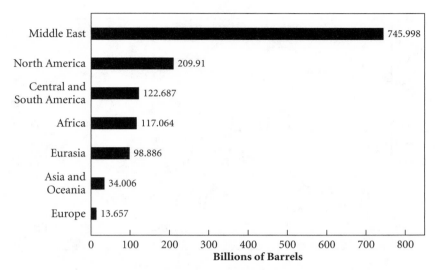

FIGURE 7. Proven reserves of oil by region (billions of barrels)
Sources: *Oil and Gas Journal,* December 22, 2008), excluding data on the
United States. Data for the United States are from the Energy Information
Administration, *U.S. Crude Oil, Natural Gas, and Natural Gas Liquids Reserves,
2007 Annual Report,* DOE/EIA-0216(2007) (February 2009). All data available
at www.eia.doe.gov/emeu/international/reserves.html.

(or around 672 billion barrels), whereas the United States, by contrast, holds
about 4 percent. Even if global oil consumption somehow decreases, the region
will still become more important as an oil supplier. As it stands, none of the
twenty-four oil-producing nations that have already extended past peak production are from the Persian Gulf region except Iran.[29]

Iraq, for its part, may peak last. Iraq could increase production to 6 mb/d by
2024, despite political and security risks.[30] The Gulf is likely to serve as the main
source of oil supply to meet rising global oil demand over the next two decades,
with its production increasing from around 30 percent of the world total to
39 percent by 2020.[31] This will make the Gulf increasingly important to the global
economy and the question of oil security even more germane.[32]

It is not just that most of the world's global reserves are in the Middle East but
also that about 80 percent of the world's spare oil capacity is there. Spare capacity

29. For data, see Duncan, "Three World Oil Forecasts Predict Peak Oil Production."
30. Jackson et al., "Pausing for Breath."
31. EIA, *International Energy Outlook 2006,* 34–35. EIA, *International Energy Outlook 2000.*
32. EIA, *International Energy Outlook 2007,* fig. 39, available at www.eia.gov/oiaf/ieo/pdf/world.
pdf.

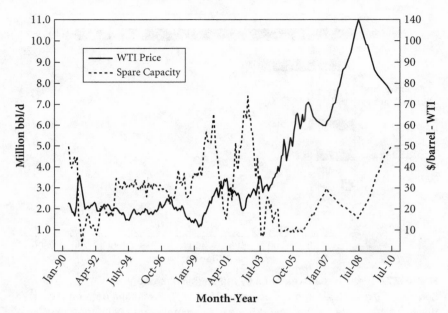

FIGURE 8.   Oil prices vs. spare capacity, 1990–2010
Source: Data drawn from Energy Information Administration (various years).

is not just about oil reserves, but about how fast and how much idle capacity can be used to bring extra oil onto the market. Saudi Arabia holds most of the world's spare capacity, which it has sought to increase.[33] As figure 8 shows, when spare capacity increases, as it did in the mid-1980s and also in the late 1990s, oil prices tend to fall. When spare capacity spikes, oil prices can collapse suddenly. As oil demand rises and oil supply declines, spare capacity will likely decrease, further highlighting the Middle East.

Oil and Globalization in the Persian Gulf

Globalization has not only affected oil demand, making the Middle East and its politics more important, but it has also made it more vital for Washington over the past decades to protect the free flow of oil. Arguably, that has made it far harder for Washington to disengage from its decades-long commitment to the

---

33. See Zawya Web site, "Saudi pledges to keep large spare oil production capacity" on http://zawya.com/printstory.cfm?storyid=ZAWYA20081110045446&l=045400081110.

Persian Gulf, even if its dependence on Middle Eastern oil or on global oil for that matter decreases.

Globalization and modern oil markets mean that a severe interruption in oil supplies will have a similar price effect across regions. The argument that America imports far less oil from the Middle East than does Europe or Asia is a modest distinction. The United States remains vulnerable to events in the Middle East. In a nonglobalized era, Washington could more easily leave the Gulf and not worry about the effects. In a globalized age, it is tied to the global economy and needs some presence in the Gulf, in the absence of serious alternatives to its security role. In turn, this presence generates a range of issues which, when interpreted through Al-Qaeda's distorted lens, contribute to anti-Americanism and terrorism. In this sense, globalization helps enable terrorism indirectly by helping ensure a forward American presence in the oil-rich Gulf.

Another reason that globalization has made it hard for Washington to leave the Gulf is that America wants to keep others from dominating oil and, in turn, influencing the entire global economy. Thus, it maintains a forward presence in and around the Persian Gulf and the capability to return to the region in full force, even after it withdraws fully from Iraq.

While the United States is less dependent on Gulf oil than are many other industrialized states, the global economy depends on Gulf oil at reasonable prices. If prices rise significantly, the price of imported goods will rise, generating inflationary pressures around the world. It would not matter if one country receives most of its oil from the Gulf or from Canada and Venezuela. In a nonglobalized world, America would depend far less on traded goods from Asia, for instance, and oil prices affected by developments in the Persian Gulf would not filter throughout the entire global economy.

These reasons help explain why America has been so involved in the region, despite the high cost in lives and other resources that protecting oil security incurs. As figure 9 reveals, the average estimate of various independent studies for the post-1990 period suggests that U.S. expenditures on Persian Gulf defense, not including the Iraq War of 2003 and the subsequent occupation, dwarfed that of other states.[34] This average for Persian Gulf expenditures alone exceeds the entire military budgets of all states except China and Britain. That comparison underscores the heavy burden that the United States has assumed for regional defense, a burden that was passed to it in the early 1970s when Britain withdrew from the Persian Gulf and has increased over time.

---

34. For a sweeping analysis of this literature, see Delucchi and Murphy, "U.S. Military Expenditures," esp. table 15-6.

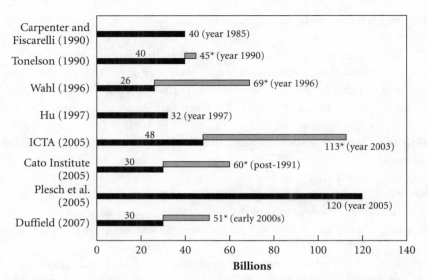

FIGURE 9. Estimates of U.S. defense spending on Persian Gulf, 1990–2007
Sources: Delucchi and Murphy, "U.S. Military Expenditures"; Duffield, *Over a Barrel*; and Hu, *Estimates*.
* Reflects the higher end of each estimate for the period on which the study focused.

The comparatively massive American expenditures on the Persian Gulf, not to mention the more important factor of significant American casualties, might be less notable if U.S. dependence on imported oil were higher than that of most other states. However, it is far lower, except in comparison to Britain and China. Figure 10 reveals this comparative oil dependence (relative to global defense expenditures as well) based on the measure of net oil imports as a percentage of total oil consumption. Arguably, this is the best measure of oil dependence, since it captures exposure to global oil price shocks and avoids the pitfall of assessing dependence in terms of how much states import from any particular region.

Globalization can explain in large part why the United States bears such a burden in the Gulf. It makes what happens in this region critical at a global level. Washington could not easily isolate itself from these effects if it seriously diminished its commitment to the region and oil prices rose as a result.

Globalizing the Afghan Jihad

Globalization and Middle Eastern oil have combined to contribute to transnational terrorism, well beyond the link between globalization and oil demand.

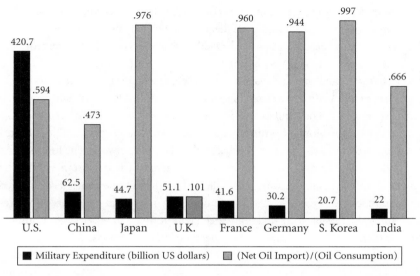

FIGURE 10. Global military expenditures vs. oil dependence, a comparison
Source: Data for this table are drawn from "U.S. Military Spending vs. the World,"
Center for Arms Control and Non-Proliferation, February 5, 2007, and from the
following two websites: www.nationmaster.com/graph/ene_oil_con-energy-oil-
consumption and www.eia.doe.gov/emeu/cabs/topworldtables1_2.htm.

Oil-related funds helped create both Al-Qaeda and the Taliban, which housed
and supported Al-Qaeda in Afghanistan. Oil money was critical not only to the
indoctrination and training of the Afghan resistance against the Soviet invasion of
Afghanistan but also to its ability to survive and to develop in Afghanistan under
Taliban control. The amount of oil money and oil-related support was massive. As
noted earlier in this book, it is estimated that while Washington committed some
4 to 5 billion dollars between 1980 and 1992 in aid to the mujaheddin resistance,
Saudi Arabia matched that amount.[35] Without such support to the resistance and
to the Taliban, it is hard to imagine Al-Qaeda being as operationally capable.

Oil money helped Al-Qaeda develop as an organization and was critical to
bolstering the Taliban in Afghanistan, but globalization played a key role as well.
Ironically, globalization can be said to have helped launch Al-Qaeda as a transnational organization, despite some of the primeval trappings of that organization.
It allowed the Afghan Arabs who would form the backbone of Al-Qaeda to transform more effectively into Al-Qaeda around the world and to emerge as a transnational force. The Afghan fighters came to fight from around the world; when

_____

35. Rashid, *Taliban*, 18.

the war ended, many went home. It is conceivable that the connections that they made in Afghanistan could have weakened substantially at such great distances. This is especially the case because Al-Qaeda became decentralized over time.

However, globalization has made it easier to organize, communicate, and remain connected across cultures and distances and at much less cost than similar undertakings earlier eras. As discussed later, high technology linked to globalization enabled terrorist cells to operate independently at significant distances. For example, the Global System for Mobile Communications standard enables predictable communications across vast distances via a reliable global phone network. The Internet and cell phones allow for coordination among many members across distances, with the ability to update instantaneously. This allows for attacks to be aborted or changed and for attacks to be coordinated as simultaneous or as separate events. Advances in semiconductors have created high-speed computing and wireless communications, which have further improved connectivity among terrorists.

The infrastructure of financial support for Al-Qaeda also went global. It started inadvertently in the 1970s with the Saudi effort to spread Wahhabism, but by the 1980s it had developed in earnest, involving over 120 countries. The largest institution for such purposes was the International Islamic Relief Organization. It claims officially that it is funded by generous Saudi donors using charity dollars, which the CIA believed were exploited by Bin Laden to run his operations in the years prior to September 11.[36]

It is doubtful that the Afghan fighters could have grown into transnational Al-Qaeda in a less globalized world. As I discuss later, they would have probably faced more state control and surveillance, tighter borders, and costlier communications in a less connected world lacking the Internet. The globalized world became a more permissive and permeable environment for a criminal organization that required such an environment to operate and remain viable across borders. Were it a local or national group, its contours would be more easily discerned and its activities addressed. But globalization has made it virtual— borrowing a notion from political scientist Richard Rosecrance, who described the rise of virtual states.[37]

Status Quo versus Change

The nexus between globalization and Middle Eastern oil is also found along a tectonic plate of regional politics—that of modernity versus status quo politics.

---

36. Brisard and Dasquie, *Forbidden Truth*, 81–84.
37. Rosecrance, *Rise of the Virtual State*.

The tension between the two constitutes a fault line in oil-rich states inside and outside the Middle East and contributes to social and economic dislocation and, quite probably, to the types of sentiments that either generate or can be exploited by terrorists.

This tension has two main sources. First, globalization and Middle Eastern oil have combined to bring the United States uncomfortably close to the political and social space of some Muslims. Both globalization and Middle Eastern oil have made it important for Washington to protect oil supplies from regional aggressors and internal threats. Meanwhile, globalization, driven by the American economic and cultural juggernaut, has brought America ever closer to Muslim societies, contributing to fears about American influence.

Second, Middle Eastern oil revenues have enabled industrialization and the economic change associated with it, but they have also helped preserve the status quo. Meanwhile, globalization has generated pressures for change, working in tandem with local economic changes.

Oil revenues have helped regimes maintain the cultural status quo in several ways. The oil economy not only gives oil-rich states control, it has also led them to create societies that can survive "as is" only with such control. Their societies are predicated on cradle-to-grave welfare in exchange for and resulting in regime dominance.

Yet while oil money and power has perpetuated the status quo, globalization has challenged the status quo on several levels. Globalization advances modernization in a manner that may threaten societies. This is certainly not just a phenomenon in the Arab or Muslim world or even in less-developed states. The major protests against globalization were on display, for instance, at the World Trade Organization summit in Seattle in 1999 and in subsequent meetings of major global economic organizations. Protestors railed against its perceived capitalist nature, the inequality that it spawns, the change that it imposes, and the threat to sovereignty it poses.[38]

Cultural globalization has also threatened societies, including those of Saudi Arabia, whose Wahhabist traditions are conservative. Globalization and the modernization that accompanies it challenge existing identities.[39] As Asaf Moghaddam asserts, "Fractured globalization is associated with major shifts in the global moral order, as the cultures and value systems of some societies spread and gain influence, and the cultures and value systems of other societies decline and lose influence. The global shifts we are experiencing, and particularly the decline of moral orders, are giving rise to counter movements and reactions; some of them

---

38. Dreher et al., *Measuring Globalisation*, 2–3.
39. Mazarr, *Unmodern Men*, ch. 1.

radical and even violent."[40] The notion of "Westoxication" is prominent among Muslim thinkers as well as jihadis who see the onslaught of Westernization as generating a loss of identity, with some seeing it as a disease that needs to be purged, a disorienting and unabating influence running against the grain of their societies and cultures.[41]

For his part, Middle East scholar Fouad Ajami illuminates the notion that anti-Americanism results from a cultural backlash against the modernity that America embodies, which is cast against the failures of Arab states.[42] Other analysts find that economic globalization may help create local grievances in less-developed areas but that cultural globalization provides the interpretive schemas that "empower" local actors with the motivation and capacity to engage in terrorist actions.[43] Political scientist Benjamin Barber and many others have argued that globalization has led to a homogenized "McWorld" where American popular culture predominates. In this view, terrorism springs from disaffected masses who are disoriented by and disgusted with American-led globalization. It destroys local cultures, traditions, and ways of life and replaces them with the homogeneity of American mass culture.[44] To what extent is this accurate? Certainly the media, Internet, and global multinational corporations have spread Western values across the world, and conservative elements fear this as an attack on religious teachings and cultural traditions. Extremist elements may be radicalized by this perceived cultural threat. At the same time, one might argue that those who participated in the Middle East uprisings and revolutions were affected, even if indirectly, by the Western model of democracy more than by any other model of governance, even if they sought to adjust it to local culture and traditions.

The combination of threats to the cultural and economic status quo can take many forms. For instance, globalization can challenge some of the precepts of both fundamentalist and jihadist Islamism. Thus, some Islamists are suspicious of the international market because they see it as manipulated by the United States. Leaders such as Sayyid Qutb and Iran's Ayatollah Khomeini saw economics as part of a broader Islamic vision. The contemporary world, dominated by Western capitalism, did not mesh well with economics suited for an Islamic state.[45]

Globalization has challenged the cultural and economic status quo, but it has also affected the political status quo. Inasmuch as globalization has weakened the state as well as national identities, it has benefited Al-Qaeda because its

---

40. Moghaddam, *How Globalization Spurs Terrorism*.
41. Mazarr, *Unmodern Men*, esp. 6–11.
42. Ajami, "Falseness of Anti-Americanism."
43. Lizardo, "Effect of Economic and Cultural Globalization."
44. Ibid., 151–52.
45. Kepel, *Jihad*, 77–79.

paradigm eclipses the state. It especially rejects states that do not subscribe to its brand of radical Islam. Al-Qaeda would like nothing better than to have globalization weaken states enough that it can gain adherents to its way of thinking. The nation-state system is antithetical to Al-Qaeda's ultimate goal, which is to establish a global caliphate.

Globalization has produced another change that cannot be underestimated: an unprecedented level of commercial and cultural penetration of societies. Such changes are hard for locals to adjust to and can breed jealousy. In the past, people in underdeveloped countries were not exposed to the lifestyles of their comparatively more wealthy Westerners. Status can create competition and leave part of these populations feeling excluded, mistreated, behind the rest of the world.

One effect of globalization may be to reinforce the importance of religion, ranging from political Islam to radical Islam.[46] Radical Islam is viewed by many as an antidote to the uncharted territory of globalization. Reza Aslan and many others have suggested that the "identity vacuum" that jihadism attempts to fill has been created by globalization and multiculturalism, which have left a generation confused and unmoored from the realities that they and previous generations had known.[47] Even if distorted by Al-Qaeda, Islam could be viewed as providing a sense of identity in a world gone amok with U.S.-dominated Westernization and globalization. In this sense, globalization contributes to a radicalized version of Islam, while Middle Eastern oil helps provide the fuel to make such ideology operational.

Global Communications: Animating the Conflict

The nexus between globalization and Middle Eastern oil extends beyond the tension between the status quo, which is reinforced by oil money and oil economies, and change, which is caused by the pressures of globalization. Middle Eastern oil issues have also stoked Al-Qaeda's grievances against Arab states, secular regimes, the United States, and the West. Meanwhile, globalization has provided the broader global context in which those grievances are presented, transmitted, amplified, and communicated to the global audience. Oil issues are well suited for such global consumption. They have been framed via global communications and media in a way that helped Al-Qaeda make its case, that generates fear, and that produces a greater perceived threat of Al-Qaeda as well.

---

46. On the rise of political Islam, see Yamani, *Changed Identities;* Al-Naqeeb, *Society and State;* and Henry and Springborg, *Globalization.*

47. Aslan, *How to Win a Cosmic War.*

Global communications have served Al-Qaeda in multiple ways. They have enhanced its ability to raise money. When Bin Laden landed in Afghanistan in May 1996 after being evicted from the Sudan, he was under significant financial pressure. Yet, he understood, perhaps partly due to knowledge he gained in the family business, the importance of global satellite television, which he saw as critical to marketing and raising funds. He himself was a global news junkie and a cellphone enthusiast. Using television and copious cellphone communications, he was able to inspire his supporters to fund his operations prior to September 11.[48] Global communications have also aided Al-Qaeda in trying to paint the United States as driven partly by oil and oil-related issues, as arrogant, crusading, and imperialist. Aspects of the historical perspective sketched in chapter 3 are reinforced among millions across borders via the transmission lines of globalization—the global media. Criticism of the United States is transferred along the transnational conveyor belt, helping shape the discursive environment in which global opinion and policy are formed. Grievances can only gain so much weight if they are not widely and repeatedly heard. If oil issues help generate a range of political, economic, and military conflicts, global communications allow Al-Qaeda to socialize these conflicts within the context of its conflict with the West. Al-Qaeda can turn this conflict into a larger struggle to try to draw in the global Muslim audience as well as anti-American groups around the world.

Globalization reflects a connection of economies but also of minds. Without the conveyor belt of globalization, the whole nature of the war on terrorism would be quite different. What would terrorism be without a large audience to try to affect? The audience would be far smaller, because it would not hear much about the conflict, see the provocative issues, and be able to connect the present with the perspectives shaped by the past. The ability to appeal to anti-Americanism would, for similar reasons, also be more limited.

Bin Laden stressed the role of the media and, most important, the role of satellite television stations as vehicles vital for stirring the Arab Street and pressuring Arab governments to detach from the United States. Understanding the importance of media, Al-Qaeda established a communications and media committee, headed for a long period by Khalid Sheikh Mohammed, the mastermind of 9/11. For his part, Bin Laden created a company called Al-Sahab, which produced professional tapes and promotional clips aimed at promoting Al-Qaeda's message around the world through key media outlets.[49]

Global communications were suited very well to Al-Qaeda's goals, which included creating a transnational ideology that would supersede states and borders.

---

48. This paragraph is based on Coll, *Bin Ladens*, 461–68.
49. Schweitzer and Ferber, "Al-Qaeda."

The Internet, satellites, cell phones, and wireless capabilities were not nationbound. Such capabilities allowed Al-Qaeda global scope, at a reasonable cost, to stir jihad among the global ummah or Muslim community.

It may well be that oil issues generate mistrust and anger and a sense of impotence in being unable to respond to perceived American domination. Meanwhile, global communications and media provide a manner of retribution. It allows jihadists to sow fear and anger in the West through terrorist acts. As key scholars have observed, "The agenda of radical Islamists appears to be driven by an information strategy of maximizing attention."[50] It is no surprise that Al-Qaeda has produced "globalized suicide missions" whose goals are not to target locals directly but to target the world and especially the United States.[51] The goal here is not to use crippling strikes but to sow significant fear. This can be done through attacks on a variety of sites no matter where they might be, because the attacks then are communicated and analyzed worldwide. Of course, targeted attacks on critical sites will produce a bigger global impact in real economic terms, but globalization allows for symbolic attacks that can alter the views of the audience. This is very different from traditional warfare, in which attacks are supposed to produce military effects—the destruction and death that weakens military capability. Small strikes on U.S. Navy ships such as the *USS Cole* or American embassies may do little irreparable damage, but they send a message of fear that reminds the global audience of the terrorist's ability and agenda. This fear is often augmented by global media, which focus enormous attention on attacks that have little or no military effects. In fact, sometimes these attacks have been accompanied by Al-Qaeda videos in which Bin Laden or al-Zawahiri railed against the United States, the Saudis or some other actor, thus creating precisely what Al-Qaeda wants: global attention and coverage and the generation of fear.

Global communications are also relevant to enhancing Al-Qaeda's WMD threat. At times, the media contributed to a specter that Al-Qaeda had or could have nuclear weapons.[52] The nuclear threat may become real, given Al-Qaeda's dogged interest in obtaining such weapons. However, the media and American pop culture aggrandize the terrorist threat. As Brian Jenkins puts it, "Key components of the audience reflect and amplify the threat, not as the terrorists' accomplices but according to their own predetermined beliefs and positions," making the "audiences themselves…the fuel feeding a self-sustaining fission of fear."[53] The WMD threat would mean far less in a world of limited global

---

50. Springer et al., *Islamic Radicalism,* 17.
51. Moghadam, "Motives of Martyrdom," esp. 74–75.
52. Jenkins, *Will Terrorists Go Nuclear?* 258–76.
53. Ibid., 303, 307.

communications. Usually threats can only become global if they are constructed for a global audience.

The media ranging from CNN to Al Jazeera with tens of millions of viewers can focus on the terrorist threat so much that they generate exaggerated fears that exceed Al-Qaeda's capabilities and potential. Even small events that are only indirectly connected to terrorism can become global news stories that shape views in important ways. Thus, the controversy over whether or not Muslims should be allowed to build an Islamic community center containing a small mosque near New York's Ground Zero became a global issue, perceived by some to be a barometer of how some Americans view Muslims in general and how some Muslims see America's sensitivities over September 11. Threats to burn the Qur'an in America in response to the New York controversy were taken seriously by American officials, including President Barack Obama, because such burnings would have been played on CNN, Al Jazeera, and other outlets and would have been perceived as hostile by many Muslim viewers. Such media phenomena would not have occurred even a few short decades ago.

While oil monies helped in the creation and transnational presence of Al-Qaeda, global communications have helped maintain and expand these transnational links. Information technologies have led to enhanced efficiency in administrative tasks, coordination of operations, communication among adherents, and attraction of sympathizers.[54] In the 1998 bombings of American embassies in East Africa, Bin Laden used his cell phone to coordinate the attacks from a remote. This represented a tactical innovation in terrorism that he may have learned from his family businesses in satellite telephony.[55] Of course, the Internet has served Al-Qaeda goals as well. Out of the approximately four thousand central Islamic websites on the Internet, about three hundred are connected to radical Islamic groups that support Al-Qaeda. These websites disseminate the organization's messages and encourage the recruitment of new suicide volunteers to join the ranks of the global jihad.[56]

The Internet has facilitated the coordination of operations, which is especially important for a dispersed, transnational operation. One website, alneda.com, has supported Al-Qaeda's effort to disperse its forces and enable them to operate independently, providing strategic guidance, theological arguments, and moral inspiration.[57] The Internet has been used for passing encrypted messages, which are hard to track, and for embedding invisible graphic codes, employing

---

54. Cronin, "Behind the Curve," esp. 46–49; and Pillar, *Terrorism and U.S. Foreign Policy,* 47.
55. Coll, *Bin Ladens,* 469.
56. Schweitzer and Ferber, "Al-Qaeda," 31.
57. Thomas, "Al-Qaeda and the Internet," 117.

the Internet to send death threats, and hiring hackers to collect intelligence such as the names and addresses of law enforcement officers from online databases.[58]

The 9/11 attacks had primitive aspects, but they also involved high technology in that the terrorists used the Internet to plan their operations. Computers seized in Afghanistan reportedly revealed that Al-Qaeda was collecting intelligence on targets and sending encrypted messages via the Internet, and Al-Qaeda cells operating in America reportedly used Internet-based phone services to communicate with cells overseas.[59] A key September 11 operative, Ali Saleh Kahlah al-Marri, filed a guilty plea agreement in federal court in April 2009. The document led to the finding that after his arrival in America on September 10, 2001, Al-Marri stored phone numbers of Al-Qaeda associates in his personal electronic device and used a simple yet hard-to-break code to communicate. He sent emails addressed to "Muk" and signed "Abdo"—the Hotmail account of 9/11 mastermind Khalid Sheikh Mohammed. The Internet was critical because, from September to November, al-Marri tried and failed to contact members of Al-Qaeda in Pakistan using prepaid calling cards and public phones, sometimes traveling 160 miles to use a different phone.[60]

Al-Qaeda has also exploited technological developments designed to shield a user's identity from unauthorized commercial or private exploitation.[61] Terrorists have exploited the Internet to disguise their identities. For instance, in addition to simple codes, which can be broken given enough time, the website spammimic.com offered tools that hide text in "spam," while speech compression technology allows users to convert a computer into a secure phone device. Network accounts can be deleted or changed as required.[62] Al-Qaeda suicide bombers and ambush units in Iraq routinely relied on the Web for training and tactical support, depending on the Internet for the type of anonymity and flexibility that is hard to track; in Qatar, Egypt, and Europe, cells affiliated with Al-Qaeda carried out or planned bombings using the Internet.[63]

The Internet has also allowed for propaganda and educational purposes (including lectures and chat sites as well as commentaries) for military training, and for multiple forms of vital communication among Al-Qaeda members. This is important because they have been dispersed around the world, especially after the U.S.-led attack on the Taliban. Peter Bergen, a terrorist expert, has described

58. On the many uses of the Internet, see Cronin, "Behind the Curve," 46–49.

59. Thomas, "Al-Qaeda and the Internet."

60. See AP/CBS News report, CBS News, May 1, 2009 "Al Qaeda Used Hotmail To Plan Attacks" available at www.cbsnews.com/stories/2009/05/01/tech/main4985597.shtml.

61. Gunartna, Inside Al-Qaeda, 35.

62. Thomas, "Al-Qaeda and the Internet," 112.

63. Coll and Glasser, "Terrorists Turn."

this global Internet connection as "Al-Qaeda 2.0."[64] It has been enabled by the rise and expansion of the World Wide Web and the revolution in computer and communications technology. Western intelligence agencies believe that the "global jihad movement," sometimes led by Al-Qaeda fugitives but increasingly made up of diverse "groups and ad hoc cells," became a "Web-directed" phenomenon. Hampered by the very nature of the Internet, governments have proven ineffective at blocking or even hindering significantly this vast online presence,[65] as was the case, for example, in the uprisings that overthrew Egyptian President Hosni Mubarak in February 2011.

Global communications facilitate recruitment and highlight oil issues. Without such issues, Al-Qaeda's videos would not be able to persuade people to its cause. Internet sites would not be able to proselytize and recruit. Images of war, of carnage, and of American attacks would not be in the living rooms of Muslims. The Internet has been vital to recruitment on a global scale and has added to the terrorist threat.[66] Al-Qaeda, however, has not dispensed with old technologies and approaches. It uses them in tandem with the new, to make them more effective. Al-Qaeda increasingly exploits communications used by states, multinational corporations, and NGOs, and it has sometimes done so with older technology, suggesting that globalization can allow old technologies to operate more effectively across open borders.[67]

Oil issues have contributed to anti-Americanism, and communications have also helped anti-Americanism develop, accelerate, and congeal in the Arab world. And that has probably benefited Al-Qaeda in recruitment, in the framing of issues, and most probably in fundraising. As Marc Lynch shows, the transnational media, reflected in organizations such as Al Jazeera, have produced a platform to tens of millions of viewers that many in the West perceive as being anti-American. Evidence drawn from analyses of this media strongly suggests that Al Jazeera has intensified an ingrained, common, anti-American narrative of the United States via massive global communications that would not have been possible in earlier decades to such a profound extent.[68] For instance, an analysis of Al Jazeera, with its fifty million viewers, reveals that it has focused increasing attention on America since 1999 and that its news and shows reflect an anti-American disposition.[69]

---

64. On its use of the Internet, see Scheuer, *Imperial Hubris*, 78–86.
65. Coll and Glasser, "Terrorists Turn."
66. Springer et al., *Islamic Radicalism*, 133, ch. 4.
67. Cronin, "Behind the Curve," 50–51.
68. For an analysis, see Lynch, "Anti-Americanisms in the Arab World," esp. 199–223.
69. Ibid., 216–23.

Porous Borders and Globalization

The oil and globalization eras have combined in another way. Globalization has made global borders more porous and allowed greater penetration.[70] Meanwhile, the oil era has provided some of the funding for the terrorist infrastructure and the issues that help motivate some terrorists to try to penetrate foreign borders. Thus, while globalization provides the highways and side roads for terrorist travel, the oil era provides some of the fuel that lights and sustains their fire and energizes elements of the global audience.

The rise of more porous borders is a hallmark of globalization and the modern era. Much thought on economics was developed many decades ago, when national economies were far more closed. In the early 1930s, for example, tariffs and their impact were, as Richard Cooper has pointed out, "considered exclusively a matter of domestic concern."[71] Increased trade and foreign direct investment has made it harder to prevent others from accessing one's society and economy. James Rosenau has referred to a mobility upheaval, recognizing that technology and globalization have enabled people to travel farther and more easily than even before.[72]

Three particular types of threats have become prominent. The globalization of commerce has expanded dramatically, creating a great many tributaries of interaction among countries, which can be traversed for positive or negative goals. These pathways have enhanced the efficiency and scope of economic interaction, but they have also increased the ability of terrorists to establish cells. The North American Free Trade Area and the European Union, for instance, resulted in less restrictive borders, which may have produced some positive economic outcomes but also allowed terrorists to move more freely and to establish cells more easily.

In addition, the volume of air travel and goods that passes through ports has increased dramatically in the past several decades, making air- and seaports more vulnerable. Laws that facilitate trade enhance efficient production and delivery of goods and services. Such efficiencies have also demanded massive expenditures aimed at addressing worst-case terrorist attacks, for globalization has increased the likelihood that Al-Qaeda will exploit open borders to smuggle in weapons, including WMD.

A third area of growing concern is cyber-attacks, which Obama identified in May 2009 as a major threat, signaling cyber protection as a national priority. Electronic attacks are increasingly seen as a cheap and easy route that is a

---

70. Goff, "Invisible Borders"; Rosenau, *Along the Domestic-Foreign Frontier;* and Haskel, "Access to Society."

71. Cooper, "Economic Globalization," 173n9.

72. Rosenau, *Distant Proximities.*

challenge to deter and contain. They may represent the next frontier for transnational terrorism, aided by a globalized environment in which it is hard to control penetration into one's economy and society and in which the profound interconnections within and among states may make them vulnerable to targeted attacks on integrated grids. Some analysts suggest the United States is vulnerable to a "digital Pearl Harbor," in which attacks on the transportation and utility networks wreak havoc on the American economy.[73]

The fears sowed by 9/11 have produced many restrictive measures aimed at shoring up porous borders and crippling the ability of terrorists and their resources to cross them. That includes greater scrutiny of the Internet, bank operations, border patrols, visa regulations, air and seaport security, and monitoring of foreign travelers. All of these changes have created a great challenge: how to ensure free trade and the countless connections across global societies that enliven the world while controlling the movement of terrorists.

Virtual Terrorists and Counterterrorism

Oil and globalization have combined to make it harder to eliminate Al-Qaeda, despite prodigious efforts by the United States and its allies to do so and despite Al-Qaeda's bankrupt ideology. Oil has provided funds to facilitate Al-Qaeda's efforts to elude attack by U.S.-led global coalition, and oil issues have decreased the proclivity of some actors to support U.S.-led efforts. At the same time, globalization has provided an interconnected haven in which Al-Qaeda can hide and become virtual.

In *The Virtual State,* Richard Rosecrance observed that territorial states had slowly transformed into virtual states whose identity and assets are harder to identify.[74] But in this transnational world, states have not become nearly as virtual as terrorist groups. States still have the characteristics that make them legal entities: territory and population that we can chart, visit, touch, and see; government with a clear headquarters; and the ability to tax. By contrast, terrorist groups really exist in the ether. We are never sure where their infrastructure lies, which makes them hard to target. In previous centuries a small number of great powers dominated world politics.

In a number of ways, Al-Qaeda exploits globalization in part by acting like an NGO.[75] NGOs are composed of numerous actors including foundations, political

---

73. Mazzetti, "Senators Warned."
74. Rosecrance, *Rise of the Virtual State.*
75. On how Al-Qaeda and other terrorist groups act as transnational advocacy networks, see Asal, et al., "Terrorism as Transnational Advocacy."

entrepreneurs, and individuals, with nebulous interactions across borders and regions but with the goal of advancing some agenda.[76] Like NGOs, it has relied on advanced telecommunications networks, and, like NGOs, its organizational structure has become decentralized in authority, with loose ties among disparate but connected groups.[77] For instance, the attacks on the transportation systems in Madrid and London in 2004 and 2005 do not appear to have been coordinated by Osama Bin Laden, although they were motivated and subsequently legitimized by him.[78] The Al-Qaeda leader in Saudi Arabia, Abdul Aziz al-Muqrin, asserted that Al-Qaeda depends on independent cells that function without "organizational cohesion."[79] Although its leaders are on the run, its decentralized organization makes it elusive.[80] However, its stealthy operations shift from one country to another, drawing on transnational contacts and recruits, and adapt when faced with setbacks.[81]

As its operational structure is shadowy, so is its virtual life in the financial arena. The U.S.-led alliance has made great strides in counterterrorism in the financial arena, trying to shut down the flow of oil and other monies, but globalization has, in some ways, complicated this effort. In previous eras, monies from commodities stayed in the coffers of kings, princes, or sheikhs and were used chiefly to raise armies, to create defensive structures, or to advance other selfish interests of autocrats and ruling families. The effect of any given currency would have been largely local or, in the case of major leaders, regional. Today, money is global. The American dollar can be easily purchased and then used to fund operations in the United States such as 9/11. If the dollar were harder to obtain, as was the case with currencies in previous eras, such operations would be more complicated.

Furthermore, in the past, currency could not move quickly. That changed with key developments such as the rise of the telegraph starting in 1844.[82] Steam power allowed ships to cross the Atlantic in a matter of days, but that was a snail's pace when telegraph allowed information to be sent in minutes. The age of cable and then satellites, followed by the advent of the Internet, fiber-optic systems, and electronic cash, created a virtual world of connectivity. By and large, money became easier to hide even though the technologies used by banks and major countries for finding money also improved. Thus, when Al-Qaeda came under severe attack in Afghanistan and Pakistan by U.S. forces, it spirited out its monies

---

76. Keck and Sikkink offer up the approach of studying international movements and organizations in terms of such networks. Keck and Sikkink, *Activists beyond Borders.*

77. Zanini, "Networking of Terror," 162.

78. Ibid., 162.

79. Cited in Abu-Nasr, "Saudi Arabia Plagued."

80. Gunaratna, "Al-Qaeda Threat," 53.

81. On Al-Qaeda's organization, see Byman, "Al-Qaeda as an Adversary," 154–56.

82. Solymar, *Getting the Message.*

in order to escape capture. Evidence suggests that the money was laundered or converted into commodities such as diamonds and gold and then hidden in different areas of the world.[83]

The integrated global economy provides transnational terrorist groups the opportunity to accumulate wealth and the ability to redistribute it quickly, all under the cloak of anonymity. Financial networks help enable terrorist operations. Loretta Napoleoni argues that a fast-growing system of terrorism-related economic activity has developed, with a turnover of $1.5 trillion.[84] This is a product of successful economic globalization in achieving deregulation, openness, privatization, and integration in the world economy. In particular, integrated financial markets and the "digitization of money," which facilitate the instantaneous transfer of funds across borders, have been exploited and adapted by terrorist organizations.[85] Whatever one believes of her estimates and analyses, Al-Qaeda has shown some effectiveness in circumventing controls on the cross-border financial transactions imposed by the United Nations. As discussed earlier, Al-Qaeda members have been in touch using email, chat rooms, websites, and satellite phones and have even used commercially available encryption software to protect their communications, making them harder to track.[86]

Terrorists have used old ways to pass money around, including cash couriers, but also new approaches. The Internet has been a boon for recruitment, fundraising, and planning. Oil money trickles down and is sometimes sent by electronic cash directly into terrorist accounts.

The spread of communications technologies combined with more porous borders has enabled terrorists to operate more or less freely across great distances. Porous borders probably have meant less control by governments, and greater communications has meant the chance to exploit lesser controls, while at the same time decreasing the chances that governments can impose controls.

Globalization and Effects

It is worth mentioning one other nexus here before discussing it more in the next chapter. Middle Eastern oil contributes to the ability of terrorists to strike at global targets while inviting them to hit oil facilities. Meanwhile, globalization generates vital, concentrated nodes in the world, which, if hit, can produce disproportionately large effects and repercussions. In this sense, globalization teams

---

83. Cronin, "Behind the Curve," 50.
84. Napoleoni, *Terror Incorporated,* xviii.
85. Li and Schaub, "Economic Globalization," 234.
86. Mannes, *Profiles in Terror,* 33.

up with Middle Eastern oil to make the outcomes of terrorist attacks potentially more serious.

The Rising American Profile

So far, we have looked at different ways in which the Middle East and globalization eras have combined to enable and worsen Al-Qaeda terrorism and to contribute more broadly to the threat of terrorism. But one last question is worth addressing here: if these eras did combine in this manner, why did it take them so long to do so? After all, these eras were well in motion far ahead of the September 9/11 attacks, which raised the specter of transnational terrorism in earnest.

The answer is that the effects of these eras did not occur overnight. As we saw throughout the book, each era developed over time, spinning off different effects as it progressed. For instance, the Middle Eastern oil era discussed in chapter 1, evolved as a function of many factors, including the rise of nation-states, nationalism, OPEC, and wars in the Middle East.

In addition, these two eras created a number of combined effects. Perhaps most important was the rising role of America in the Middle East. To some extent, the United States became more involved in the region reluctantly. A number of factors drove its presence in the region, but threats to Middle Eastern oil were most salient. They pushed Washington into the region especially due to the fall of the Shah of Iran, the Soviet invasion of Afghanistan, the Iran-Iraq War, and then Iraq's stunning invasion of Kuwait in August 1990. Meanwhile, Washington's profile in the region also increased due to globalization. It brought American culture, economics, and politics directly into the space of Muslims in the Persian Gulf. At times, the globalization and Middle Eastern oil eras combined to penetrate the region even as each contributed its own effects. Thus, America's interest in democratizing the region reflected globalization in that its values were being exported around the world, and its desire to democratize the Middle East was also tied to oil and terrorism. The George W. Bush administration believed that a democratized Iraq and Middle East would be less conflict-ridden, less threatening to oil, less likely to develop WMD, and less likely to incubate and to support terrorists.

Al-Qaeda versus the United States: The Globalization Factor

While Al-Qaeda has benefited from globalization, so have major states, in important ways. It is therefore important to explore which side has benefited more and how so. I argue that globalization has largely militated in favor of Al-Qaeda, chiefly because it has made it cheaper and easier to buy and use high technology and to move and operate across borders.

Communications technology, including computers, the Internet, and satellites, makes it cheaper to communicate at long distances, while the "digitization" of money enables the wide use of credit cards and smart cards and the instantaneous transfer of funds worldwide, with less chance of being prosecuted for laundering and other crimes. In this sense, global technologies help level the playing field. Richard Holbrooke, former U.S. Ambassador to the United Nations, asked how a man in a cave can "outcommunicate the world's leading communications society."[87] Part of the answer is simple: global communications enmeshed in globalization allow the weak to spread their message and, in a sense, play the role of the great equalizer, at least in the communications realm. You do not have to be powerful, rich, and supported by an armada of planes and ships to get on the Internet or television.

Global media also benefit the United States due to their global reach and influence. Washington uses communications to appeal to and manipulate its audience. But great access to media does not always mean great effects. How receptive are Muslim audiences to America's messages? Polling data suggest a problem. Washington's message can get garbled, chewed up, and processed to fit existing perspectives that are not positive about America.[88] Of course, Al-Qaeda's message is also viewed as vile by most Muslims, but Al-Qaeda needs to draw a relatively small percentage of people to its side in order to cause major trouble. Meanwhile, arguably, the United States needs to convince a relatively high percentage of people to act against Al-Qaeda in order to prevent or check terrorism.

Microelectronic technologies have also enabled massive global communications via the storage and nearly simultaneous transmission of vast amounts of information around the globe. In the past, these technologies or ones like them would have been monopolized by the rich states. However, globalization has allowed for them to spread, giving underdeveloped societies the potential to interact in previously unforeseen ways.[89]

Globalization also makes penetration easier and less costly, disproportionately helping Al-Qaeda, which otherwise would be shut out of Western countries or face far greater difficulties accessing them. This represents a sea change across areas of world politics.

Until at least the end of the nineteenth century, it was very hard to access elites, security sensitive area, and borders altogether. The diplomatic corps was

---

87. *9/11 Commission Report*, 377.
88. Mannes, *Profiles in Terror*, 33.
89. Rosenau, *Distant Proximities*.

small; the elite were chosen from the nobility and gentry; and the borders were well controlled to prevent penetration by outsiders. Interest groups, lobbyists, foreign agents, the media, high technology, telecommunications, transnational businesses, and other tools of penetration were comparatively absent. Political penetration was difficult to achieve, except at the highest levels, where cross-border familial ties made it as much a tool of elite domination as one of statecraft. Nonstate actors would have had little chance of seriously penetrating great powers. Over time, the nature, intensity, and consequences of political penetration have changed. The increasing volume of social, political, and economic interaction has made penetration a much more important phenomenon.[90]

While strong states have significant means by which to use penetration, weaker actors like terrorist groups have some advantages. Penetration suits them, because it is usable by actors of all sizes and capabilities.

Globalization also has made terrorism less costly and easier to execute, in part due to the huge increase in financial transactions, which complicate the efforts of governments to crack down on those illegal transactions that fund terrorist operations.[91] As political scientists Quan Li and Drew Schaub point out, financial markets have also experienced a drastic increase in the volume of cross-national transactions. The daily turnover in the foreign exchange market is nearly $2 trillion, exceeding the value of all traded goods and services and threatening to overwhelm the enforcement officers who attempt to intercept money meant to sponsor acts of terrorism.[92]

As a network, Al-Qaeda has structural limitations and vulnerabilities. It can be weakened by reducing the flow of information, hampering its decisionmaking abilities, and undermining collective action.[93] In a less globalized past, Al-Qaeda would not have had the ability to elude and confound America's use of globalized communications. Now it may have some chance to do so, thanks to lowered costs. High technology is no longer the exclusive province of wealthy states.

In the nineteenth century, transnational problems such as terrorism and global warming were minor, if present at all; but they now drive the revolution that links the interests, needs, and fates of nations worldwide. Middle Eastern oil and globalization have had separate effects on terrorism, but they are also important to consider together. The overlap of these two eras is defining world

---

90. Haskel, "Access to Society."
91. For an extensive discussion, see Li and Schaub, "Economic Globalization and Terrorism," 234–36.
92. Ibid., 231.
93. Eilstrup-Sangiovanni and Jones, "Assessing the Dangers of Illicit Networks."

politics in a manner not well appreciated or even understood, partly because it is so broad and abstract.

Globalization has had positive effects, which I will explore, but it has also benefited terrorists. Of course, great powers can also exploit globalization to fight terrorism. But the real issue in understanding the rise of transnational terrorism is whether the terrorists or the great powers have benefited more from globalization. When we consider the combined effects of oil and globalization, it appears that globalization has lowered the costs of and barriers to Al-Qaeda's entry onto the global stage. It has helped level the playing field, which otherwise would have overwhelmingly favored the great powers. And globalization has made it less costly for Al-Qaeda to engage in terrorism—terrorism that is linked to oil in various ways.

7

HOW GLOBALIZATION AMPLIFIES THE TERRORIST THREAT

Imagine, for a moment, a massive terrorist attack at a less globalized moment. A bomb goes off in the heart of seventeenth-century Madrid. The bomb kills only twenty people because the lack of mass transportation deprives terrorists of deadlier targets. The media are limited in technology and cannot even imagine what real-time coverage would mean. The global impact is likely modest, because a limited number of actors are connected to Madrid economically and are therefore insulated from its travails. No videos are broadcast repeatedly around the world, allowing the terrorists to spread their message and to instill fear. Stock markets are not shaken because the web of markets is not well developed, unlike in modern times when globalization ties one market to another in a web that includes global oil dependence and oil trade and which can be highly sensitive to faraway geopolitical events.[1]

Had the September 11 attacks occurred in 1750, they would not have been known to much of the world for weeks, and even then their effects would not have cascaded along numerous interconnected dimensions to other parts of the world. It was not until the invention of the telegraph in the nineteenth century and its broader adoption by the mid- to late nineteenth century that communications allowed for some speed at great distances, and even then, communication to the broader public faced additional delays, especially to the undereducated.

---

1. On how oil dependence has created a repeating pattern of banking, currency, and energy-price crises, see El-Gamal and Jaffe, *Oil, Dollars, Debt, and Crises.*

Globalization generates vital, concentrated nodes in the world, which, if hit, can produce disproportionately large effects and repercussions. Global communications allow for such effects to be further communicated to a global audience and dramatized. Meanwhile, the oil era has offered much potential for precisely these types of shocks, not only by contributing to terrorism but also because the global oil infrastructure is a target for terrorists, and strikes on it or even near it can have major effects in a globalized world. Together, globalization and the oil era have offered terrorists a means by which to strike. They can exploit the nature of globalization and the nodes offered by the global energy infrastructure.

The Butterfly Metaphor

The butterfly metaphor captures the notion that a butterfly flapping its wings in Brazil today could affect the atmosphere in ways that bring a snowstorm in Alaska tomorrow.[2] The metaphor of the butterfly effect has numerous incarnations, but at the core it refers to the idea that in dynamic nonlinear systems, a butterfly's wings might create tiny changes in the atmosphere which, in turn, ultimately generate or prevent a massive storm. The flapping wing represents a small change in the initial condition of the atmospheric system. That small change produces a cascade of events that produce big consequences. The notion is that such massive changes would not have occurred, had the butterfly not flapped its wings. The butterfly effect is a somewhat overused and not always persuasive metaphor, but its theme is of cross-disciplinary salience, ranging from the study of chemical, atmospheric, biological, and political systems.[3]

In the field of international relations, the notion that in interconnected systems, small perturbations might reverberate or cause cascading disruptions is an important one. Dynamics of this kind have been observed in various forms of globalization.[4] As political scientist James Rosenau suggests, a belief has now emerged that "unexpected events are commonplace, that anomalies are normal occurrences, that minor incidents can mushroom into major outcomes."[5] Globalization scholars are fundamentally interested in such effects, including "contagion," "the boomerang," and the butterfly effect.[6]

---

2. Casti, *Complexification.*

3. Ibid.; and Lorenz, "Deterministic Nonperiodic Flow." On complex systems, see Harrison, ed., *Complexity in World Politics.*

4. Rosenau, *Turbulence in World Politics;* Rosenau, *Distant Proximities;* Jervis, *System Effects;* and Maoz, "Network Polarization."

5. Rosenau, *Distant Proximities,* 209.

6. Lorenz, "Deterministic Nonperiodic Flow"; and Walt, "Fads, Fevers, and Firestorms."

The East Asian financial crisis that affected much of Asia in the summer of 1997 took scholars and others by surprise and created fears of a global economic meltdown or contagion. The crisis had modest beginnings. It started in tiny Thailand with the collapse of the Thai currency, the baht. But that small action created a cascade of ripple effects around the global economy. Not dissimilarly, many feared that the U.S. financial meltdown of 2008 would spread to the broader American and global economies. The perception was that if one major bank or brokerage house was allowed to fail, or even a major multinational corporation, like American International Group, then the financial system itself might be at risk. The failure of the financial firm Lehman Brothers seemed to reinforce this fear, causing a serious drop in stock prices. But at its core, this was a concern about butterfly effects or something akin to them; it was about the potential for the financial system to unravel if one of its parts were damaged. It was believed that America's ills might not affect the rest of the world, but the American economic crisis quickly went global. To what extent we actually witnessed a butterfly effect is not fully clear, though a case can be made that the financial meltdown in the United States resulted in part from the government's willingness to let Lehman Brothers fail, after which there were global effects due to this failure and to America's general economic travails. Without question, the effects on markets and psychology were larger than one might expect in a system less interconnected, both financially and by media.

One might argue that another type of butterfly effect was on display in the first months of 2001, when uprisings in little Tunisia appeared to spur revolutionary zeal in Egypt, Libya, Bahrain, and Yemen, and stirred additional, smaller revolts elsewhere in the Middle East. Although this type of butterfly effect was not driven by the economic links of globalization as was the case with the financial meltdown, global media were critical in placing events in Tunisia in an international fish bowl and suggesting the idea of revolt to peoples across the region. Meanwhile, globally linked oil and stock markets were highly sensitive to events in the region, and concerns emerged that regional developments might even stall global economic growth if oil prices spiked and remained at high levels.

Globalization and the Butterfly Effect

Globalization can contribute to butterfly effects in several ways, of which, I argue, two are key. First, it does so by virtue of its interconnections across economic, political, and cultural space. In a globalized context, it is fair to say that interactions between two actors often affect third parties who have interconnected relations with either or both of the actors in the dyad as well as issue areas that overlap the conflict.[7] Carried by more developed and complex political, socioeconomic, strategic, and cultural connections, the effects of these events are likely to be more far-reaching. As the global system has become more tightly knit and more permeated by powerful technologies, the ramifications of any event have become more numerous, significant, and instantaneous. The combination of developed trade links, exchange rate sensitivity, foreign direct investment, and capital and labor mobility increases the probability that events will produce butterfly-like, broader, and quicker effects.

Second, while interconnections produce cascading effects under certain conditions, these various effects are communicated to a regional and global audience via another aspect of globalization: communications. Globalization creates what terrorists seek: the ability to gain global attention for events that might be ignored in a world less connected by the media. Such a world allows for the terrorist to jump onto a global stage decked out with lighting and cameras, secure in the knowledge that the inexhaustible channels of the global communications empire will sow fear at great distances. Even small attacks gain symbolic meaning, not just by virtue of the possibility that they will create real, butterfly-like effects, but also because those effects—real or not—will have a potentially serious impact on the audience, which then becomes part of the drama, adding fire to the threat.[8]

The inherent potential for butterfly effects in the context of globalization creates the potential for terrorist attacks to produce damage that is disproportionate to the size of the attack or the power of the attacker. It is fair to say that we are living in special times the likes of which William the Conqueror, Genghis Khan, and Frederick the Great could never have imagined. We can take great trips to meccas of culture and sophistication—New York, Sydney, Paris—that offer so much in one place. We can enjoy the excitement of feeling at the heart of it all and actually experience countless global cross-currents in one metropolis. As captured in the oft-repeated notion of a "global village," globalization ties together these wonderful places, whereas in the past they were distant, separate, and much more removed from one another.

At the same time, what happens in one city can be known immediately in another and cause global impacts. And that also has a downside. Benjamin Barber argues that "Jihad's war has been less with democracy than with McWorld," that it does battle with the modern, the secular, and the cosmopolitan.[9] Globalization may strengthen the enemies of jihad economically, but it can also make them more vulnerable to terrorist attacks. The two are not mutually exclusive,

---

7. Rosenau, "A Pre-Theory Revisited," 256–62; Keohane and Nye, *Power and Interdependence;* and Jervis, *Coping with Complexity.*

8. Jenkins, *Will Terrorists Go Nuclear?* 307.

9. Barber, *Jihad vs. McWorld,* 210.

and certainly the United States has been well aware of the potential for the cascading effects of terrorist attacks in an interconnected world.

September 11 and Beyond

The terrorist attacks of 9/11 were minor events from a military standpoint. They produced no damage to military assets, with the exception of easily repaired damage to the Pentagon. No soldiers were killed in battle, no tanks destroyed, no ships disabled. By historical military standards, even the nearly three thousand civilian casualties, while heartbreaking, were small in number compared to casualties in even minor wars.

However, that these attacks occurred in a globalized world made them serious in other ways. The attacks produced a major, though brief, economic impact on American markets. When the stock markets reopened on September 17, the Dow Jones Industrial Average fell 684.81 points, or 7.13 percent, to 8920.70, at the time a record-setting one-day point decline. By the end of the week, it had fallen 14.3 percent. Stocks eventually bounced back, as they always do, and the economic impact may have been chiefly limited to the short term, but it was very serious at the time of the attacks.

The attacks also generated fear around the world. September 11 was a signal that Al-Qaeda had greater capability than believed. America was its chief target, but others around the world also had to worry about the advent of such audacious terrorism. And because of global interconnectedness, others also had to be concerned that even if they were not the target, they would suffer the repercussions of an attack on the United States. An attack could hurt their economies by virtue of ripple effects throughout the world economy. Of course, they might also get caught in the crossfire between a vengeful United States and terrorists on the run worldwide.

The attacks also altered world history in a manner that will not be fully known for many years, if at all. They led to the Afghanistan War and were fundamentally linked to the 2003 invasion of Iraq. And they led to numerous changes associated with the broader war on terrorism—a multi-billion-dollar effort spanning every continent in the world.

American and Global Security

Especially in the post–September 11 period, American policymakers have become concerned about the implications of globalization for American and world security. The U.S. government has prioritized the protection of the transportation infrastructure, as underscored by numerous national security documents including the National Strategy for Maritime Security, Homeland Security Presidential Directive 7 (HSPD-7: Critical Infrastructure Identification, Prioritization, and Protection), and Department of Defense Directive 3020.40 (Defense Critical Infrastructure Program).[10] The Defense Department has been tasked with studying vulnerabilities to infrastructure. Indeed, Title X of the Implementing Recommendations of the 9/11 Commission Act of 2007 (which became P.L. 110-53 with President Bush's signature on August 3, 2007) calls for a national database on U.S. transportation assets whose loss "would have a negative or debilitating effect on the economic security, public health, or safety of the United States." Similarly, the U.S. National Infrastructure Protection Plan raised the possibility of cascading failures and their effects on U.S. infrastructure. Appendix 1B.3.2 of the plan notes specifically the issue of interdependency and the "potential cascading and escalating effects of disruption or destruction of foreign assets, systems, and networks; critical foreign technology; goods; resources; transit routes; and chokepoints."[11] The butterfly metaphor is interesting in theory, but what it suggests is also important in real-world planning.

These concerns may be justified. While speculation exists on what globalization means for the actors that dwell in its interconnected maze, one simulation study finds that a small disruption to ports in the global shipping system, represented by limited but targeted hostile attacks on these ports, can cause major effects on the vulnerability of the system. Indeed, the disruption of just three ports, affecting a small percentage of the system's cargo, can undermine the entire system's operations. Removing the port of Rotterdam provides the biggest impact to the network. If Rotterdam is removed and then Bremerhaven is removed in addition, the impact increases significantly. If Gioia Tauro, on the southwestern coast of Italy, is removed in addition to the other two nodes, the network fractures by nearly 20 percent. That would represent extraordinary challenges to global shipping and trade.[12] If this simulation is on target, it underscores a central dynamic in globalization. While interconnectivity often increases efficiency and enhances growth, the downside is that these efficient links can also generate vulnerabilities if exploited effectively. As suggested above, this may be the case with global trade through ports, much of which is oil trade, and it may also be the case in other areas, including the targeting of the global oil infrastructure itself.

---

10. U.S. Department of Homeland Security, *National Infrastructure Protection Plan.*
11. Ibid., 127.
12. Carmel et al., "Globalization and State Vulnerability."

Inviting Attack on Oil Facilities: Butterfly and Non-Butterfly

Globalization is also related to the effects of Al-Qaeda attacks on Middle Eastern oil facilities. Middle Eastern oil invites Al-Qaeda attacks on oil facilities, a phenomenon that especially developed in earnest in Saudi Arabia in 2003 and 2004. Meanwhile, globalization makes the effects of such attacks potentially more serious. Thus, terrorist attacks on oil facilities can produce larger effects by virtue of massive global communications, the importance of Persian Gulf oil to the global economy in general, and their impact on global oil markets and oil pricing. Global oil markets can be conveyor belts for political, economic, and security events, especially in the oil-rich Middle East.

Based on a database of global terrorist attacks, global oil facilities have not been a primary target of terrorists, accounting for only 262 of 5,000 incidents from 1922 to 1999.[13] Nor has Al-Qaeda focused on them in particular, although its attacks on oil facilities have increased since September 11. These facilities have invited attack for a variety of reasons. Al-Qaeda doctrine on this subject is specifically related to the oil and gas industry, as demonstrated by an Al-Qaeda document entitled, "The Laws of Targeting Petroleum-Related Interests and a Review of the Laws Pertaining to the Economic Jihad."[14] Terrorist attacks on oil fields have become common, though none so far have been of major scale.[15] U.S. intelligence has intercepted messages among the fifty-five thousand workers of Saudi Aramco, the world's largest oil company, indicating that terrorists are among their ranks and have sought to plan terrorist sabotage.[16] On the day that the French-flagged supertanker *Limburg* was bombed in the Arabian Sea off Yemen's southeastern Hadramaut coast on October 6, 2002, the Al Jazeera network in Qatar broadcast a Bin Laden audio tape in which he warned that Islamic forces were preparing to attack the crusader's "economic lifeline."[17]

A spate of attacks related to Saudi oil facilities raised the specter of a broader attack that might cripple or hinder oil production. Bin Laden ordered these attacks roughly at the same time that the United States invaded Iraq. Subsequent accounts from the Al-Qaeda leadership in the kingdom suggest that they felt the order was premature and that they needed more time to prepare. Bin

---

13. Lia and Kjok, "Energy Supply as Terrorist Targets?"
14. Matheson, "Terrorism and the Oil and Gas Industry."
15. Adams, *Terrorism and Oil*, 11–12.
16. "The Saudi Oil Industry and Terrorism," United Press International, November 17, 2003.
17. "Tanker Terror," *The Middle East* (December 2002).

Laden, however, was determined to initiate the uprising against the House of Saud immediately, in the spring of 2003.[18]

The targeting of oil infrastructure represented a change in Al-Qaeda strategy. In a 1994 declaration, Bin Laden stated that he was seeking to "alert my brothers, the mujaheddin, the sons of the nation, to protect this [oil] wealth and not to include it in the battle, as it is a great Islamic wealth and a large economic power essential for the soon-to-be-established Islamic state, by God's permission and grace."[19] However, in a mid-December 2004 speech, he asserted that "one of the main causes for our enemies' gaining hegemony over our country is their stealing our oil; therefore, you should make every effort in your power to stop the greatest theft in the history of the natural resources of both present and future generations, which is being carried out through collaboration between foreigners and [native] agents....Focus your operations on it [oil production], especially in Iraq and the Gulf area, since this [lack of oil] will cause them to die off [on their own]."[20] For his part, al-Zawahiri has called on the "mujaheddin to concentrate their attacks on Muslims' stolen oil, from which most of the revenues go to the enemies of Islam while most of what they leave is seized by the thieves who rule our country."[21]

The new generation of Al-Qaeda saw targeting oil supplies in the Arabian Peninsula as a priority.[22] In 2004, Al-Qaeda began to act on its rhetoric by deliberately targeting oil-related facilities in Saudi Arabia for the first time.[23] After the terrorist bombing of the Khobar Towers in Saudi Arabia in the summer of 2004, a group connected to or part of Al-Qaeda released a statement indicating that it would target Americans involved in Saudi oil, which America wanted to steal for the West, and that it was seeking to undermine global oil markets and the Saudi regime.[24] In an audio recording, the Al-Qaeda affiliate responsible for the 2004 Khobar Towers attacks blamed the Saudi government for providing "America with oil at the cheapest prices according to their masters' wish, so that their economy does not collapse."[25] The killing on May 1, 2004, of six Western contractors in Saudi Arabia's western oil hub of Yanbu, a petrochemical complex on the Red Sea, created fears in Saudi Arabia and around the world that Al-Qaeda may have

18. Hegghammer, "Terrorist Recruitment," 41.

19. Zambelis, "Attacks in Yemen."

20. Gartenstein-Ross, "Al-Qaeda's Oil Weapon."

21. Marriott, "Oil Back above $60."

22. Johnsen, "Attacks on Oil Industry."

23. On the nature and implications of attacks by Al-Qaeda affiliates in Saudi Arabia after 2003, see al-Rasheed, *Contesting the Saudi State*, 134–210; Hegghammer, "Terrorist Recruitment," 39–60; Teitelbaum, "Terrorist Challenges"; and Obaid and Cordesman, *Al-Qaeda in Saudi Arabia*.

24. CNN, May 29, 2004.

25. Quoted in Whitlock, "Commandos Free Hostages."

penetrated Saudi security forces. Although the attacks did not affect oil facilities, Crown Prince Abdullah moved quickly to pledge to crush the terrorists.[26]

That attack was followed in late May 2004 by attacks on three complexes used largely by Americans and other foreigners in Saudi Arabia's oil-rich Eastern Province. The attack coincided with already heightened fears over oil prices, which the Saudis wanted to address by using excess capacity produced in this region. The attacks underscored the intent of Al-Qaeda, as stated earlier in May 2004 by its leader in Saudi Arabia, Abdul Aziz al-Muqrin, to overthrow the royal family.[27]

The attacks were not successful in damaging oil facilities, but they continued to reflect sentiment about how Saudi oil facilities benefited the "enemies of Islam," as al-Zawahiri put it, or, in the words of al-Muqrin, served a blow to the "occupying American oil companies…which are plundering Muslims' resources," and to the Saudi government which provides oil according to its "master's wish."[28] The attacks, even though they did not disrupt a single drop of oil, did cause oil prices to rise and may have added to the "risk premium" in the price of oil—that part of the price that reflects geopolitical threats to oil supplies.

The targeting of oil facilities was guided by a rough set of goals that Abd al Aziz bin Rashid al-Anzi, a former Al-Qaeda leader in Saudi Arabia, posted on a British website. In line with Bin Laden's views, Al-Anzi stated that the targeting of oil facilities is a part of economic jihad, as it is "one of the most powerful ways in which we can take revenge on the infidels during the present stage."[29] Like Bin Laden, he asserted that oil wealth belongs to the ummah, and not to Saudi Arabia as a state, and that it is acceptable "to destroy Muslim property if infidels have seized control of it, or if there are fears that something like this may happen…as long as the potential damage of the infidels making use of this property is greater than the potential benefit that can be obtained when this property is returned to Muslim hands."[30] Al-Anzi enumerated four types of oil target—oil wells, oil pipelines, oil facilities, and petroleum industry personnel—and discussed the extent to which attacking each of them would hurt non-Muslims more than Muslims. Thus, he noted that oil industry personnel are the easiest targets to attack but advised that non-Muslims should be the priority targets. The targeting of a Muslim is, however, permissible if their death can be considered "necessary and beneficial."[31]

26. Watkins, "ABB Lummus Vacates Yanbu," 26.
27. MacFarquhar, "Militants Attack in Saudi Oil Area," A1, A6.
28. Fattah, "Suicide Attacks Foiled"; and "Al-Qaeda Targets."
29. Al Shishani, "Al-Qaeda and Oil Facilities."
30. Ibid.
31. Ibid.

One major threat to global oil security in a globalized world with connected markets and communications is that Al-Qaeda or one of its affiliates will launch a conventional or WMD terrorist attack on these facilities. While such threats are often exaggerated, they are not impossible by any means. There are a range of possible and probable attack scenarios. Terrorists could try to close down the Strait of Hormuz, a fear that arose after the 9/11 attacks, or attack key oil fields directly.[32] While the facilities are very well protected from land and air and while much has been learned about how to fix damaged facilities, a lucky hit could be devastating to the global economy. Most dangerously, they could hit sensitive points in Saudi Arabia's eight most significant oil fields, both onshore and offshore, and cause major problems in supply that could last months. Loading terminals such as that at Ras Tanura, which transfers 5 million barrels of oil each day; according to credible reports, Al-Qaeda has already targeted it.[33]

The extra light crude complex at Abqaiq, with a capacity of 7 mb/d, is the "mother of all processing facilities" and therefore a grand target, because a moderate-to-severe attack could create a loss of oil to the West equal to that of the 1973 embargo.[34] Its stabilizing towers remove sulfur from oil by using hydrogen to convert sulfur into hydrogen sulfide gas, thus turning it from sour to sweet. An attack on the ten tall towers that process 6 to 7 mb/d could cripple oil operations for some time, doubling or even tripling prices if the damage were severe. The Abqaiq scenario is not fantasy. Worst-case-scenario planners in the Reagan era speculated that it would remove as many as 5.8 mb/d from global markets, which is double the amount of oil lost during the 1973 Arab oil embargo. And the Abqaiq facility is just one of several highly rich targets.[35] Terrorists could also hijack ships and use them to attack ports and facilities or try to destroy tankers in sensitive ports outright.[36] The tanker threat is serious insofar as the world's oil supply is transported by only 435 tankers, and not many new ones have been built. However, as the Iran-Iraq War showed, it is very difficult to damage a tanker seriously. Tankers hit by missiles developed holes but could be repaired. Terrorists could also hit large oil reservoirs such as Kuwait's Burgan Field.[37] Reportedly, Al-Qaeda has targeted such facilities. Speaking on condition of anonymity, U.S. intelligence officials reportedly revealed that Al-Qaeda has sought volunteers for precisely such attacks.[38]

Al-Qaeda could also hit large facilities in other oil-exporting states such as Iraq. An attempted suicide bombing of Iraq's main oil export terminals on April 24,

---

32. Banerjee, "Fears Again," sec. 3, p. 1.
33. Lia and Kjok, "Energy Supply as Terrorist Targets?" 111.
34. Baer, *Sleeping with the Devil*, prologue.
35. Ibid.
36. "Sea Terrorists Threaten Oil," *Oil and Gas Journal*, June 18, 2007, 30.
37. Adams, *Terrorism and Oil*, 102.
38. "Report: al Qaida May Sabotage."

2004, generated major fears of future attacks and drove up the price of crude oil. Of course, hundreds of attacks on Iraq's oil facilities impeded its ability to increase its production capacity. They were directed chiefly at its major oil pipelines, but terrorists also attempted, without success, to knock out its offshore oil terminals through which much of its oil flows. The facilities are well guarded, but a lucky hit could reduce Iraq's output by more than 50 percent for several weeks, if not more.

It is also conceivable that terrorist groups will seek to disrupt global energy, not within the Mideast context but at other choke points. These range from Texas oil refineries to the Alaskan and other pipelines around the world. The United States alone has over two hundred thousand miles of oil and gas pipelines and numerous storage facilities. The National Infrastructure Protection Center, which became part of the U.S. Department of Homeland Security, issued information bulletins on February 7 and 12, 2003, that warned that the energy sector should be considered an Al-Qaeda target. Terrorist acts against American and global oil facilities, especially if simultaneously conducted in different areas, could produce significant spikes in oil prices.[39]

The American and global power grid could also be attacked, which would indirectly affect oil stability. Al-Qaeda could shut down key oil refineries and other relevant facilities around the world that run on electricity, causing massive economic problems. We saw the real potential for such attacks in August 2003 when the United States and Canada faced major blackouts after a failure of the electrical grid. The September 11 attacks and their aftermath also raise the potential that terrorists may use WMD, possibly in connection with a major blackout that disrupts security, against targets linked to key perceived adversaries.

Even small attacks on oil facilities could spook global oil markets, pushing oil prices higher. This would be especially likely if an attack happens when global spare capacity is low, when concerns about peak oil are more serious, and when OPEC hawks who prefer higher oil prices than do OPEC doves have more power in OPEC. Any attacks would be more effective if oil markets believe that they presage even more serious attacks in the future.

Beyond the Butterfly: Weapons of Mass Destruction

Globalization may well create greater potential for butterfly effects, but it also increases the potential that attacks that are quite large, rather than small, will produce massive effects. The same interconnectedness that allows small attacks

---

39. "Big Oil Ready for Possible Terror Strike," *Oil Daily*, February 18, 2003.

to create disproportionate effects also allows large attacks to produce even more massive effects.

Future attacks could make 9/11 pale in comparison. In our ability to control WMD, globalization has cut both ways.[40] But when combined with the effects of the oil era, globalization engenders a more problematic outcome. Oil has provided some of the money to fuel defense programs aimed at obtaining and deploying weapons of mass destruction. Meanwhile, globalization has left the global economy and population centers highly vulnerable to WMD use. Whether used by terrorists or states, a well-placed nuclear weapon could permanently alter the course of history.

Globalization assures that a nuclear explosion would set off seismic shocks, careening up and down the very tectonic plates of global economic and political life. Destroying a major city is tantamount to attacking an organ of the body. When one part fails, others cannot function as well, and the organism, if attacked repeatedly, may die. In past, agrarian eras of lower globalization and higher isolation, the world probably would have been far safer from the scourge of WMD terrorism. We would have been far harder to attack, and an attack in one area would not have affected so many others so decisively.

But the temporal overlap of globalization and oil-related terrorism has made us more vulnerable to terrorism and less able to address it. The two together have produced a unique vulnerability. Concentrated population centers are partly a function of globalization, and they leave millions of people in harm's way.

Globalization is also related to the ability of terrorists to obtain WMD. Chapter 4 laid out the connection between oil and WMD, but globalization adds to the threat inasmuch as it provides the labyrinth within which WMD can be pursued with less chance of being blocked. WMD proliferation has taken a different turn in the age of Al-Qaeda. In the past, we focused on the problem of states seeking WMD under conditions of anarchy in world politics, which fueled mistrust and arms races. But the advent of the nuclear supply network pieced together by the Pakistani scientist A. Q. Khan represents a departure from this model, involving a variety of organizations not directly connected to a state.[41]

Countering Terrorism under Globalization

If terrorist acts can generate butterfly effects in a globalized context, so can the responses to them as political statements, economic warfare, or aspects of military

---

40. Hoyt and Brooks, "A Double-Edged Sword."
41. Russell and Wirtz, eds., *Globalization*.

actions. We can argue that under globalization, events are more likely to generate unintended effects, which are harder to predict and to control.[42] Unlike linear systems, which are predictable, logical, and incremental, dynamic systems can be more unpredictable, sensitive, and confounding.[43] Neither scholars nor the general public tend to think of the world in these terms, and scholars seldom actually analyze world politics in this manner. Thus, with the partial exception of works that examine the relationship between globalization and conflict,[44] few studies systematically explore how globalization produces unintended effects, with the exception of a few sporadic references,[45] despite a long pedigree of work on unintended consequences in the human condition.[46] As James Rosenau observed two decades ago, rising globalization and interconnectedness dated even his own seminal work on "Pre-Theory" and foreign policy.[47]

It is important to consider not just that terrorist acts will produce unintended effects tied to nonlinear dynamics but also that the response to them will do so. They create a chain reaction of events which produce their own effects in a globalized world.

The Al-Qaeda threat is part real, part perceived, and part a function of this reactivity on the part of the United States. By reactivity, I mean that Al-Qaeda has forced the United States to respond to its threat; sometimes the American response has been measured, and at other times its reaction has been perceived to be excessive. Whether or not it was truly excessive is another matter. The perception that it has sometimes been excessive has hurt its reputation and position in some quarters. The Iraq invasion of 2003 is such a case in that it significantly increased anti-Americanism. The point of this book is not to argue that it was a major mistake. That is a subject for others to consider. But the invasion and aspects of the occupation did generate significant costs for the United States, as will be examined in greater detail in the conclusion.

Al-Qaeda, by provoking America, has triggered responses both large and small that have been carried globally via the media. Even relatively small actions (when compared to a war) such as targeting Al-Qaeda leaders have resulted in civilian casualties abroad that have lost America some support. For example,

---

42. Kelly and Thibaut, *Interpersonal Relations,* ch. 9. They have shown as much in their work on social globalization. See also Perrow, *Normal Accidents.*

43. Casti, *Complexification.*

44. On the literature that argues that globalization does not often generate cooperation or increases conflict, see McMillan, "Globalization and Conflict," 33–58; and Barbieri, "Economic Globalization."

45. For a rare systematic effort to examine the links between interconnectedness and unintended dynamics, see Jervis, *System Effects.*

46. See ibid., 61–67.

47. Rosenau, "A Pre-Theory Revisited," 245–305.

Afghanistan-based U.S. predators carried out a dozen or more missile strikes in the tribal areas of Pakistan in January 2010, some of which went awry and killed dozens of Pakistani civilians. It may make great sense to target Al-Qaeda leaders and to try to disrupt their ability to organize attacks in Afghanistan and against the United States, but news of major civilian casualties travels fast, via local and global media, and that can hurt America's ability to claim the high ground in Afghanistan and Pakistan and to gain support from locals.

Global interconnectedness helps shape activities that occur under its maze of connections. Butterfly-type effects are arguably more likely under conditions of interconnectedness, as reflected in globalization. We see these types of dynamics repeatedly in world politics, in various crises ranging from interruptions to electric grids to the global financial crisis, to the uprisings in the Middle East in 2011. If such dynamics are more common nowadays, they make terrorism a potentially more dangerous phenomenon, be it directed against cyber-networks, oil facilities, airplanes, trains, or targets of symbolic importance whose destruction would capture the attention of the global media and generate fear.

In some measure, this butterfly-like threat presumes that terrorists will be able to discover where the vulnerable nodes in the world system are and attack them, in order to produce cascading effects. Yet even if they do not hit particularly vulnerable nodes, their actions under globalization are more likely to produce broader and quicker effects on actors and on issue areas than would have been the case in a less globalized world. Globalization adds a wild card to the impact of terrorism. It makes it harder to predict just what its effects will be whether the terrorism involves an actual attack or an attempt to sow fear. The central point is that a small band of terrorists can cause effects that are disproportionate to the size of their attack and that enhances their real and perceived threat, well beyond their actual capabilities. Of course, major powers can also cause disproportionate effects in modern world politics, but that is not so notable. They have always had the resources to generate a larger impact. They did not really need the interconnectedness of globalization in order to do so. What is more notable is that globalization has enabled weaker actors without major economic and military capabilities to generate disproportionate effects. That would not have been the case in previous eras and, partly for that reason, it is very unlikely that we would have been as concerned with such a small band of terrorists in the past.

CONCLUSION

When oil held great promise as the unabashed driver of the industrializing world economy, the great robber barons, the Rockefellers and the Gettys, were celebrated. They were heroes, pioneers of a new age. Their companies would move the world, and they would become enormously wealthy. But their fortunes would slowly begin to change. Once viewed as bold capitalists, the major oil companies and their chief executives would over time start to be viewed in some quarters with greater skepticism, as price gougers and polluters, as repositories of inequitable wealth beholden to dangerous regimes, as managers of a dirty good. The British Petroleum oil spill in the Gulf of Mexico in the summer of 2010 may well have captured this slow-moving change in world politics, with its seemingly hapless chief executive, Tony Hayward, vilified for BP's slow response to stem the flow of oil.

Whatever the merits of these claims, it is hard not to notice the schizophrenic nature of global oil. It is at once a global menace and the fuel of the global economy. We would freeze or die without it. The world would come to a standstill. Economies would sputter. Oil-rich states would fall into chaos, causing regional instabilities. And yet, despite its centrality to human existence, oil and the issues that it generates can stir scandal, protest, intrigue, jealousy, rivalry, hate, war, and violence, as the story of oil and terror laid out in this book suggests. The many elusive and direct links within the petroleum triangle of oil, globalization, and terrorism help tell a tale. They explain why and how a small band of terrorists could become such a real and perceived threat to American and global security and could survive even against the dogged efforts of the strongest power that the world has known, Osama Bin Laden's death notwithstanding.

The Net Effect of Globalization on Terror

This book does not argue that, on the whole, globalization has produced negative effects in world politics. It would require a much more involved enterprise and probably several volumes to even venture an educated guess about the overall impact of globalization. Rather, this book has argued that globalization is not, by and large, a positive force with regard to the issue of transnational terrorism, especially when we take into account Middle East oil and oil-related issues. The most likely positive effects of globalization do not seem to mitigate the negative impact of Middle East oil and globalization on terrorism much.

The first likely positive effect of globalization is that it has raised overall global wealth—a point that some would question.[1] If we assume that it is a fair point, we can still ask whether greater wealth reduces transnational terrorism. It can be argued that the people who benefit from globalization have not tended to become terrorists. Studies suggest that advanced nations have gained more from globalization than the less-developed countries from which most terrorists come. The Middle East has not benefited nearly as much from globalization as the developed world.

We must also consider that while globalization has generated global economic growth, it may have exacerbated the gap between the rich and the poor. It may reinforce the problem created by oil of the haves and have-nots in the Middle East and generate resentment that contributes to terrorism. Globalization may reduce terrorism in some cases, but that reduction may depend on particular factors such as economic development and trade levels.[2]

A similar but different consideration is that globalization may well decrease poverty around the world, although these positive effects may not be equal across regions of the world. Economist Joseph Stiglitz, for instance, argues that globalization has not yielded economic benefits for the poorest countries, such as Pakistan and Afghanistan, where Al-Qaeda operates.[3] It still remains unclear, as

---

1. On this literature, see Li and Schaub, "Economic Globalisation and Transnational Terrorism," 237–39.

2. Li and Schaub discovered, based on a sample of 112 countries from 1975 to 1997, a statistical association between economic globalization and transnational terrorist incidents. They argue that, in general, the trade, foreign direct investment and portfolio investment of a country do not directly increase the number of transnational terrorist incidents inside its borders. The economic development of the country and its top trading partners reduces the number of terrorist incidents inside the country. Ibid.

3. Stiglitz, *Globalization and Its Discontents*.

discussed in chapter 2, whether or not poverty increases terrorism. The evidence is spotty. In particular, has Al-Qaeda been aided by global poverty? Did it attack on September 11 because of poverty at one level or another, even if the attackers themselves were not poor? Chapter 2 suggests that other motivations were more important, although we cannot know for sure to what extent poverty has created sympathy for Al-Qaeda and increased anti-Americanism, thus aiding Al-Qaeda in a broad sense.

Second, some scholars believe that interdependence reduces war between states.[4] Economic liberalism argues that economic exchange creates vested interests in peace. By recognizing that their own wealth and prosperity depend on others, states think twice about cheating and engaging in conflict and will prefer to cooperate, all other things being equal.

One might say that globalization creates vested interests, that since we are all interconnected, we have a common interest in defeating terrorism, lest terrorist acts hurt the global economy on which we all depend. There may be truth in this argument insofar as states see themselves as part of a globalized world in which terrorism can hurt them. However, they may also see America as the main target and wonder why they should expend resources to protect the United States. In addition, for some states, attacks on America may not be a negative outcome: they may help keep the global hegemon in check or increase other states' prospects of gaining power relative to the United States. In such a case, failure to cooperate against terrorism may represent a new form of balancing against the strongest actor. It would be a form of balancing via noncooperation, rather than through alliances or arms buildups or even soft balancing.

For its part, sociological liberalism emphasizes that increased contact among individuals in a globalized world creates a sense of community, producing salutary effects.[5] In one version, this hinges on the notion that the better we know and understand others, especially those of different cultures, the easier it will be to get along with them and to avoid conflict. That may or may not be the case, but it is unlikely that such general effects will decrease terrorist behavior. Greater interaction with the West, in fact, may produce the opposite outcome. We might recall the radicalization of Sayyid Qutb following his stay in the United States. He found Western society anti-Arab, materialistic, unjust, and corrupt and its women shockingly promiscuous.[6]

---

4. Key works include Keohane and Nye, *Power and Interdependence;* Russett and Oneal, *Triangulating Peace;* and Mansfield and Pollins, eds., *Economic Globalization.*

5. For a good description of liberalism and globalization, see Barbieri, *Liberal Illusion.*

6. Qutb, *Social Justice in Islam.*

Political liberalism has argued that domestic and international political institutions, generated by and embedded in a context of globalization, decrease the potential for militarized disputes and increase prospects for cooperation.[7]

There are other problems with the argument that these three forces can decrease terrorism. Even if interdependence decreases prospects for war, it is not clear how this outcome would reduce terrorism, which emerges at the nonstate level. Indeed, whether or not states go to war may not affect the prospects for terrorism at all. Some wars may be linked to terrorism, such as Iraq's invasion of Kuwait, while other wars may have little to do with terrorism.

Nor is it fully clear that interdependence, which may be viewed as the economic dimension of globalization, reduces prospects for war. Some scholars have contested these findings or tried to qualify them.[8] Realists are not only more skeptical about the notion that globalization prevents inter-state war but also stress that interdependence can slide into unequal dependence.[9] Inequality has serious power implications, as Albert Hirschman reminded us, wherein one side exploits another.[10] It can lead, as Robert Gilpin has pointed out, to insecurity about the continued supply of goods, which can increase prospects for conflict.[11] When dependence on others is high, the dependent state may feel uncomfortable and insecure. It may seek to escape that condition in order to decrease vulnerability, and that may generate conflict with others.[12]

Third, some argue that better-educated people are less likely to be radicalized. Inasmuch as globalization enhances education around the world, and not just in advanced countries, it can diminish the prospects for individual or collective radicalization, which can contribute to terrorism. This sensible argument may well be true, although the current evidence supporting it is not strong.[13] What may be more true is that eliminating ideological education can diminish terrorism, but it is not clear that globalization diminishes the role of such education as much as it might enhance global education worldwide. Radical madrassas may be unaffected by the tide of globalization, which occurs at a level that does not affect the dynamics that generate and sustain them.

---

7. On how democracy, globalization, and international organizations do so, see Russett and Oneal, *Triangulating Peace*.

8. Barbieri, *Liberal Illusion*. For historical examples, see Mearsheimer, "Back to the Future," 45–46. On the broader literature, see McMillan, "Globalization and Conflict"; and Mansfield and Pollins, eds., *Economic Globalization*.

9. Waltz, "The Myth of Globalization." See also McMillan, "Globalization and Conflict," 33–58.

10. Hirschman, *National Power*.

11. On the realist view, see McMillan, "Globalization and Conflict," 40–42.

12. For historical examples, see Mearsheimer, "Back to the Future."

13. Krueger and Malečková, "Education, Poverty, and Terrorism."

Fourth, it can be argued that globalization has increased international cooperation against terrorism. It has reduced the barriers to international cooperation by breaking down notions of nationalism and territoriality and strengthening international laws and institutions. It has been said that networked liberal institutions across the globe provide the best means to defeat the networked terrorist cells of radical extremists. That may well be true, but the flip side is that terrorists can also use networks to their advantage. Witness the range of responses against terrorists. Those responses are aimed at curtailing their ability to move people and resources across territories, through banking systems, and on the highways of global capital.[14] These are networks—highways and mazes of links that terrorists are trying to learn how to exploit and anti-terrorist authorities are trying to learn how to check, with each adapting to the motives and strategies of the other.

State Power Revisited

The petroleum triangle also carries with it broader implications for the study of world politics. Globalization and Middle Eastern oil mean something for state power—an area of thought that is important to understanding world politics.[15] I have not argued that globalization in and of itself weakens the power of states— that is beyond the purview of this book—but rather that the effects of globalization on state power may well be contingent on other factors, such as Middle Eastern oil. If we examine factors emerging from both the globalization and Middle Eastern oil eras, we find some evidence that globalization weakens the power of particular states. I define "power" here in line with the Correlates of War project, which uses these indicators of capability: industrial strength, military capability, gross national product, elite competence, and political organization and legitimacy.[16] I also define power in terms of the ability to bring about desired outcomes or to get others to do something they otherwise would not do. The second definition is also important because counting capabilities may not tell us how effective the actor is in actually using those capabilities to achieve desired outcomes.[17]

The Middle Eastern oil and globalization eras appear to have weakened the power of the United States, as they related to transnational terrorism, though

---

14. Arquilla and Ronfeldt, eds., *Networks and Netwars.*

15. Held and McGrew, *Globalization/Anti-Globalization,* 24.

16. For more on this, see Singer, "Reconstructing Correlates of War Dataset." While the dataset is designed to estimate the probability of victory in military disputes, it can also serve to estimate capability.

17. On power and its definitions, see Nye, *The Future of Power.*

so far not in any major way or in any discernable, lasting manner. They have helped Al-Qaeda and its affiliates become a major real and perceived threat to American and global security, and they have made Al-Qaeda harder to eliminate. American power has been weakened in the sense that Washington has been forced to expend monies, to divert attention away from developing and using power in novel ways, and to react to Al-Qaeda in ways that have generated anti-Americanism. All three effects have probably made it harder for Washington to get others to do what they otherwise would not do.

In bolstering terrorism, these eras have pushed Washington to spend significant amount of monies to address Al-Qaeda. It is hard to know what the United States would have spent on defense and national security had Al-Qaeda not attacked on September 11. However, it would not have invaded and engaged in nation-building in Afghanistan, nor is it likely that it would have invaded Iraq. Moreover, it most probably would not have created numerous, expensive security agencies at home, including the Department of Homeland Security, and made many costly quid pro quo agreements with other countries to enlist them against Al-Qaeda. If we also consider that it could have spent such monies on economic growth or on decreasing the national debt, and we examine the multiplier benefits of such moves, the costs of fighting Al-Qaeda rise even more. If one continues this thought experiment, one could argue that the deep recession that began in 2008–9 might have been mitigated had such monies been deployed effectively in the American economy. That recession, in turn, has produced its own costs, not least a trillion dollars in American stimulus spending to prevent a depression and to restart the economy.

What we do know is that while Al-Qaeda's real threat matters, so does the perception of this threat. That threat has caused America to expend much in terms of the lives of soldiers as well as treasure. One book puts a conservative estimate of the cost of the Iraq War at $3 trillion.[18] That seems high. Nonetheless, if one believes that the United States would not have invaded Iraq were it not for September 11, or even that it would have invaded Iraq but not remained there for so many years, then the costs of the Iraq War become part of fighting the war on terrorism.

Al-Qaeda's strategy, in fact, has revolved in part around economic warfare. As Bruce Hoffman points out, Al-Qaeda has sought to bankrupt the United States because it realizes that it cannot defeat it militarily.[19] As suggested in chapter 2, Bin Laden drew lessons from the Soviet War in Afghanistan in the 1980s. He saw Soviet withdrawal as a victory for his jihadists and believed that they had bled

18. Stiglitz and Blimes, *Three Trillion Dollar War.*
19. Hoffman, "American Jihad."

Moscow economically through protracted rebel warfare. He said as much in his now-infamous October 2004 videotape in which he also made an analogy to the United States: "We are continuing in the same policy to make America bleed profusely to the point of bankruptcy," said Bin Laden.

On March 11, 2005, the independent pan-Arab daily newspaper *Al-Quds Al-Arabi* published extracts from a document by Saif al-Adel, an Egyptian by birth and a senior member of Al-Qaeda. The document, "Al Qaeda's Strategy to the Year 2020," summarized Al-Qaeda's strategy as consisting of five stages:

- Provoke the United States into invading a Muslim country;
- Incite local resistance to occupying forces;
- Expand the conflict to other countries so as to engage the United States in a long war of attrition;
- Convert Al-Qaeda into an ideology that can be adopted without requiring direct command and control, and can be used by franchises to attack countries allied with the United States until they withdraw from the Middle East; and
- Similarly to the Soviet war in Afghanistan, the U.S. economy will finally collapse under the strain of too many engagements in too many places. Arab regimes supported by the United States will collapse, and a Wahhabi Caliphate will be installed across the region.[20]

The combined effect of Middle Eastern oil and globalization also appear to have enhanced the potential for devastating future attacks. Such attacks, while extremely hard to carry out, could employ weapons of mass destruction, wreaking great economic, political, and human upheaval. Such potential costs must be accounted for in assessing the real and perceived threat of Al-Qaeda terrorism. If such attacks occur with WMD, American power and freedom of action will decrease. The costs would probably exceed those related to the American response to September 11. America would be a different country the day after a serious WMD attack. This does not mean that the United States would not remain a powerful country, nor does it mean that Al-Qaeda cannot be crippled. It means only that Middle Eastern oil and globalization have on the whole weakened state power more than strengthened it.

The United States is robust despite the challenges of fighting transnational terrorism, and Al-Qaeda's impact may well be transient. Nor do most Muslims or others around the world believe that Al-Qaeda has anything to offer other than violence and hate. That significantly undermines its already slight ability to

---

20. This paragraph is based on Atwan, "Secret History of Al Qaeda," 221.

trigger a real clash of civilizations and competing ideas, as it so desires. Al-Qaeda certainly could not get hundreds of thousands of Arabs to march against their own governments as they did, for instance, in Tunisia, Egypt, and Bahrain. They marched for political and economic rights, and for freedom from oppression, but not to become members of a transnational terrorist organization that sought to impose Taliban-like governments in their countries.

However, in addition to imposing high costs on the United States, Al-Qaeda terrorism has diverted American attention from other critical issues. The opportunity cost is impossible to estimate, but one need only accept that the time of American leaders for dealing with various issues is limited and that a lot of time has been spent focusing on the Al-Qaeda threat to understand that these costs are also high.

The war on terror has put Washington at odds with other countries. The 2003 invasion of Iraq was unpopular around the world and caused an increase in anti-Americanism. Such effects could not have been good for American power. The Middle Eastern oil era has created its own effects, which on the whole have probably not militated in favor of American power. Oil dependence has made America vulnerable to the vagaries of regional politics and costly interventions. Were the world not dependent on Middle Eastern oil but instead received energy in other forms or from other places, states would have more control over oil security. While perceived and real threats to oil security appear to have been exaggerated over the past twenty or so years, such threats certainly do exist, and when exaggerated, they create serious volatility in oil prices and generate greater potential for oil price spikes.[21]

This book is not about how to fight Al-Qaeda and its franchises and off-shoots around the world, but it does suggest that U.S. expenditures in this fight have been high and carry serious costs. While American power remains robust, even as it is being challenged by rising countries such as China and India, such expenditures have taken their toll. Middle Eastern oil and globalization have combined to help Al-Qaeda develop into a serious perceived and real threat, but more needs to be done to assess how much of this threat is perceived and how much is real. In turn, such research can help in assessing to what extent the massive expenditures to fight Al-Qaeda are warranted. At some point, the high costs may become a greater national security threat for the United States, with its already large budget deficit, than the actual threat from Al-Qaeda. But that remains to be seen, even with the death of Bin Laden.

---

21. This argument is developed in Yetiv, *Crude Awakenings*.

The Future of Energy Policy

While this book has aimed to contribute to our understanding of state power, it also offers several modest policy ideas on energy. Hydrocarbon Man, to which we referred in the introduction, will strain to keep all of the benefits of the oil era, especially as he emerges in earnest in industrializing countries such as India and China. Indeed, China has expanded its presence and involvement in regions around the world, and especially in the Middle East, in the effort to secure oil.[22] Beijing's voracious appetite for oil, driven by a consumer culture that is buying inefficient vehicles by the millions, could offset the gains of any serious American energy policy, if China continues along its current path.[23]

This book underscores the importance of diminishing oil dependence. We run greater risks in continuing on our current trajectory, not chiefly because of supply security issues, which are real if often exaggerated, but because Middle Eastern oil and globalization have combined to worsen transnational terrorism.

Oil and globalization have produced effects that factor into the price of energy. The American and global publics are increasingly aware of the various costs of burning carbon fuels. There is a large literature on the direct and indirect costs of global dependence on oil, but it does less to connect these various costs (political, military, environmental) to the immediate cost of a barrel of oil.[24] This may be because adding up the costs requires interdisciplinary analysis, which is difficult to achieve. Whatever the reason, we have become accustomed to thinking that the price of a barrel of oil reflects only the economic costs of producing and delivering oil.

In any case, the "true" costs of using oil are much higher than we think. They include the protection of Middle Eastern oil and, in part, responses to the real and perceived threat of Al-Qaeda terrorism. When we add globalization to the mix, the costs rise even higher. Should Al-Qaeda ever manage to use WMD, the cost of using oil will rise higher yet. In fact, to be precise, we should already be factoring in the threat of such an eventuality into the price of oil.

The upshot for policy is fairly clear. We need oil for the foreseeable future, and oil has done much to help the world industrialize. But if the cost of oil is higher than we think in the form of its links to terrorism, we should move more zealously toward conserving and developing alternatives. In other walks of life,

22. See Yetiv and Lu, *China and Global Energy.*
23. See Yetiv and Fowler, *Global Oil Dependence and the Common.*
24. For instance, see Moran and Russell, eds., *Energy Security and Global Politics;* Duffield, *Over a Barrel;* Klare, *Rising Powers;* Rutledge, *Addicted to Oil;* and Smil, *Energy at the Crossroads.* One exception to the rule is Duffield, *Over a Barrel.*

we constantly make an effort to reduce risk, whether it involves big things like buying insurance or small things like putting on more clothes when the weather gets cold. Those of us who fail to do so sometimes pay a hefty price. If we spend so much time minimizing risk in our personal lives, we ought to do the same about the global threats.

Shifting to other sources of energy will be a great challenge and, if successful, will represent a slow-motion revolution for global politics, economics, development, and security. Oil has created an entire infrastructure, a way of life built around its discovery, production, and use. Changes will alter production across a great many areas of global business, creating complex new relationships, reshaping or severing established ones, and affecting fundamental transnational problems such as global warming, arms proliferation, and terrorism. In this sense, the Age of Hydrocarbon Man and the oil/globalization eras will share something in common. As Daniel Yergin points out, the "abundance of oil begat the proliferation of the automobile, which begat a completely new way of life."[25] Likewise, the ubiquitous effects of the end of the oil/globalization eras will yield new realities in the human condition.

This book is not intended to explore how we can reduce oil dependence, but it cannot hurt to suggest a few basic ideas.[26] Given that the United States is projected to import approximately 25 mb/d of oil by year 2020, the nation certainly needs to develop a plan for efficient oil use.[27] As one energy analyst put it, it will take "fairly heroic efforts to get U.S. import dependence down by even 25%, and Washington is not as oil dependent as many other states."[28] As a result, such an energy strategy will have to be planned at least in part with other nations. Less dependence on oil will not insulate America from an oil shock and its effects on the global economy.[29] But a comprehensive national plan, one that does not wreck the U.S. economy in the process, will be a start.

Studies show that culture plays a key role in consumption habits and in conditioning the preferences of consumers.[30] To shift culture and, in effect, to alter the paradigm of oil consumption, leaders will have to think creatively, offer serious

---

25. Yergin, *Prize*, 550.

26. For an excellent and accessible analysis of our oil dependence problems, including a plan for dealing with it, see Friedman, *Hot, Flat, and Crowded*.

27. Butler interview.

28. Butler interview. We should note that U.S. oil resources have been tapped for decades and are largely mature.

29. The United States is required to share imports under the monitoring of the IEA as the representative of consumer countries. This is mandated if a disruption of petroleum supplies of at least 7 percent of IEA supplies occurs, and if a majority of the IEA governing board votes for import sharing.

30. Becker, *Accounting for Tastes;* and Settle and Alreck, *Why They Buy,* 224–32.

economic incentives that make it painful to use oil abundantly, and change the discursive environment that shapes how we think about oil use. For example, efforts to move toward the wide adoption of fuel-efficient vehicles—an excellent goal given that most of the world's oil goes into gas tanks—will matter little if they rely on the appetite of consumers or if they are done in a piecemeal fashion. However, they can make a major difference if accompanied by incentives and penalties.

The United States has moved in this direction. The massive 2008 stimulus program, for instance, encouraged a move to hybrid, electric and other more efficient vehicles. However, the American approach toward the development of a comprehensive energy policy has been slow and not on a mass scale. Nor have the industrializing states, especially China, done enough to move their fleets toward more efficient vehicles.

Various studies underscore above all the value of carbon and gasoline taxes. For instance, one OECD study has suggested that a broad carbon tax on fuels would reduce oil use and in turn, carbon emissions by over 10 percent, a result confirmed by a subsequent OPEC Secretariat study. Combined with other approaches, such a tax could meet the reduction in greenhouse gases mandated by the 1997 Kyoto Protocol.[31] Meanwhile, a 2008 Congressional Budget Office study showed that the 100 percent increase in real U.S. gasoline prices since 2003 pushed American motorists to change how they drove and the types of vehicles they bought. Data on trips and speeds on several California highways from 2003 to 2006 were gathered, as well as on U.S. sales of new and used vehicles over the same period. The data show that consumers responded to higher gasoline prices, and that while the effect was small, it increased if prices remained high.[32] Since higher gasoline taxes are unpopular and politicians are therefore reluctant to support them, one approach might offset higher carbon taxes with lower taxes in other areas, such as payroll. In this way, carbon would face higher taxes but the overall tax bill of Americans would not go up. This is sometimes referred to as a "revenue-neutral" tax.

This book has explored the myriad connections among Middle Eastern oil, globalization, and terrorism, but it does not argue that terrorism will be an inevitably dangerous feature of the twenty-first century.[33] If Middle Eastern oil and globalization contribute to terrorism, changes in these two factors might

---

31. On these studies, see *Global Energy Outlook*, 26.

32. For graphs and analysis, see www.cbo.gov/ftpdocs/88xx/doc8893/Summary.4.1.shtml.

33. On the challenges that terrorist groups eventually face, see Fettweis, "Freedom Fighters and Zealots." On Al-Qaeda in particular, see Cronin, "How Al Qaeda Ends."

work against terrorism. Several such changes are developing. They may well be transitory, but they are worth noting so as to offer a rounded view of the oil-globalization-terror triangle.

The first positive change is that, the Saudis since around 2003–4 have become more cooperative in fighting terrorism and cutting off the flow of funds to Al-Qaeda. This occurred after they realized that Al-Qaeda was targeting the House of Saud. It is unclear to what extent this change has staying power. Nor did the Saudis even come close to the level of cooperation that Washington sought, as the evidence presented in chapter 4 showed. However, they at least improved over time, and Bin Laden's death may accelerate this trend.

Another positive change is that Iraq stabilized from 2007 to 2010. Al-Qaeda suffered a defeat as Iraqi Sunnis turned on the terrorist organization. The reversal of American fortunes in Iraq appeared to be associated with the change of strategy in Washington referred to as "the Surge." In a nationally televised address on January 10, 2007, President George W. Bush stated that "America will change our strategy to help the Iraqis carry out their campaign to put down sectarian violence and bring security to the people of Baghdad. This will require increasing American force levels."[34] In line with this speech, the United States increased the number of American troops by twenty thousand in order to improve security, in particular in Baghdad and Al Anbar province while extending the tours of duty of thousands of other soldiers. The strategy aimed to help Iraqis secure violent neighborhoods, protect the local population against insurgents and Al-Qaeda–related elements, increase Iraq's ability to secure Iraq after the American presence is decreased, and provide conditions that could promote reconciliation among political and ethnic factions.[35]

Iraq's increasing stability and the election of President Barack Obama led to an American decision to withdraw its forces from Iraq. Will Iraq remain stable after the exit of U.S. combat forces in 2011? It remains to be seen. But Iraq's improved stability has been a positive development. Depending on events, Washington's withdrawal may well decrease anti-American sentiment among Iraqis and others in the Muslim world, depriving Al-Qaeda of potential sources of support.

America has become better at using the channels of globalization, including international banking, to check terrorist financing, and it has become more aware of the importance of global media in winning the hearts and minds of Middle

---

34. President George W. Bush, "President's Address to the Nation," Office of the Press Secretary, January 10, 2007. Available athttp://georgewbushwhitehouse.archives.gov/news/releases/2007/01/20070110-7.html.

35. President George W. Bush, "Fact Sheet: The New Way Forward in Iraq," Office of the Press Secretary, January 10, 2007. Available at http://georgewbushwhitehouse.archives.gov/news/releases/2007/01/20070110-3.html.

Easterners. Globalization still reduces the cost of information, access, and communications for Al-Qaeda and its affiliates, but Washington has become more effective in using globalization to its benefit and in understanding and negotiating its complex pathways.

Another positive factor is that systematic polling data from 2002 to 2008, discussed earlier in the book, as well as surveys in 2011 from the Pew Research Center's Global Attitudes Project,[36] showed that confidence in Bin Laden and Al-Qaeda had waned in the Muslim world. Despite his death, this data can tell us something about transnational terrorism. The data suggest that the ideas that animated Al-Qaeda and brought it sympathy in some quarters lost luster. Of course, even smaller percentages of support for Bin Laden and Al-Qaeda among those surveyed still translate into many millions of people. Moreover, polling numbers can change over time and vary substantially across countries. For instance, an April 2010 survey of two thousand Pakistanis conducted by the Pew Global Attitudes Project found that roughly 59 percent of Pakistanis described the United States as an "enemy" of Pakistan. About 15 percent viewed the Taliban favorably, up from 10 percent a year earlier. Al-Qaeda beat out both the United States and the Taliban with an 18 percent favorable rating, up from 9 percent a year earlier.[37] It is no surprise that Bin Laden took refuge in Pakistan to try to elude American military forces.

On the whole, these surveys strongly suggest that the message of Al-Qaeda and Bin Laden was increasingly ignored. The data are also important inasmuch as they may well indicate that radicals in the Muslim world, beyond just the terrorists, have lost influence relative to moderates. In turn, this suggests that the uprisings and revolutions in the Middle East, even if fraught with setbacks in the coming years, may have a greater chance of success than would otherwise be the case.

Al-Qaeda also appears to have faced increasing financial stress in recent times, albeit it has also shown signs of adaptation. Witness the moves toward a partial diversification of income including drug money and toward the partial morphing of the organization into local various affiliates. While Al-Qaeda continued to gain monies in the oil-rich Persian Gulf, global cooperation in shutting down its funding also improved.

---

36. "Osama bin Laden Largely Discredited among Muslim Publics in Recent Years," available at http://pewglobal.org/2011/05/02/osama-bin-laden-largely-discredited-among-muslim-publics-in-recent-years/.

37. "Concern about Extremist Threats Slips in Pakistan," available at http://pewglobal.org/2010/07/29/concern-about-extremist-threat-slips-in-pakistan.

Adding to its problems, Al-Qaeda also largely lost its base in Afghanistan and was on the move. Dennis Blair, the director of national intelligence, told the U.S. Senate Select Committee on Intelligence on January 22, 2009, that Pakistan's tribal areas remained home to the core leadership of Al-Qaeda but that its leadership had been battered by "a succession of blows as damaging to the group as any since the fall of the Taliban in 2001." Terrorism analyst Marc Sageman suggests that Al-Qaeda leaders have been on the run, leaving a less talented cadre of terrorists at play.[38]

Even before Bin Laden's death, it would have been fair to say that the developments discussed above had constrained Al-Qaeda and its affiliates. Some U.S. government officials had tended to reach that conclusion.[39] For example, National Intelligence Officer for Transnational Threats, Ted Gistaro, asserted that "greatly increased worldwide counterterrorism efforts" had constrained Al-Qaeda's ability to attack the United States and its allies and "have led terrorist groups to perceive the homeland in particular as a harder target to strike than on September 11."[40]

The death of Bin Laden hurt Al-Qaeda and may well accentuate the developments discussed above. However, it will take time for its longer run effects to unfold and be understood. Myriad questions will need to be answered in order to understand these effects: Can Al-Qaeda raise enough money to run its infrastructure? In what measure were Bin Laden's many contacts in the oil-rich Persian Gulf his exclusively? Will his death have a sizable impact on America's ability to cut off terrorist funding? Will Al-Qaeda be riven by internal conflict over leadership and goals? What leaders can take the helm and can they exploit globalization to Al-Qaeda's advantage? To what extent can they play Bin Laden's varied roles? Will Al-Qaeda's affiliates, old and new, continue to develop as new wheels of transnational terrorism? Will they decide to focus more on enemies at home than on America? Can Washington develop more effective foreign, defense, and energy policies that increase its welfare and power and diminish grist for the distorted cognitive lenses of jihadi terrorists? How well can America navigate globalization's pathways and side roads and check the ability of terrorists to exploit them? Will it understand better the difference between the real and perceived threat of terrorism and respond accordingly? Can America succeed better in altering how it is viewed by many in the Muslim world?

On that score, the struggle within the Muslim world and the perspective through which some Muslims see the United States and the West is important. Al-

---

38. Sageman, *Leaderless Jihad.*
39. See, for instance, Bergen, *The Long War.*
40. See The Washington Institute for Near East Policy, Washington, DC. "Remarks by Mr. Ted Gistaro" on August 12, 2008 available at www.dni.gov/speeches/20080812_speech.pdf.

Qaeda and its affiliates cannot function without some support or sympathy or at least indifference from others. For instance, Al-Qaeda's ability to hide from U.S.-led forces has depended on the extent to which locals help counterterrorism forces locate Al-Qaeda operatives. Moreover, its potential to attract funding also depends on support from individuals and groups in the regional and global audience.

The Middle East revolutions and revolts of 2011 may generate positive change, alter how many Muslims see the United States, and hurt Al-Qaeda further. But it is too soon to tell. The extent of that change will depend on many factors, including what types of governments replace the former autocratic regimes and how America and its regional and global allies respond to the changing Middle East landscape over the coming years. Real democratization in the region may well deprive Al-Qaeda and its affiliates of one of their central rallying cries against corrupt and autocratic regimes in the region. By contrast, the rise of new autocrats or radical factions or power vacuums may not produce this effect and may create greater openings for radical jihadis in some countries, such as Yemen.

It is also conceivable that Al-Qaeda or some incarnation of it may be able to regroup in Afghanistan, if the U.S.-led forces fail to stabilize that country. Reportedly, President Obama became concerned enough about a Vietnam-like morass that he began to explore an exit strategy; he even wrote a six-page "terms sheet" in November 2009 to contain the military's push for a larger force, and he appeared to downgrade nation-building in Afghanistan and to stress the more limited goals of denying Al-Qaeda a safe haven and diminishing instead of defeating the Taliban insurgency.[41]

While Al-Qaeda has faced serious setbacks, we should remain cautious about predicting its demise and that of its affiliates. Some analysts have argued that Al-Qaeda has struck against American interests even when it was supposed to have been seriously constrained.[42] And it has shown some ability to morph in order to escape counterterrorist efforts,[43] and to adjust to those efforts.[44]

Overall, the fate of Al-Qaeda, its affiliates, and transnational terrorism in the twenty-first century is impossible to predict. A race is on between the factors that embolden and strengthen Al-Qaeda and its affiliates and those that sap their energies and weaken them. Although Al-Qaeda has certainly been diminished by various developments in recent years, including the death of Bin Laden, it may take years or even decades before we know the ultimate outcome of this race. What occurs in the Petroleum Triangle may well shape important contours of this unfolding tale.

---

41. Woodward, *Obama's Wars*.
42. Hoffman, *American Jihad*.
43. See "Remarks by Mr. Ted Gistaro," available at www.dni.gov/speeches/20080812_speech.pdf.
44. Quoted in Hess, "Intel Chief."

References

INTERVIEWS

Aufhauser, David. Former general counsel for the Treasury Department. Via phone: August 10, 2005.

Birol, Fatih. Chief economist and head of the Economic Analysis Division, International Energy Agency. Paris, France: March 11, 2010.

Butler, G. Daniel. Senior U.S. energy analyst. Washington, D.C.: April 1, 2004.

Glaser, Daniel. Office director for the Executive Office for Terrorist Financing and Financial Crimes, Department of the Treasury. Via phone: July 16, 2004.

BIBLIOGRAPHY

"A Selection From the Cache of Diplomatic Dispatches," *New York Times,* February 23, 2011, at www.nytimes.com/interactive/2010/11/28/world/20101128-cables-viewer.html?hp#report/financing-09STATE131801.

Abadi, Jacob. *Britain's Withdrawal from the Middle East, 1947–1971: The Economic and Strategic Imperatives.* Princeton, NJ: Kingston Press, 1982.

ABC News, "Clinton's Biggest Fear: Libya As a Big Somalia, Says Al Qaeda Affiliates Are Biggest Threat," March 2, 2011.

Abdallah, Abdel Mahdi. "Causes of Anti-Americanism in the Arab World: A Socio-Political Perspective." *Middle East Review of International Affairs* 7 (December 2003).

Abelson, Robert P., and John B. Black. "Introduction." In *Knowledge Structures,* ed. James A. Galambos, Robert P. Abelson, and John B. Black. Hillsdale, NJ: Lawrence Erlbaum Associates, 1986.

Abu-Nasr, Donna. "Saudi Arabia Plagued by New Wave of Terror." Associated Press, June 2, 2004.

——. "Yemen Tries New Tactics to Combat Terrorism." Associated Press, May 3, 2002.

Abuza, Zachary. "Funding Terrorism in Southeast Asia: The Financial Network of Al-Qaeda and Jemaah Islamiya." *Contemporary Southeast Asia* 25 (August 2003): 169–99.

Adams, James. *The Financing of Terror.* New York: Simon and Schuster, 1986.

Adams, Neal. *Terrorism and Oil.* Tulsa, OK: PennWell Corporation, 2003.

Adelman, M. "My Education in Mineral (Especially Oil) Economics." *Annual Review of Energy and the Environment* 22 (1997): 13–46.

Ait-Laoussine, Nordine. "Pricing of Oil: The Need for a New Stabilizing Mechanism." *Middle East Economic Survey* 34 (September 1991).

Al Khilewi, Mohammed. "Saudi Arabia Is Trying to Kill Me" *Middle East Quarterly* 5 (September 1998): 66–77.

Albrecht, Holger, and Oliver Schlumberger. "Waiting for Godot: Regime Change without Democratization in the Middle East." *International Political Science Review* 25 (October 2004): 371–92.

Albright, Madeleine. *Madam Secretary: A Memoir.* New York: Hyperion, 2003.

Al-Chalabi, Issam. *Iraqi Oil Policy: Present and Future Perspectives.* Cambridge: Cambridge Energy Research Associates, 2003.

Alden, Edward. "The Money Trail." *Financial Times,* October 18, 2002.

Al-Issawi, Tarek. "Tape Urges Young People to Strike U.S." Associated Press, October 2, 2004.

Allison, Graham. *Nuclear Terrorism: The Ultimate Preventable Catastrophe.* New York: Henry Holt, 2004.

Al-Naqeeb, Khaldoun Hasan. *Society and State in the Gulf and Arab Peninsula: A Different Perspective.* New York: Routledge, 1991.

Al-Rasheed, Madawi. *Contesting the Saudi State: Islamic Voices from a New Generation.* New York: Cambridge University Press, 2007.

——. *A History of Saudi Arabia.* Cambridge, U.K.: Cambridge University Press, 2002.

Al-Shishani, Murad Batal. "Al-Qaeda and Oil Facilities in the Midst of the Global Economic Crisis." *Journal of Energy Security,* vol. 23, April 23, 2009.

Al-Yassini, Ayman. *Religion and State in the Kingdom of Saudi Arabia.* Boulder, CO: Westview Press, 1985.

Ambah, Faiza Saleh. "Saudi Raids Uncover Network of Extremists' Sleeper Cells." Associated Press, August 14, 2003.

——. "Saudis Hint Al-Qaeda Presence." Associated Press, July 30, 2003.

Amuzegar, Jahangir. *Managing the Oil Wealth: OPEC's Windfalls and Pitfalls.* London: I.B. Tauris, 1999.

Andersen, Roy, Jon G. Wagner, and Robert F. Seibert. *Politics and Change in Middle East.* Upper Saddle River, NJ: Prentice Hall Professional, 9th ed., 2009.

Anderson, Irvine H. *ARAMCO, the United States, and Saudi Arabia.* Princeton, NJ: Princeton University Press, 1981.

Anderson, Lisa. "Shock and Awe: Interpretations of the Events of September 11." *World Politics* 56 (January 2004): 303–25.

Arena, Michael P., and Bruce A. Arrigo. *The Terrorist Identity: Explaining the Terrorist Threat.* New York: New York University Press, 2006.

Armanios, Febe. "Islamic Religious Schools, Madrassas: Background." CRS Report for Congress, CRS-4, October 29, 2003.

——. "The Islamic Traditions of Wahabbism and Salafiyya." CRS Report for Congress, CRS-6, December 22, 2003.

Arquilla, John, and David Ronfeldt, eds. *Networks and Netwars: The Future of Terror, Crime, and Militancy.* Santa Monica, CA: RAND, 2001.

Asal, Victor, Brian Nussbaum, and William Harrington. "Terrorism as Transnational Advocacy: An Organizational and Tactical Examination." *Studies in Conflict and Terrorism* 30 (2007): 15–39.

Aslan, Reza. *How to Win a Cosmic War: God, Globalization, and the End of the War on Terror.* New York: Random House, 2009.

Atwan, Abdel Bari. *The Secret History of Al Qaeda.* Berkeley: University of California Press, 2006.

Aufhauser, David D. "Keynote Address to the Securities Industry Association's Anti-Money Laundering Compliance Conference." Department of the Treasury, March 27, 2003.

Ayubi, Nazih N. *Over-Stating the Arab State: Politics and Society in the Middle East.* London: I.B. Tauris, 1995.

Bacevich, Andrew J., and Elizabeth H. Prodromou. "God Is Not Neutral: Religion and U.S. Foreign Policy after 9/11." *Orbis* 48 (Winter 2004): 43–54.

Baer, Robert. *Sleeping with the Devil: How Washington Sold Our Soul for Saudi Crude.* New York: Crown, 2003.

Banerjee, Neela. "Fears Again, of Oil Supplies at Risk." *New York Times,* October 14, 2001, section 3.

Barber, Benjamin R. *Jihad vs. McWorld.* New York: Random House, 1995.

Barbieri, Katherine. "Economic Globalization: A Path to Peace or a Source of International Conflict?" *Journal of Peace Research* 33 (1996): 29–49.

Barbieri, Katherine. *The Liberal Illusion.* Ann Arbor: University of Michigan Press, 2002.

Barkin, J. Samuel. *Realist Constructivism: Rethinking International Relations Theory.* New York: Cambridge University Press, 2010.

Barnett, Michael N. *Dialogues in Arab Politics: Negotiations in Regional Order.* New York: Columbia University Press, 1998.

Baron, Jonathan. *Thinking and Deciding.* New York: Cambridge University Press, 2000.

Barzilai, Gad. "War, Democracy, and Internal Conflict: Israel in a Comparative Perspective." *Comparative Politics* 31 (April 1999): 317–36.

Basile, Mark. "Going to the Source: Why Al-Qaeda's Financial Network Is Likely to Withstand the Current War on Terrorist Financing." *Studies in Conflict and Terrorism* 27 (2004): 169–85.

Beblawi, Hazem, and Giacomo Luciani, eds. *The Rentier State.* New York: Croom Helm, 1987.

Becker, Gary, *Accounting for Tastes.* Cambridge, MA: Harvard University Press, 1996.

Bell, David A. *The Cult of the Nation In France: Inventing Nationalism, 1680–1800.* Cambridge, MA: Harvard University Press, 2001.

Bengio, Ofra. *Saddam Speaks on the Gulf Crisis: A Collection of Documents.* Tel Aviv, Israel: Tel Aviv University Press, 1992.

———. *Saddam's Word: Political Discourse in Iraq.* Oxford: Oxford University Press, 1998.

Benjamin, Daniel, and Steven Simon. *The Age of Sacred Terror.* New York: Random House, 2002.

Berenson, Alex. "An Oil Enigma: Production Falls Even as Reserves Rise." *New York Times,* June 12, 2004.

Bergen, Peter L. *Holy War, Inc.: Inside the Secret World of Osama bin Laden.* New York: Free Press Publications, 2002.

———. *The Longest War: The Enduring Conflict Between America and Al-Qaeda.* New York: Free Press, 2011.

Beyer, Lisa. "Inside the Kingdom." *Time,* September 15, 2003.

Bhagwati, Jagdish. *In Defense of Globalization.* New York: Oxford University Press, 2004.

Bhalla, Surjit S. "Imagine There's No Country: Poverty, Inequality, and Growth in the Era of Globalization." Washington, DC: Institute for International Economics, 2001.

Biersteker, Thomas J., and Sue E. Eckert, eds. *Countering the Financing of Terrorism.* New York: Routledge, 2008.

Bill, James A. *The Eagle and the Lion.* New Haven, CT: Yale University Press, 1988.

Bin Sultan, Khaled. *Desert Warrior: A Personal View of the Gulf War by the Joint Forces Commander.* New York: HarperCollins, 1995.

Bloomberg, Brock S., and Gregory D. Hess. "The Lexus and the Olive Branch." In *Terrorism, Economic Development, and Political Openness,* ed. Philip Keefer and Norman Loayza. Cambridge, U.K.: Cambridge University Press, 2008.

Bodansky, Yossef. *Bin Laden: The Man Who Declared War on America.* New York: Random House, 2001.

———. *The Secret History of the Iraq War.* New York: HarperCollins, 2004.

Bowman, Steve. "Weapons of Mass Destruction: The Terrorist Threat." CRS Report for Congress, March 7, 2002.

Brady, Aaron F. "Peak Oil Demand in the Developed World: It's Here." New York: Cambridge Energy Research Associates (CERA), 2009.

Brecher, Michael. "State Behavior in a Crisis: A Model." *Journal of Conflict Resolution* 23 (1979): 446–80.

Brewer, Garry D., and Peter DeLeon. *The Foundations of Policy Analysis.* Homewood, IL: Dorsey Press, 1983.

Brisard, Jean-Charles. *Zarqawi: The New Face of Al-Qaeda.* New York: Other Press, 2005.

Brisard, Jean-Charles, and Guillaume Dasquie. *Forbidden Truth: U.S.-Taliban Secret Oil Diplomacy and the Failed Hunt for Bin Laden.* New York: Thunder's Mouth Press, 2002.

Bronson, Rachel. *Thicker Than Oil.* New York: Oxford University Press, 2006.

Brown, Anthony C. *Oil, God, and Gold: The Story of ARAMCO and the Saudi Kings.* New York: Houghton Mifflin, 1999.

Brune, Nancy, and Geoffrey Garrett. "Globalization Rorschach Test: International Economic Integration, Inequality, and the Role of Government." *Annual Review of Political Science* 8 (June 2005): 399–423.

Brynen, Rex, Bahgat Korany, and Paul Noble, eds. *Political Liberalization and Democratization in the Arab World: Theoretical Perspectives.* Boulder, CO: Lynne-Rienner, 1995.

Brynjar, Lia, and Ashild Kjok. "Energy Supply as Terrorist Targets?" In *Oil in the Gulf,* ed. Daniel Heradstveit and Helge Hveem. London: Ashgate, 2004.

Bueno De Mesquita, Ethan. "The Quality of Terror." *American Journal of Political Science* 49 (July 2005): 515–30.

Bunce, Valerie. "Comparative Democratization: Big and Bounded Generalizations." *Comparative Political Studies* 33 (August–September 2000): 703–34.

Button, Ken. "The Impact of Globalization on International Air Transport Activity: Past Trends and Future Perspective." Organization for Economic Cooperation and Development, Global Forum on Transport and Environment in a Globalising World, November 2008. Available at www.oecd.org/dataoecd/51/53/41373470.pdf, accessed September 27, 2010.

Byman, Daniel L. "Al-Qaeda as an Adversary: Do We Understand Our Enemy?" *World Politics* 56 (October 2003): 139–63.

——. *Deadly Connections: States that Sponsor Terrorism.* New York: Cambridge University Press, 2007.

Campbell, C. J., and J. H. Laherrere. "The End of Cheap Oil." *Scientific American,* March 1998.

Carmel, Steven, David C. Earnest, and Steve A. Yetiv. "Globalization and State Vulnerability to Terrorist Attack." International Studies Association Meeting, San Francisco, California, March 2008.

Carroll, James. *House of War: The Pentagon and the Disastrous Rise of American Power.* New York: Houghton Mifflin, 2006.

Casti, John L. *Complexification: Explaining a Paradoxical World through the Science of Surprise.* New York: HarperCollins, 1984.

Central Intelligence Agency. *National Intelligence Estimate: Iraq's Continuing Programs for Weapons of Mass Destruction.* National Intelligence Estimate 2002-16HC, October 2002.

——. "Moscow and the Persian Gulf." IR00766, May 12, 1972.

Cerny, Philip G. *Rethinking World Politics: A Theory of Transnational Neopluralism.* New York: Oxford University Press, 2010.

Chabris, Christopher, and Daniel Simons. *The Invisible Gorilla: And Other Ways Our Intuitions Deceive Us*. New York: Crown, 2010.

Chalabi, Fadhil J. "Iraq and the Future of World Oil." *Middle East Policy* 7 (October 2000): 163–73.

Chalmers, Johnson. *Blowback: The Costs and Consequences of American Empire*. New York: Metropolitan Books, 2000.

Chaudhry, Kiren Aziz. "Economic Liberalization and the Lineages of the Rentier State." *Comparative Politics* 27 (October 1994): 1–25.

Chiozza, Giacomo. *Anti-Americanism and the American World Order*. Baltimore: Johns Hopkins University Press, 2009.

Churchill, Winston Spencer. *Visions of Glory, 1874–1932*. Boston: Little, Brown, 1983.

Cirincione, Joseph (with Hon B. Wolfsthal and Miriam Rojkumar). *Deadly Arsenals: Tracking Weapons of Mass Destruction*. Washington, DC: Carnegie Endowment, 2002.

Clarke, Richard A. *Against All Enemies: Inside America's War on Terror*. New York: Free Press, 2004.

Clement, M. Henry, and Robert Springborg. *Globalization and the Politics of Development in the Middle East*. Cambridge, U.K.: Cambridge University Press, 2001.

Coll, Steve. *The Bin Ladens: An Arabian Family in the American Century*. New York: Penguin Press, 2008.

———. *Ghost Wars: The Secret History of the CIA, Afghanistan, Bin Laden*. New York: Penguin Press, 2004.

Coll, Steven, and Susan B. Glasser. "Terrorists Turn to Web as a Weapon." *Washington Post*, August 7, 2005.

Combatting Terrorism. General Accounting Office, NSIAD-99-163, September 1999.

Comras, Victor. "Al-Qaeda Finances and Funding to Affiliated Groups." In *Terrorism Financing and State Responses: A Comparative Perspective*, ed. Jeanne K. Giraldo and Harold A. Trinkunas. Stanford, CA: Stanford University Press, 2007.

Congressional Research Service, *U.N. Security Resolutions on Iraq: Compliance and Implementation*, Report to the Committee on Foreign Affairs. Washington, D.C.: GPO, March 1992.

Contributions by the Department of the Treasury to the Financial War on Terrorism. Washington, DC: United States Treasury Department, September 2002.

Cooley, Alexander. "Globalization and National Security after Empire: The Former Soviet Space." In *Globalization and National Security*, ed. Jonathan Kirshner. New York: Routledge, 2006.

Cooper, Richard N. "Economic Globalization and Foreign Policy in the Seventies." *World Politics* 24 (January 1972): 159–81.

Cooperative Defense Initiative Against Weapons of Mass Destruction in Southwest Asia. Washington, DC: Department of Defense, United States Central Command, 2002.

Cordesman, Anthony H. *The Gulf and the Search for Strategic Stability*. Bolder, CO: Westview Press, 1984.

———. *Saudi Arabia Enters the Twenty-First Century: The Political, Foreign Policy, Economic, and Energy Dimensions*. Westport, CT: Praeger, 2003.

"Court Testimony of Al-Qaeda Operative Jamal al-Fadl." Transcript available at http://cns.miis.edu/pubs/reports/pdfs/binladen/060201.pdf.

Crescenzi, Mark J. C. "Economic Exit, Interdependence, and Conflict." *Journal of Politics* 65 (August 2003): 809–32.

Cronin, Audrey Kurth. "Behind the Curve: Globalization and International Terrorism." *International Security* 27 (Winter 2002–2003): 30–58.

——. "How Al Qaeda Ends: The Decline and Demise of Terrorist Groups." *International Security* 31 (Summer 2006): 7–48.

——. "Sources of Contemporary Terrorism." In *Attacking Terrorism: Elements of a Grand Strategy,* ed. Audrey Kurth Cronin and James M. Ludes. Washington, DC: Georgetown University Press, 2004.

Croucher, Sheila L. *Globalization and Belonging: The Politics of Identity in a Changing World.* Lanham, MD: Rowman and Littlefield, 2004.

Crystal, Jill. *Oil and Politics in the Gulf: Rulers and Merchants in Kuwait and Qatar.* New York: Cambridge University Press, 1990.

Curzon, George N. *Russia in Central Asia in 1889 and the Anglo-Russian Question.* London: Frank Cass, 1967.

Dahl, Robert. *Democracy and Its Critics.* New Haven, CT: Yale University Press, 1989.

Deane, Claudia, and Darryl Fears. "Negative Perception of Islam Increasing." *Washington Post,* March 9, 2006.

De Borchgrave, Arnaud. "Pakistan, Saudi Arabia in Secret Nuke Pact; Islamabad Trades Weapons Technology for Oil." *Washington Times,* October 22, 2003.

De Novo, John A. "The Movement of an Aggressive American Oil Policy Abroad, 1918–1920." *American Historical Review* 61 (1956): 854–67.

Deffeyes, Kenneth. *Hubbert's Peak: The Impending World Oil Shortage.* Princeton, NJ: Princeton University Press, 2001.

Delucchi, Mark A., and James Murphy. "U.S. Military Expenditures to Protect the Use of Persian-Gulf Oil for Motor Vehicles." Institute of Transportation Studies, University of California, Davis, October 2006.

Diamond, Larry, ed., *Political Culture and Democracy in Developing Countries.* Boulder, CO: Lynne Rienner, 1993.

Diamond, Stephen A. "Messiahs of Evil." *Psychology Today,* May 20, 2008.

Donadio, Rachel. "U.S. Plans New Course for Antidrug Efforts in Afghanistan." *New York Times,* June 28, 2009.

Downs, Erica S. "The Chinese Energy Security Debate." *China Quarterly* 177 (March 2004): 21–41.

Dreher, Axel. "Does Globalization Affect Growth? Evidence from a New Index of Globalization." *Applied Economics* 38 (2007): 1091–10.

Dreher, Axel, Noel Gaston, and Pim Martens. *Measuring Globalisation: Gauging Its Consequences.* New York: Springer, 2008.

Driody, Dan. *The Halliburton Agenda: The Politics of Oil and Money.* New York: John Wiley and Sons, 2004.

Duffield, John S. "Oil and the Iraq War: How the United States Could Have Expected to Benefit, and Might Still." *Middle East Review of International Affairs* 9 (June 2005).

——. *Over a Barrel: The Costs of U.S. Foreign Oil Dependence.* Stanford, CA: Stanford University Press, 2008.

Dunn, Michael Collins. "Is the Sky Falling? Saudi Arabia's Economic Problems and Political Stability." *Middle East Policy* 3 (1995): 29–39.

Eckholm, Erik. "Now You See It: An Audit of KBR." *New York Times,* March 20, 2005.

Eilstrup-Sangiovanni, Mette, and Calvert Jones. "Assessing the Dangers of Illicit Networks: Why Al-Qaeda May Be Less Threatening Than Many Think." *International Security* 33 (Fall 2008): 7–44.

El-Gamal, Mahmoud, and Amy Myers Jaffe. *Oil, Dollars, Debt, and Crises: The Global Curse of Black Gold.* Cambridge: Cambridge University Press, 2009.

Elm, Mostafa. *Oil, Power, and Principle: Iran's Oil Nationalization and Its Aftermath.* Syracuse, NY: Syracuse University Press, 1992.

Emerson, Steven. "Testimony of Steven Emerson." *Terrorism Financing,* Before the United States Senate Committee on Governmental Affairs, July 31, 2003.

Enders, Walter, and Todd Sandler. "Patterns of Transnational Terrorism, 1970–99: Alternative Time Series Estimates." *International Studies Quarterly* 46 (June 2002): 145–65.

Energy Information Administration, Annual Energy Outlook (Various years; US Department of Energy).

Energy Information Administration, International Energy Outlook (Various years; US Department of Energy).

Engdahl, William F. "Oil and the Origins of the Great War." *History Compass* 5/6 (November 2007): 2041–60.

Entelis, John P. "Oil Wealth and the Prospects for Democratization in the Arabian Peninsula: The Case of Saudi Arabia." In *Arab Oil: Impact on the Arab Countries and Global Implications,* ed. Naiem A. Sherbiny and Mark A. Tessler. New York: Praeger, 1976.

Esposito, John. *The Islamic Threat: Myth or Reality?* New York: Oxford University Press, 1999.

———. *Unholy War: Terror in the Name of Islam.* New York: Oxford University Press, 1999.

"Excerpts from Iraqi Document on Meeting with U.S. Envoy." *New York Times,* September 23, 1990.

Fair, Christine. *The Madrassah Challenge: Militancy and Religious Education in Pakistan.* Washington, DC: United States Institute of Peace Press, 2008.

Fandy, Mamoun. *Saudi Arabia and the Politics of Dissent.* New York: St. Martin's Press, 1999.

Farah, Douglas. "Al Qaeda's Road Paved with Gold." *Washington Post,* February 17, 2002.

———. *Blood from Stones: The Secret Financial Network of Terror.* New York: Broadway Books, 2004.

Farrall, Leah. "How al Qaeda Works." *Foreign Affairs* (March–April, 2011): 128–38.

Fattah, Hassan M. "Suicide Attacks Foiled at Two Oil Sites, Yemen Says." *New York Times,* September 16, 2006.

Ferguson, Charles D., and William C. Potter. *The Four Faces of Nuclear Terrorism.* London: Routledge, 2005.

Ferguson, Charles, Tahseen Kazi, and Judith Perera. *Commercial Radioactive Sources: Surveying the Security Risks.* Center for Nonproliferation Studies, January 2003.

Fettweis, Christopher J. "Freedom Fighters and Zealots: Al Qaeda in Historical Perspective." *Political Science Quarterly* 124 (Summer 2009): 269–96.

Freedman, Lawrence. "War In Iraq: Selling the Threat." *Survival* 46 (Summer 2004): 7–50.

Friedman, Thomas L. *Hot, Flat, and Crowded: Why We Need a Green Revolution—And How It Can Renew America.* New York: Picador Paperback, 2009.

Fukuyama, Francis. *America at the Crossroads: Democracy, Power, and the Neoconservative Legacy.* New Haven, CT: Yale University Press, 2006.

———. *The End of History and the Last Man.* New York: Free Press, 1992.

Fuller, Graham E. *The Future of Political Islam.* New York: Palgrave, 2003.

Gannon, Kathy. "Taliban Gains Money, Al-Qaeda Finances Recovering." Associated Press, June 21, 2009.

Gartenstein-Ross, Daveed. "Al-Qaeda's Oil Weapon." *Daily Standard,* October 3, 2005.

Gartzke Erik, Quan Li, and Charles Boehmer. "Investing in the Peace: Economic Interdependence and International Conflict." *International Organization* 55 (Spring 2001): 391–438.

Gause, Gregory F. "Can Democracy Stop Terrorism?" *Foreign Affairs* (September/October 2005): 62–76.

——. *Oil Monarchies: Domestic and Security Challenges in the Gulf States.* New York: Council on Foreign Relations, 1994.

——. "Saudi Arabia Challenged." *Current History* 103 (January 2004).

Gerges, Fawaz A. *America and Political Islam: Clash of Cultures or Clash of Interests?* Cambridge, U.K.: Cambridge University Press, 1999.

——. *The Far Enemy: Why Jihad Went Global.* Cambridge, U.K.: Cambridge University Press, 2005.

Gerth, Jeff, and Judith Miller. "A Nation Challenged: On the List; Philanthropist, or Fount of Funds for Terrorists?" *New York Times,* October 13, 2001.

——. "Saudi Arabia Is Called Slow in Helping Stem the Flow of Cash to Militants." *New York Times,* December 1, 2002.

Gilboy, George. "China's Energy Security Policy after September 11: Crossing the River When the Stones are Moving." Private report, CERA, February 2009.

Glanz, James. "Army Plans to End Contentious Halliburton Logistics Pact and Split Work among Companies." *New York Times,* July 13, 2006.

Goff, Patricia M. "Invisible Borders: Economic Liberalization and National Identity." *International Studies Quarterly* 44 (December 2000): 533–62.

Goldberg, Jacob. *The Foreign Policy of Saudi Arabia.* Cambridge, MA: Harvard University Press, 1986.

Goodstein, David. *Out of Gas: The End of the Age of Oil.* New York: W.W. Norton, 2001.

Gordon, Michael R., and General Bernard E. Trainor. *Cobra II: The Inside Story of the Invasion and Occupation of Iraq.* New York: Pantheon Books, 2006.

Gordon, Philip H. "Iraq: The Transatlantic Debate." *Institute for Security Studies Occasional Papers* 39 (November 2002).

"The Great Divide: How Westerners And Muslims View Each Other," *13-Nation Pew Global Attitudes Survey.* June 22, 2006.

Gueli, Richard. "Bin Laden and Al-Qaeda: Challenging the Assumptions of Transnational Terrorism." *Strategic Review of Southern Africa,* November 25, 2003.

Gulick, Edward V. *Europe's Classical Balance of Power.* Ithaca, NY: Cornell University Press, 1955.

Gunaratna, Rohan. "The Al-Qaeda Threat and the International Response." In *Globalisation and the New Terror: The Asia-Pacific Dimension,* ed. David Martin Jones. Northampton, MA: Edward Elgar, 2004.

——. "The Evolution of Al-Qaeda." In *Countering the Financing of Terrorism,* ed. Thomas J. Biersteker and Sue E. Eckert. New York: Routledge, 2008.

——. *Inside Al-Qaeda: Global Network of Terror.* New York: Columbia University Press, 2002.

Gunning, Jeroen. "Terrorism, Charities, Diasporas." In *Countering the Financing of Terrorism,* ed. Thomas J. Biersteker and Sue E. Eckert. New York: Routledge, 2008.

Gurses, Mehmet, "State-Sponsored Development, Oil, and Democratization." *Democratization* 16: 508–29.

Gustafson, Thane. *Changing Course? Iraq and the "New" U.S.-Russian Relationship.* Cambridge, MA: Cambridge Energy Research Associates, 2003.

Haddad, Yvonne Yazbeck. "Islamist Perceptions of U.S. Policy in the Middle East." In *The Middle East and the United States,* ed. David W. Lesch. Boulder, CO: Westview Press, 2003.

Hafez, Mohammed M. *Why Muslims Rebel: Repression and Resistance in the Islamic World.* Boulder, CO: Lynne Rienner, 2003.

Halliday, Fred. *Two Hours That Shook the World: September 11, 2001, Causes and Consequences.* London: Saqi Books, 2002.

Haqqani, Husain. "Islam's Medieval Outposts." *Foreign Policy* (November/December 2002).

Harrison, Neil E. ed. *Complexity in World Politics: Concepts and Methods of a New Paradigm.* New York: State University of New York Press, 2006.

Hart, Parker T. *Saudi Arabia and the United States: Birth of a Security Relationship.* Bloomington: Indiana University Press, 1998.

Haskel, Barbara G. "Access to Society: A Neglected Dimension of Power." *International Organization* 34 (Winter 1998): 89–120.

Hauner, Milan. "The Last Great Game." *Middle East Journal* 38 (Winter 1984): 72–84.

Hegghammer, Thomas. "Terrorist Recruitment and Radicalisation in Saudi Arabia." *Middle East Policy* 13 (Winter 2006): 39–60.

Held, David, and Anthony McGrew. *Globalization/Anti-Globalization: Beyond the Great Divide.* Malden, MA: Polity Press, 2007.

Held, David, Anthony McGrew, Davis Goldblatt, and Jonathan Perraton. *Global Transformations: Politics, Economics and Culture.* Stanford, CA: Stanford University Press, 1999.

Helms, Christine Moss. *The Cohesion of Saudi Arabia.* Baltimore: Johns Hopkins University Press, 1981.

Herb, Michael. *All in the Family: Absolutism, Revolution, and Democracy in the Middle Eastern Monarchies.* New York: State University of New York Press, 1999.

Herbst, Jeffrey. "War and the State in Africa." *International Security* 14 (Spring 1990): 117–49.

Hirshman, Albert. *National Power and the Structure of Foreign Trade.* Berkeley: University of California Press, 1980.

Hoeber, Susanne Rudolph, and James Piscatori, eds. *Transnational Religion: Fading States.* Boulder, CO: Westview Press, 1997.

Hoffman, Bruce. *Inside Terrorism.* New York: Columbia University Press, 1998.

Hourani, Albert. *A History of the Arab Peoples.* Cambridge, MA: Belknap Press of Harvard University Press, 1991.

Hoyt, Kendall, and Stephen G. Brooks. "A Double-Edged Sword: Globalization and Biosecurity." *International Security* 28 (Winter 2003/04): 123–48.

Hu, Patricia S. "Estimates of 1996 U.S. Military Expenditure on Defending Oil Supplies from the Middle East: Literature Review." Prepared for the US Department of Energy under contract DE-AC05-960R22464, August 1997.

Huntington, Samuel P. *The Clash of Civilizations and the Remaking of World Order.* New York: Simon and Schuster, 1996.

——. *The Third Wave: Democratization in the Late Twentieth Century.* Norman: University of Oklahoma Press, 1991.

——. *Who Are We? The Challenges to America's National Identity.* New York: Simon and Schuster, 2004.

——. "Will More Countries Become Democratic?" *Political Science Quarterly* 99 (Summer 1984): 203–35.

Hurtado, Patricia. "Financial Institutions Warned by FBI of Al-Qaeda Terror Threat." Bloomberg, February 02, 2011.

Ibrahim, Raymond ed. *The Al-Qaeda Reader.* New York: Broadway Books, 2007.

Ibrahim, Saad Eddin. "An Open Door." *Wilson Quarterly* 28 (Spring 2004): 36–46.

Ignatieff, Michael. *The Lesser Evil: Political Ethics in an Age of Terror.* Princeton, NJ: Princeton University Press, 2004.

Inside 9-11. New York: St. Martin's Press, 2002.

Jacquard, Roland. *In the Name of Osama Bin Laden.* Durham, NC: Duke University Press, 2002.

Jackson, Peter. "Why the Peak Oil Theory Falls Down: Myths, Legends, and the Future of Oil Resources." Decision Brief, CERA, November 2006.

Jackson, Peter, Jonathan M. Craig, Samia Razak, and Leta Smith. "Pausing for Breath: Liquids Production Capacity to 2030." CERA, October 2009.

Janis, Irving L., and Leon Mann. *Decision Making: A Psychological Analysis of Conflict, Choice, and Commitment.* New York: Free Press, 1977.

Jenkins, Brian Michael. *Will Terrorists Go Nuclear?* New York: Prometheus Books, 2008.

Jensen, Nathan, and Leonard Wantchekon. "Resource Wealth and Political Regimes in Africa." *Comparative Political Studies* 37 (September 2004): 816–41.

Jensen, W. G. "The Importance of Energy in the First and Second World Wars." *Historical Journal* 3 (1968): 538–54.

Jervis, Robert. *System Effects: Complexity in Political and Social Life.* Princeton, NJ: Princeton University Press, 1997.

Jervis, Robert, and Jack Snyder, eds. *Coping with Complexity in the International System.* Boulder, CO: Westview Press, 1993.

Johnsen, Gregory D. "Attacks on Oil Industry Are First Priority for al-Qaeda in Yemen" *Terrorism Focus* 5 (February 2008).

Johnson, Thomas H. "Financing Afghan Terrorism." In *Terrorism Financing and State Responses: A Comparative Perspective,* ed. Jeanne K. Giraldo and Harold A. Trinkunas. Palo Alto, CA: Stanford University Press, 2007.

Johnston, David. "Classified Section of Sept. 11 Report Faults Saudi Rulers." *New York Times,* July 26, 2003.

Juergensmeyer, Mark. "Religious Terror and Global War." In *Understanding September 11,* ed. Craig Calhoun, Paul Price, and Ashley Timmer. New York: New Press, 2002.

———. *Terror in the Mind of God: The Global Rise of Religious Violence.* Berkeley: University of California Press, 2003.

Kamp, Karl-Heinz. "WMD Terrorism: An Exchange." *Survival* 40 (Winter 1998/1999): 168–83.

Kaplan, David E., and Joshua Kurlantzick. "How a Terror Network Funds Attacks— And Hides its Tracks." *U.S. News and World Report,* October 1, 2001.

Karam, Azza, ed., *Transnational Political Islam.* London: Pluto Press, 2004.

Karl, Terry L. "Oil-Led Development: Social, Political, and Economic Consequences." CDDRL Working Paper no. 80. Stanford, CA: Stanford University, 2007.

———. *The Paradox of Plenty: Oil Booms and Petro-States.* Berkeley: University of California Press, 1997.

Karsh, Efraim. *Islamic Imperialism.* New Haven, CT: Yale University Press, 2006.

Kassman, Laurie. "U.S. Prepares New Relationship with Sovereign Iraq." Voice of America, June 21, 2004.

Katzenstein, Peter J., and Robert O. Keohane, eds. *Anti-Americanisms in World Politics.* Ithaca, NY: Cornell University Press, 2007.

———. "Political Consequences of Anti-Americanism." In *Anti-Americanisms in World Politics,* ed. Katzenstein and Keohane. Ithaca, NY: Cornell University Press, 2007.

———. "Varieties of Anti-Americanism." In *Anti-Americanisms in World Politics,* ed. Katzenstein and Keohane. Ithaca, NY: Cornell University Press, 2007.

Katzman, Kenneth. "Iraq: U.S. Efforts to Change the Regime." Congressional Research Service, Washington, DC, October 3, 2002.

———. "Iraq: U.S. Regime Change Efforts and Post-Saddam Governance." Congressional Research Service, Washington, DC, August 23, 2005.

Kaufmann, Chaim. "Threat Inflation and the Failure of the Marketplace of Ideas: The Selling of the Iraq War." *International Security* 29 (2004): 5–48.

Kechichian, Joseph A. "Can Conservative Arab Gulf Monarchies Endure a Fourth War in the Persian Gulf?" *Middle East Journal* 61 (Spring 2007): 283–306.

——. *Succession in Saudi Arabia.* New York: Palgrave, 2001.

Keck, Margaret, and Kathryn Sikkink. *Activists beyond Borders.* Ithaca, NY: Cornell University Press, 1998.

Kelly, H. H., and John. W. Thibaut. *Interpersonal Relations: A Theory of Globalization.* New York: Wiley, 1978.

Keohane, Robert O., and Joseph S. Nye. *Power and Interdependence.* New York: Longman, 2001.

Kepel, Gilles. *Jihad: The Trail of Political Islam.* Cambridge, MA: Harvard University Press, 2002.

——. *The War for Muslim Minds: Islam and the West.* Cambridge, MA: Harvard University Press, 2004.

Kepel, Gilles, and Jean-Pierre Milelli, eds. *Al-Qaeda in Its Own World.* Cambridge, MA: Harvard University Press, 2008.

Khan, M. A. Muqtedar. "Liberal Islam, Radical Islam, and American Foreign Policy." *Current History* 102 (December 2003): 417–21.

Khong, Foong Y. *Analogies at War.* Princeton, NJ: Princeton University Press, 1992.

Kida, Thomas. *Don't Believe Everything You Think: The Six Basic Mistakes We Make in Thinking.* Prometheus Books, 2006.

Kirshner, Jonathan, ed. *Globalization and National Security.* New York: Routledge, 2006.

Kissinger, Henry. *White House Years.* Boston: Little, Brown, 1979.

Klare, Michael T. *Blood and Oil: The Dangers and Consequences of America's Growing Petroleum Dependency.* New York: Metropolitan Books, 2004.

Kohut, Andrew. "Testimony of Andrew Kohut: How the United States is Perceived in the Arab and Muslim Worlds." U.S. House of Representatives, International Relations Committee, Subcommittee on Oversight and Investigations, November 10, 2005.

Krasner, Stephen D. *Sovereignty: Organized Hypocrisy.* Princeton, NJ: Princeton University Press, 1999.

Kroll, John A. "The Complexity of Interdependence." *International Studies Quarterly* 37 (1993): 321–48.

Krueger, Alan B., and David D. Laitin. "Kto Kogo: A Cross-Country Study of the Origins and Targets of Terrorism." In *Terrorism, Economic Development, and Political Openness,* ed. Philip Keefer and Norman Loayza. Cambridge, U.K.: Cambridge University Press, 2007.

Krueger, Alan B., and Jitka Maleckova Malečková. "Education, Poverty, and Terrorism: Is There a Causal Connection?" *Journal of Economic Perspectives* 17 (Fall 2003): 119–44.

Labeviere, Richard. *Dollars for Terror: The U.S. and Islam.* New York: Algora Publishing, 2000.

Lacroix, Stephanie. "Between Islamists and Liberals: Saudi Arabia's New Islamo-Liberal Reformists." *Middle East Journal* 58 (Summer 2004).

Laqueur, Walter, ed. *Voices of Terror: Manifestos, Writings and Manuals of Al-Qaeda, Hamas, and Other Terrorists from Around the World and Throughout the Ages.* New York: Reed Press, 2004.

Lawson, Fred. "Hegemony and the Structure of International Trade Reassessed: A View from Arabia." *International Organization* 37 (March 1983): 317–37.

Leader, Stefan. "Usama Bin Laden and the Terrorist Search for Weapons of Mass Destruction." *Jane's Intelligence Review* 11 (June 1998).

Leblond, Doris. "ASPO Sees Conventional Oil Production Peaking by 2010." *Oil and Gas Journal* (June 2003).

Lebow, Richard N. *Between Peace and War: The Nature of International Crisis.* Baltimore: John Hopkins University Press, 1984.

Levi, Michael. *On Nuclear Terrorism.* Cambridge, MA: Harvard University Press, 2007.

Levi, Michael, and Henry Kelly. "Weapons of Mass Disruption." *Scientific American* 287 (November 2002): 76–81.

Levy, Adrian, and Catherine Scott-Clark. *Nuclear Deception: The Dangerous Relationship between the United States and Pakistan.* New York: Walker and Company, 2008.

Lewis, Bernard. *What Went Wrong: Western Impact and Middle Eastern Response.* Oxford: Oxford University Press, 2002.

Li, Quan. "Does Democracy Promote or Reduce Transnational Terrorist Incidents?" *Journal of Conflict Resolution* 49 (April 2005): 278–97.

Li, Quan, and Rafael Reuveny. "Economic Globalization and Democracy: An Empirical Analysis." *British Journal of Political Science* 33 (2003): 29–54.

Li, Quan, and Drew Schaub. "Economic Globalization and Transnational Terrorism." *Journal of Conflict Resolution* 48 (April 2004): 230–58.

——. "Poverty Causes Terrorism." In *At Issue: Is Poverty a Serious Threat?* ed. Mercedes Munoz. Detroit: Greenhaven Press, 2006.

Lieven, Anatol. *America Right or Wrong: An Anatomy of American Nationalism.* New York: Harper Collins, 2004.

Linzer, Dafna. "Iraq Approves Inspectors' Use of U-2 Surveillance Planes, Iraqi Ambassador Says." Associated Press, February 6, 2003.

Lizardo, Omar. "The Effect of Economic and Cultural Globalization on Anti-U.S. Transnational Terrorism 1971–2000." *Journal of World-Systems Research* 12 (July 2006): 149–86.

Lorenz, Edward N. "Deterministic Nonperiodic Flow." *Journal of Atmospheric Sciences* 20 (1963): 130–41.

Lorenzetti, Maureen. "U.S. Firms Say Timetable May Slip on Saudi Gas Deals." *Oil and Gas Journal,* January 21, 2002.

Luciani, Giacomo. "Allocation vs. Production States: A Theoretical Framework." In *The Rentier State,* ed. Hazem Beblawi and Giacomo Luciani. New York: Croom Helm, 1987.

Lustick, Ian S. "The Absence of Middle Eastern Great Powers: Political 'Backwardness' in Historical Perspective." *International Organization* 51 (Autumn 1997): 658–83.

Lynch, Marc. "Anti-Americanisms in the Arab World." In *Anti-Americanisms in World Politics,* ed. Peter J. Katzenstein and Robert O. Keohane. Ithaca, NY: Cornell University Press, 2007.

MacFarquhar, Neil. "Anti-Western and Extremist Views Pervade Saudi Schools." *New York Times,* October 19, 2001.

——. "Militants Attack in Saudi Oil Area; At Least Ten Dead." *New York Times,* May 30, 2004.

Mahajan, Rahul. *The New Crusade: America's War on Terrorism.* New York: Monthly Review Press, 2002.

Mango, Andrew. *Ataturk: The Biography of the Founder of Modern Turkey.* New York: The Overlook Press, 1999.

Mann, James. *Rise of the Vulcans: The History of Bush's War Cabinet.* New York: Penguin, 2004.

Mannes, Aaron. *Profiles in Terror: A Guide to Middle East Terrorist Organizations.* Lanham, MD: Rowman and Littlefield, 2004.

Mansfield, Edward D., and Brian M. Pollins, eds. *Economic Globalization and International Conflict: New Perspectives on an Enduring Debate.* Ann Arbor: Michigan University Press, 2003.

Maoz, Zeev. "Network Polarization, Network Interdependence, and International Conflict, 1816–2002." *Journal of Peace Research* 43 (July 2006): 391–411.

Matheson, George A. "Terrorism and the Oil and Gas Industry." *Journal of Counterterrorism and Homeland Security International* 14 (Spring 2008).

Mattair, Thomas R. "Mutual Threat Perceptions in the Arab/Persian Gulf: GCC Perceptions." *Middle East Policy* 14 (Summer 2007): 133–40.

Maugeri, Leonardo. "Not in Oil's Name." *Foreign Affairs* 82 (July/August 2003).

Mazarr, Michael J. *Unmodern Men in the Modern World.* Cambridge, U.K.: Cambridge University Press, 2007.

Mazo, Eugene. "What Causes Democracy?" Center for Democracy, Development and the Rule of Law, Stanford University, Working Paper, 2005.

McCullough, David. *Truman.* New York: Simon and Schuster, 1992.

McMillan, Susan M. "Globalization and Conflict." *Mershon International Studies Review* 41 (1997).

Mearsheimer, John J. "Back to the Future: Instability in Europe after the Cold War." *International Security* 15 (Summer 1990): 5–56.

Medalia, Jonathan. "Terrorist 'Dirty Bombs': A Brief Primer." CRS Report for Congress, October 29, 2003.

Michael, Maggie. "Purported Al-Qaeda Tape Accuses U.S. of Trying to Replace Arab Governments." Associated Press, June 12, 2004.

Miller, Judith. "Nuclear Monitor Sees Treaties Weakening." *New York Times,* May 15, 2004.

Moghadam, Assaf. "Motives of Martyrdom: Al-Qaeda, Salafi Jihad, and the Spread of Suicide Attacks." *International Security* 33 (Winter 2008/2009): 46–78.

Moghaddam, Fathali. *How Globalization Spurs Terrorism: The Lopsided Benefits of "One World" and Why That Fuels Violence.* Westport, CT: Praeger, 2008.

Mohapatra, Aswini K. "Democratization in the Arab World: Relevance of the Turkish Model." *International Studies* 45 (October 2008): 271–94.

Montgomery, Dave. "FBI Chief Links Al-Qaeda to Deadly Blast, Praises Saudis." Knight Ridder, June 2, 2003.

Moran, Daniel, and James A. Russell, eds. *Energy Security and Global Politics: The Militarization of Resource Management.* New York: Routledge, 2009.

Morrow, James D. "How Could Trade Affect Conflict." *Journal of Peace Research* 36 (1999): 481–89.

Mottahedeh, Roy P. "The Clash of Civilizations: An Islamicist's Critique." *Harvard Middle Eastern and Islamic Review* 2 (1995): 1–26.

Mowatt-Larssen, Rolf. "Al Qaeda Weapons of Mass Destruction Threat: Hype or Reality?" Belfer Center for Science and International Affairs, Harvard University, 2010. Available at http://belfercenter.ksg.harvard.edu/publication/19852/al_qaeda_weapons_of_mass_destruction_threat.html, accessed September 26, 2010.

Mueller, Karl P. "The Paradox of Liberal Hegemony: Globalization and U.S. National Security." In *Globalization and National Security,* ed. Jonathan Kirshner. New York: Routledge, 2006.

Mullins, Martin, and Finbarr Murphy. "Financial Globalisation, State Autonomy, and Modern Financial Instruments: The Case of Brazil." *Globalizations* 4 (December 2009): 433–49.

Munoz, Mercedes, ed. *At Issue: Is Poverty a Serious Threat?* Detroit: Greenhaven Press, 2006.

Munson, Henry. "Lifting the Veil: Understanding the Roots of Islamic Militancy." *Harvard International Review* 25 (Winter 2004): 20–24.

Murawiec, Laurent. *The Mind of Jihad.* Cambridge, U.K.: Cambridge University Press, 2008.

Myers, Richard. *Eyes on the Horizon: Serving on the Front Lines of National Security.* New York: Simon and Schuster, 2009.

Naimi, Ali. "Globalization and the Future of the Oil Market." *Middle East Economic Survey* (May 2005).

Napoleoni, Loretta. *Modern Jihad.* London: Pluto Press, 2003.

———. *Terror Incorporated: Tracing the Dollars behind the Terror Networks.* New York: Seven Stories Press, 2005.

National Commission on Terrorist Attacks upon the United States, "Monograph on Terrorist Financing." Available at www.9-11commission.gov/staff_statements/911_TerrFin_Monograph.pdf.

National Military Strategy to Combat Weapons of Mass Destruction (Washington, DC: Chairman, Joint Chiefs of Staff, February 13, 2006).

National Security Archive. "Casual Conversation." May 13, 2004. Washington, D.C., National Security Archive and Chadwyck-Healey, 2009, available at www.gwu.edu/~nsarchiv/NSAEBB/NSAEBB279/index.htm, accessed on 9/27/2010.

Nau, Henry R. *Identity and Power in American Foreign Policy.* Ithaca, NY: Cornell University Press, 2002.

Nehme, Michel G. *Fear and Anxiety in the Arab World.* Gainesville: University Press of Florida, 2003.

Nisbett, Richard, and Lee Ross. *Human Inference: Strategies and Shortcomings of Social Judgment.* Englewood Cliffs, NJ: Prentice Hall, 1980.

Nixon, Richard. *U.S. Foreign Policy in the 1970s.* Report to the Congress, February 18, 1970 (Washington, DC: GPO, 1970).

Nye, Joseph S., Jr. *Soft Power: The Means to Success in World Politics.* New York: Public Affairs, 2004.

———. *The Future of Power.* New York: Public Affairs, 2011.

Obaid, Nawaf, and Anthony Cordesman. *Al-Qaeda in Saudi Arabia: Asymmetric Threats and Islamic Extremists.* Washington, DC: Center for Strategic and International Studies, 2005.

"Pakistani Scientist Credits Saudi Arabia for N-Test Help." Rawalpindi Nawa-i-Waqt, translated from Urdu, September 23, 2000.

Palmer, Michael A. *Guardians of the Gulf.* New York: Simon and Schuster, 1999.

Pape, Robert. *Dying to Win: The Strategic Logic of Suicide Terrorism.* New York: Random House, 2006.

Perl, Raphael. "Terrorism, the Future, and U.S. Foreign Policy." CRS Issue Brief for Congress, CRS-7, April 11, 2003.

Perrow, Charles. *Normal Accidents: Living with High-Risk Technologies.* New York: Basic Books, 1984.

Perry, George L. "Oil and Terrorism." *International Economist* (November/December 2001).

Peters, Edward. "The Firanj Are Coming—Again." *Orbis* 48 (Winter 2004): 3–19.

Peters, Gretchen. *Seeds of Terror: How Heroin is Bankrolling the Taliban and Al Qaeda.* New York: St. Martin's Press, 2009.

Phillips, Kevin. *American Dynasty: Aristocracy, Fortune, and the Politics of Deceit in the House of Bush.* New York: Viking, 2004.

———. *American Theocracy: The Peril and Politics of Radical religion, Oil, and Borrowed Money in the 21st Century.* New York: Viking, 2006.

Piazza, James A. "Incubators of Terror: Do Failed and Failing States Promote Transnational Terrorism?" *International Studies Quarterly* 52 (2008): 469–88.

Pillar, Paul R. *Terrorism and U.S. Foreign Policy.* Washington, DC: Brookings, 2001.

Pincus, Walter. "Secret Presidential Pledges over Years Erected U.S. Shield for Saudis." *Washington Post,* February 9, 1992.

Pollack, Josh. "Saudi Arabia and the United States, 1931–2002." *Middle East Review of International Affairs* 6 (September 2002): 77–102.

Prokop, Michaela. "Saudi Arabia: The Politics of Education." *International Affairs* 79 (2003): 77–89.

Putnam, Robert D. *Making Democracy Work: Civic Traditions in Modern Italy.* Princeton, NJ: Princeton University Press, 1993.

Qutb, Sayyid. *Milestones.* In translation. Indianapolis: American Trust Publications, 1990.

———. *Social Justice in Islam.* 1948.

Ramazani, Ruhi K. *The United States and Iran: The Patterns of Influence.* New York: Praeger, 1982.

Rashid, Ahmed. *Taliban: Islam, Oil, and the New Great Game in Central Asia.* New Haven, CT: Yale University Press, 2000.

Ratner, Michael, Jennie Green, and Barbara Olshansky. *Against War in Iraq: An Anti-War Primer.* New York: Seven Stories Press, 2003.

Reagan, Ronald. *Public Papers of the Presidents of the United States: Ronald Reagan.* Washington, DC: GPO, 1981.

Renshon, Jonathan. "Stability and Change in Belief Systems: The Operational Code of George W. Bush." *Journal of Conflict Resolution* 52 (2008): 771–94.

"Report: Al Qaida May Sabotage Saudi Oil." United Press International, March 11, 2003.

"Reshaping U.S.-Russian Threat Reduction." *RANSAC Report,* November 2002.

Rice, Condoleezza. "Testimony." 9/11 Commission, April 8, 2004. Hart Senate Office Building in Washington, DC.

Richards, Alan. "At War with Utopian Fanatics." *Middle East Policy* 8 (2001): 5–9.

Ripsman, Norrin M., and T. V. Paul. *Globalization and the National Security State.* Oxford: Oxford University Press, 2010.

Risen, Jane, and Thomas Gilovich. "Informal Logical Fallacies." In *Critical Thinking in Psychology,* ed. Robert J. Sternberg, Henry L. Roediger III, and Diane F. Halpern. Cambridge, U.K.: Cambridge University Press, 2007.

Risse-Kappen, Thomas. *Bringing Transnational Relations Back In.* New York: Cambridge University Press, 1995.

Road to War: American Decision Making During the Gulf Crisis. Princeton: Films for the Humanities & Sciences, 1993.

Roberts, Paul. *The End of Oil: On the Edge of a Perilous New World.* New York: Houghton Mifflin, 2004.

Rosati, Jerel A. "The Power of Human Cognition in the Study of World Politics." *International Studies Review* 2 (2000): 45–75.

Rosecrance, Richard. *The Rise of the Trading State: Commerce and Conquest in the Modern World.* New York: Basic Books, 1986.

Rosenau, James N. *Along the Domestic-Foreign Frontier.* Cambridge, U.K.: Cambridge University Press, 1997.

———. *Distant Proximities: Dynamics Beyond Globalization.* Princeton, NJ: Princeton University Press, 2003.

——. "A Pre-Theory Revisited: World Politics in the Era of Cascading Interdependence." *International Studies Quarterly* 28 (1984): 245–305.

——. *Turbulence in World Politics: A Theory of Change and Continuity.* Princeton, NJ: Princeton University Press, 1990.

Ross, Michael. "Does Oil Hinder Democracy?" *World Politics* 53 (April 2001): 325–61.

Rubin, Barry, and Judith Colp Rubin, eds. *Anti-American Terrorism and the Middle East.* New York: Oxford University Press, 2002.

Rumsfeld, Donald H. "Testimony by Secretary of State Donald H. Rumsfeld." U.S. Senate, Armed Services Committee, July 9, 2003. Available at www.defenselink.mil/speeches/2003/, accessed September 27, 2010.

Russell, James A., and James J. Wirtz, eds. *Globalization and WMD Proliferation: Terrorism, Transnational Networks, and International Security.* London: Routledge, 2007.

Russett, Bruce, and John O'Neal. *Triangulating Peace: Democracy, Interdependence, and International Organizations.* New York: W.W. Norton, 2001.

Rutledge, Ian. *Addicted to Oil.* London: I.B. Tauris, 2005.

Sachar, Howard M. *Europe Leaves The Middle East, 1936–1954.* New York: Alfred A. Knopf, 1972.

Safran, Nadav. *Saudi Arabia: The Ceaseless Quest for Security.* Cambridge, MA: Harvard University Press, 1985.

Sageman, Marc. *Leaderless Jihad: Terror Networks in the Twenty-First Century.* Philadelphia: University of Pennsylvania Press, 2008.

Sanger, David E. "Bush Officials Praise Saudis for Aiding Terror Fight." *New York Times,* November 27, 2002.

——. "Pakistan Found to Aid Iran Nuclear Efforts." *New York Times,* September 2, 2004.

Schattschneider, E. E. *The Semi-Sovereign People: A Realist's View of Democracy in America.* New York: Holt, Rinehart, and Winston, 1960.

Scheuer, Michael. *Imperial Hubris: Why the West Is Losing the War on Terror.* London: Brassey's, 2004.

——. *Through Our Enemies' Eyes: Osama bin Laden, Radical Islam, and the Future of America.* Washington, DC: Potomac Books, 2002.

Schmidt, Susan. "Spreading Saudi Fundamentalism in U.S." *Washington Post,* October 2, 2003.

Schofield, Richard. *Kuwait and Iraq: Historical Claims and Territorial Disputes.* London: Royal Institute of International Affairs, 1991.

Scholte, Jan Aart. *Globalization: A Critical Introduction.* New York: Palgrave, 2000.

Schweitzer, Yoram, and Sari Goldstein Ferber. "Al-Qaeda and the Internationalization of Suicide Terrorism." Jaffe Center for Strategic Studies Memorandum no. 78, November 2005.

Schweitzer, Yoram, and Shaul Shay. *The Globalization of Terror: The Challenge of Al-Qaeda and the Response of the International Community.* New Brunswick, NJ: Transaction, 2003.

Sedgwick, Mark. *Against the Modern World: Traditionalism and the Secret Intellectual History of the 20th Century.* New York: Oxford University Press, 2004.

Settle, Robert, and Pamela Alreck, *Why They Buy: American Consumers Inside and Out.* New York: John Wiley, 1986.

Seyyid, Abdulai Y. "The OPEC Fund and Development Cooperation in a Changing World." OPEC Fund for International Development, Vienna, Austria, 2003.

Seznec, Jean-Francois. "Stirrings in Saudi Arabia." *Journal of Democracy* 13 (October 2002): 33–40.

Shambayati, Hootan. "The Rentier State, Interest Groups, and the Paradox of Autonomy: State and Business in Turkey and Iran." *Comparative Politics* 26 (April 1994): 307–31.

"Shaikh Saud Hits Govt's Support for U.S. War on Terrorism." *APS Diplomatic Recorder,* October 20, 2001.

Shapiro, Robert. *Futurecast.* New York: St. Martin's, 2008.

Shushan, Debra, and Chris Marcoux. "Arab Generosity Not Keeping Up with Arab Prosperity." ForeignPolicy.com, April 23, 2010.

Sick, Gary. *All Fall Down: America's Tragic Encounter with Iran.* New York: Random House, 1985.

Simmons, Matthew. *Twilight in the Desert: The Coming Saudi Oil Shock and the World Economy.* New York: Wiley, 2005.

Simon, J. L. *The Ultimate Resource.* Princeton: Princeton University Press, 1996.

Sivan, Emmanuel. *Radical Islam: Medieval Theology and Modern Politics.* New Haven, CT: Yale University Press, 1985.

Slevin, Peter. "U.S. Promises Democracy in Middle East." *Washington Post,* August 8, 2003.

Smil, Vaclav. *Energy at the Crossroads.* Cambridge, MA: MIT Press, 2003.

Snyder, Jack. *From Voting to Violence: Democratization and Nationalist Conflict.* New York: W.W. Norton, 2000.

Solymar, Laszlo. *Getting the Message: A History of Communications.* Oxford: Oxford University Press, 1999.

Sorensen, Georg. *Democracy and Democratization: Process and Prospects in a Changing World.* Boulder, CO: Westview Press, 1998.

Speth, James. *Red Sky at Morning: America and the Crisis of the Global Environment.* New Haven, CT: Yale University Press, 2004.

Springer, Devin R., James L. Regens, and David N. Edger. *Islamic Radicalism and Global Jihad.* Washington, DC: Georgetown University Press, 2009.

Stern, Jessica. *The Ultimate Terrorists.* Cambridge, MA: Harvard University Press, 1999.

Stiglitz, Joseph E., and Linda J Bilmes. *The Three Trillion Dollar War: The True Cost of the Iraq Conflict.* New York: W. W. Norton, 2008.

Suskind, Ron. *The One Percent Doctrine: Deep Inside America's Pursuit of Its Enemies since 9/11.* New York: Simon and Schuster, 2006.

———. *The Price of Loyalty: George W. Bush, the White House, and the Education of Paul O'Neill.* New York: Simon and Schuster, 2004.

Taber, Charles S. "The Interpretation of Foreign Policy Events: A Cognitive Process Theory." In *Problem Representation in Political Decision Making,* ed. Donald A. Sylvan and James F. Voss. New York: Cambridge University Press, 1998.

Tarrow, Sidney. *The New Transnational Activism.* New York: Cambridge University Press, 2005.

Teitelbaum, Joshua. "Terrorist Challenges to Saudi Arabian Internal Security." *Middle East Review of International Affairs* 9 (2005).

Telhami, Shibley, and Fiona Hill. "America's Vital Stakes in Saudi Arabia." *Foreign Affairs* 81 (November/December 2002).

Tenet, George J. "Converging Dangers in a Post 9/11 World." Testimony of the Director of Central Intelligence before the Senate Select Committee on Intelligence, www.au.af.mil/au/awc/awcgate/cia/worldwidethreatbriefing2002.htm.

Tenet, George, and Bill Harlow. *At the Center of the Storm: My Years at the CIA.* New York: HarperCollins, 2007.

"Terrorism Financing: Origination, Organization, And Prevention." U.S. Senate, Committee on Governmental Affairs, 108th Cong., 1st Sess., July 31, 2003. Washington,

DC: GPO, 2004, available at http://purl.access.gpo.gov/GPO/LPS44946, accessed February 2, 2011.

The Global Reach of Al-Qaeda. U.S. Congress. Senate. Committee on Foreign Relations. Subcommittee on International Operations and Terrorism. 107th Cong., 1st Sess., December 18, 2001. Washington, DC: GPO, 2002. Available at http://purl.access.gpo.gov/GPO/LPS19421.

The 9/11 Commission Report: Final Report of the National Commission on Terrorist Attacks upon the United States. New York: W.W. Norton, 2004.

Thomas, Timothy L. "Al-Qaeda and the Internet: The Danger of 'Cyberplanning.'" *Parameters* 117 (Spring 2003): 112–23.

Thornberry, Patrick. "On the Legal Case for Invading Iraq." In *The Iraq War and Democratic Politics,* ed. Alex Danchev and John MacMillan. New York: Routledge, 2005.

Tilly, Charles. "Reflections on the History of European State-Making." In *The Foundation of National States in Western Europe,* ed. Charles Tilly. Princeton, NJ: Princeton University Press, 1975.

Treisman, Daniel. *Oil and Democracy in Russia.* National Bureau of Economic Research, Working Paper no. 15667, January 2010.

Tripathi, Dwijendra, and Prithi Misra. *Towards a New Frontier: History of the Bank of Varoda.* New Delhi: Manohar, 1985.

Tsui, Kevin K. "More Oil, Less Democracy: Evidence from Worldwide Crude Oil Discoveries." *Economic Journal* (January 2010).

Tucker, David. "What Is New about the New Terrorism and How Dangerous Is It?" *Terrorism and Political Violence* 13 (Autumn 2001): 1–14.

Unger, Craig. *House of Bush, House of Saud: The Secret Relationship Between The World's Two Most Powerful Dynasties.* New York: Scribner, 2004.

United Nations Development Programme. "*Arab Human Development Report 2009.*" Available at www.arab-hdr.org/publications/other/ahdr/ahdr2009e.pdf, accessed September 26, 2010.

Update on the Global Campaign against Terrorist Financing. Second Report of an Independent Task Force on Terrorist Financing. New York: Council on Foreign Relations, June 15, 2004.

U.S. Department of Homeland Security. *National Infrastructure Protection Plan.* Washington, DC: GPO, 2006.

Van Natta, Don, Jr., and Timothy L. O'Brien. "Flow of Saudis' Cash to Hamas Is Scrutinized." *New York Times,* September 17, 2003.

Vance, Cyrus. *Hard Choices: Critical Years in America's Foreign Policy.* New York: Simon and Schuster, 1983.

Vandewalle, Dirk. *Libya since Independence: Oil and State-Building.* Ithaca, NY: Cornell University Press, 1998.

Veliotes, Nicholas. "U.S. Policy toward the Persian Gulf." Hearing before the Subcommittee on Foreign Affairs and the Joint Economic Committee, U.S. House of Representatives, 97th Cong., 2nd Sess., May 10, 1982.

Verleger, Phillip K. *Adjusting to Volatile Energy Prices.* Washington, DC: Institute for International Economics, January 1993.

Von Hippel, Karin. "The Roots of Terrorism: Probing the Myths." *Political Quarterly* 73 (August 2002): 25–39.

Wald, Matthew L. "Approval Is Seen for Military Action against Iraq." *New York Times,* September 23, 2002.

——. "Nuclear Weapons Program Could Get Own Police Force." *New York Times,* May 8, 2004.

Wallace, Michael D., Peter Suedfeld, and Kimberley Thachuk. "Political Rhetoric of Leaders under Stress in the Gulf Crisis." *Journal of Conflict Resolution* 37 (March 1993): 94–107.

Walt, S. M. "Fads, Fevers, and Firestorms." *Foreign Policy* 121 (December 2000): 34–42.

Watkins, Eric. "ABB Lummus Vacates Yanbu; Saudis Vow to Crush Terrorists." *Oil and Gas Daily*, May 10, 2004.

Wayne, E. Anthony. "Testimony before the Senate Committee on Banking, Housing, and Urban Affairs." *Money Laundering and Terrorist Finance Issues in the Middle East*, July 13, 2005. Available at http://banking.senate.gov/_Wles/ACFAA.pdf.

Wedeen, Lisa. "Beyond the Crusades: Why Huntington, and Bin Laden, Are Wrong." *Middle East Policy* 10 (Summer 2003): 54–61.

Weisman, Steven R. "Rice Urges Egyptians and Saudis to Democratize." *New York Times*, June 21, 2005.

——. "U.S. Doesn't Seek to Impose Reforms, Powell Tells Kuwaitis and Saudis." *New York Times*, March 12, 2004.

White House. *Fact Sheet on Terrorist Financing Executive Order.* Press release, September 24, 2001. Available at www.whitehouse.gov/news/releases/2001/09/print/20010924-2.html.

White House, "National Strategy to Combat Weapons of Mass Destruction," December 2002, at http://www.fas.org/irp/offdocs/nspd/nspd-wmd.pdf

Whitlock, Craig. "Commandos Free Hostages Being Held in Saudi Arabia." *Washington Post*, May 30, 2004.

Wiktorowicz, Quintan. "Civil Society as Social Control: State Power in Jordan." *Comparative Politics* 33 (October 2000): 43–61.

——. "The New Global Threat: Transnational Salafis and Jihad." *Middle East Policy* 8 (2001): 18–38.

Windsor, Jennifer L. "Promoting Democratization Can Combat Terrorism." *Washington Quarterly* 26 (Summer 2003): 43–58.

Wines, Michael, and Sabrina Tavernise. "Russian Oil Production Still Soars, for Better and Worse." *New York Times*, November 21, 2001.

Winthrop, Rebecca, and Corinne Graff. "Beyond Madrasas: Assessing the Links Between Militancy and Education in Pakistan." Center for Universal Education, Brookings Institution, June 2010. Available at www.brookings.edu/papers/2010/06_pakistan_education_winthrop.aspx, accessed September 27, 2010.

Woodward, Bob. *Bush at War.* New York: Simon and Schuster, 2002.

——. *Obama's Wars.* New York: Simon and Schuster, 2010.

Wright, Lawrence. *The Looming Tower: Al-Qaeda and the Road to 9/11.* New York: Alfred Knopf, 2006.

Wright, Robin. *Sacred Rage: The Wrath of Militant Islam.* New York: Simon and Schuster, 2001.

"Written Statement for the Record of the Director of Central Intelligence before the National Commission on Terrorist Attacks upon the United States." March 24, 2004.

Yamani, Mai. *Changed Identities: Challenge of the New Generation.* Washington, DC: Brookings Institution, 2002.

Yashar, Deborah J. *Demanding Democracy: Reform and Reaction in Costa Rica and Guatemala, 1870s–1950s.* Stanford: Stanford University Press, 1997.

Yergin, Daniel. *The Prize: The Epic Quest for Oil, Money, and Power.* New York: Simon and Schuster, 1991.

Yetiv, Steve A. *America and the Persian Gulf: The Third Party Dimension in World Politics.* New York: Praeger, 1985.

——. *Crude Awakenings: Global Oil Security and American Foreign Policy.* Ithaca, NY: Cornell University Press, 2010.

——. *Explaining Foreign Policy: U.S. Decision-Making and the Persian Gulf War.* Baltimore: Johns Hopkins University Press, 2004; 2nd ed., 2011.

Yetiv, Steve A., and Chunlong Lu. "China, Global Energy and the Middle East." *Middle East Journal* (Spring 2007): 199–218.

Yetiv, Steve A., and Eric Fowler, "Global Oil Dependence and the Commons: The Challenges of Decreasing Oil Consumption." *Political Science Quarterly* (Summer 2011).

Zambelis, Chris. "Attacks in Yemen Reflect al-Qaeda's Global Oil Strategy Publication." *Terrorism Monitor,* September 4, 2008.

Zanini, Michele. "The Networking of Terror in the Information Age." In *Globalisation and the New Terror: The Asia-Pacific Dimension,* ed. David Martin Jones. Northampton, MA: Edward Elgar, 2004.

Index